On the Edge

Will Hutton is the author of the bestselling *The State We're In* and *The State to Come*. He is Chief Executive of the Industrial Society.

Anthony Giddens, the 1999 BBC Reith Lecturer, is the Director of the London School of Economics. He is the author of more than twenty books, including *Beyond Left and Right: The Future of Radical Politics* and *The Third Way: The Renewal of Social Democracy*.

ON THE EDGE
Living with Global Capitalism

EDITED BY
Will Hutton and Anthony Giddens

VINTAGE

Published by Vintage 2001

2 4 6 8 10 9 7 5 3 1

First published in Great Britain in 2000 by
Jonathan Cape

Vintage
Random House, 20 Vauxhall Bridge Road,
London SW1V 2SA

Random House Australia (Pty) Limited
20 Alfred Street, Milsons Point, Sydney
New South Wales 2061, Australia

Random House New Zealand Limited
18 Poland Road, Glenfield,
Auckland 10, New Zealand

Random House (Pty) Limited
Endulini, 5A Jubilee Road, Parktown 2193,
South Africa

The Random House Group Limited Reg. No. 954009
www.randomhouse.co.uk

A CIP catalogue record for this book
is available from the British Library

ISBN 0 09 927368 3

Papers used by Random House are natural, recyclable products
made from wood grown in sustainable forests. The manufacturing processes conform to the environmental regulations of the
country of origin

Printed and bound in Great Britain by
Bookmarque Ltd, Croydon, Surrey

Contents

Preface

Every generation believes it is living through great change, and our generation is no different. If we believe that information technology and digitalisation are likely to transform our lives, earlier generations thought that flight, or electricity, or steam power would do the same for them: and they were right. And if we think the pace of social change is breathtaking, then the most radical transformation of all is in the position of women – and that made its fastest and most dramatic progress in the first twenty-five years of this century when women moved from being essentially male chattels to winning the vote. We are not alone in living through change.

But whatever went before, it remains true that a new century begins at a moment when everything seems in question. What gives contemporary change its power and momentum is in the economic, political and cultural change summed up by the term 'globalisation'. It is the interaction of extraordinary technological innovation combined with world-wide reach driven by a global capitalism that gives today's change its particular complexion. It has now a speed, inevitability and force that it has not had before.

It is this change that the debates and essays assembled in this book try to assess. There is a clear quantum leap in the scale and nature of risk and opportunity. It is possible, for example, to manipulate the genetic composition of food fundamentally and then for the change to be reflected in the pattern of world food production and trade within a few years. The remotest Asian farmer, for example, is as likely to be affected as the European consumer from the farming of genetically modified (GM) wheat in the American Midwest. Giant corporations with turnovers that dwarf the GDP of all but a dozen countries in the world

vii

can deploy the latest technology globally - whether in mobile phones or biotechnology.

On the other hand, the power of these companies does not go unchallenged – not only by states, which seek to regulate them, but by activist groups and consumer organisations, often themselves now globalised. Only about a year ago, one of the world's largest biotechnology corporations, Monsanto, seemed to be in an impregnable market position, a leader in the promotion of GM crops. Protest movements, beginning in Europe and spreading world-wide, have changed all that. As of November 1999, there is talk of the Monsanto group having to break up and dispose of its agricultural chemicals division, the market value of which has dropped to almost zero.

The transmission system for all these changes is a market capitalism, combined with global advances in communications, which is now unchallenged as the means through which the world organises its economy and society. The collapse of communism, which for all its grotesque defects and brutalities had the unsung merit of taking the more brutal edge off capitalism in its effort to triumph in its great ideological battle with its enemy, has allowed a resurgence in a tougher, harder and more global capitalism. The quest for markets is as relentless as the growth of private corporate power; inequality has widened, especially in the Anglo-Saxon economies in the vanguard of globalisation, as the rewards for managerial and technological skills have exploded while those at the bottom have been exposed to an emerging world market in labour.

But there are important opportunities and benefits that can be gained from this new world. In Asia and parts of Latin America the pace of economic development has reached levels that would have been unthinkable in earlier times. Access to capital and foreign markets, along with the transfer of technology via inward investment and the free dissemination of information, have allowed rapid industrialisation and a sharp rise in living standards – frequently helped by judicious public investment in human capital. The dynamism and growth of the American economy over the last decade has been remarkable, and acted as a locomotive for the world economy as a whole.

There has been a wholesale reinvention of the cultural perception of business and capitalism. Business, particularly business associated with the new technologies, is now seen as the embodiment of modernity. It has shed its old image as being inherently exploitative. The capacity to restructure, to reorganise, and to translate ideas into products is seen as an essential component of economic dynamism. High financial rewards, although criticized when seen to be undeserved or excessive, are increasingly accepted as the proper return for risk; profit has been relegitimised. Whatever we may think about the results, the emerging truth is that we live not merely in a business civilisation, but one that is going global.

This has been refracted throughout the political economy of the West. Governments and states everywhere are less confident about the merits of the public domain and the effectiveness of public action, and increasingly abdicate initiative to the private sector or seek out the private sector as a partner. Government, too, has to be reinvented and become more enterprising. And there are signs that some workers are becoming more entrepreneurial and risk-taking in their attitude towards employment, building 'portfolio' jobs and small businesses. There is, of course, an accompanying intensification and insecurity of work as companies seek to maximise shareholder value. The more activist spirit is informing the actions of those at the bottom; the poor are forming self-help organisations, bartering and aiming to lift themselves out of poverty. Even the poor resist being described as poor. On the other hand, the diminishing role of the welfare state and competitive pressures at the bottom of the labour market make life for the poor as relatively harsh as in the more unregulated periods of capitalism in the nineteenth century. But the situation is complex, offset by some of the trends described above.

This book brings together some of the best and most interesting writers and thinkers in the world to reflect upon these trends. Paul Volcker and George Soros are both concerned about the destabilising impact of global financial markets, and argue that the Asian crisis emerged from the structure of the financial system rather than from embedded weaknesses in the economies concerned. Both, despite the recent recovery, urge reform. Manuel Castells agrees that the financial markets are a source of an instability that menaces global prosperity, but also sees them as one of the transmission mechanisms of global capitalist values. Castells does not rest there; he restates his analysis about the new 'info-capitalism' of which the financial markets are part, tracing its rise and benefits along with the new risks; he explains that the various new fundamentalisms, ranging from religion to the green movement, are arising in reaction to globalisation as societies around the world come to terms with the new forces.

Jeff Faux, Larry Mishel and Robert Kuttner trace the way globalisation has affected the growth of income inequality and job insecurity in the USA along with the growth of private monopoly power, with Kuttner asserting the continuing if evolving role of government. Richard Sennett reflects upon how people's experience of work is changing. Work was once a source of identity and biography; now its shifting patterns means that it can no longer serve as a basis for organising community or people's personal biography. This is a preoccupation echoed by Arlie Hochschild, who shows how First World mothers are employing Third World mothers to care for their children – and the Third World mothers give the First World children better care than their own. There is an international care chain, so that even motherhood and parenting are being shaped by globalisation.

Vandana Shiva widens Hochschild's critique; the Third World is being environmentally despoiled by the First World, which uses its power to ensure that the international rules of the game benefit it. Ulrich Beck in another sophisticated analysis argues that with every-thing up in the air, individuals are compelled to become activists in living their lives; they have to reinvent themselves and every social construct, permanently rewriting and rethinking their biographies. In this sense globalisation is entering the intimacies of personal life. And Polly Toynbee assesses the globalisation of the media through which we interpret ourselves; she dismisses the doom-sayers who fear for the future of local culture before the advance of popular capitalism, but she simultaneously worries that some transnational media magnates have too much political and market power – and calls for close attention and possible regulation over how that power is used.

The writers range from the broadly optimistic (Toynbee and Beck) to the broadly pessimistic (Vandana Shiva, and Faux and Mishel), but all agree that the global system needs more governance if individuals and core social and cultural needs are not to be diminished and swallowed up by the new trends. A concluding chapter by the two editors reviews what can be done, and calls for nothing less than the establishment of a global civil society on which global regulation and government can be based.

We thought we should begin the book with a debate on what globalisation is about. Rather than synthesise our different views, we present our arguments that we recorded, drafted and redrafted in response to each other over the summer and early autumn of 1999; we hope you find the result interesting and helpful. For the record we both think we convinced the other of the merits of our respective cases. Tony Giddens, as he says, tends to be on the side of the 'Gee-whizzers' who think the world has turned on its axis; Will Hutton is more cautious, recognising the force of the pressure of change but seeing it as being as much a product of a shareholder-value-driven capitalism and the old-fashioned political power of the USA as associated with the new technologies and knowledge economy. The discussion, we hope, offers the reader some insight into the principal issues and arguments. The key point on which we both agree is that globalisation has to be taken seriously; it is an agent for economic, social and political transformation. The world is on the edge.

Our thanks to our understanding publishers, who saw successive deadlines come and go; our contributors who delivered on time unlike their editors; and our personal assistants, Angela Burton, Miriam Clarke and Anne de Sayrah. Chris Stevens copy-edited the entire manuscript with great sensitivity. Jörg Hensgen, our editor at Jonathan Cape, saw through the project with enthusiasm, charm and professionalism. And of course a big thank-you to Will's wife and family and Tony's partner Alena Ledeneva, who once again found themselves besieged and beleaguered by the 'book'. We hope you enjoy the result.

Will Hutton
Anthony Giddens

December 1999

ON THE EDGE

ANTHONY GIDDENS and WILL HUTTON
in Conversation

What is Changing?

WILL HUTTON: So what is the meaning of globalisation? What is changing? What is qualitatively different about today and contemporary capitalism from what went before?

ANTHONY GIDDENS: First of all there is the term 'globalisation' itself. Only a few years ago the word was hardly used. Now one comes across it everywhere. I doubt if there is a single country in the world where globalisation isn't being extensively discussed. The global spread of the term is evidence of the very changes it describes. Something very new is happening in the world.

That 'something new' isn't just a single set of changes. A number of overlapping trends are involved. The first, and in my opinion in some ways the most important one, is the world-wide communications revolution. It has its origins in the late 1960s, when the first satellite was sent up above the earth, making instantaneous communication possible from any part of the world to any other. The past thirty years or so have seen an enormous intensification of global communications, the latest and most profoundly important being the internet.

The second big change is the arrival of the 'weightless economy', itself increasingly globalised. The new knowledge economy almost certainly operates according to different principles from the industrial economy that preceded it. For the moment, financial markets make up its leading edge. Financial markets today are stunning in their scope, their instantaneous nature and their enormous turnover.

Globalisation refers, thirdly, to a post-1989 world. The fall of Soviet communism is without any doubt at all one of the momentous

1

transformations of the century. It went largely unpredicted by the legions of academics and others who specialised in the study of Soviet society. In retrospect, we can see that the most powerful influences over the dissolution of communism were the two factors I just mentioned. The Soviet Union was making pretty reasonable progress in the old industrial economy. It simply couldn't compete in the new global electronic economy.

Finally, globalisation refers to transformations happening on the level of everyday life. One of the biggest changes of the past thirty years is the growing equality between women and men, a trend that is also world-wide, even if it still has a long way to go. This development is connected with changes affecting the family and emotional life more generally, not only in Western societies but to a greater or lesser degree almost everywhere. If one puts together these four sets of influences, the level of global transformation they signal is nothing short of spectacular.

WH: Very few would dispute that account of what is changing; it's almost the new common sense. But why is there so much talk about globalisation *now*? What do we think is new about the year 2000, compared, say, with 1975? What's going on in our society and the economy that's qualitatively different and represents a discontinuity? We had pretty global financial markets twenty-five years ago in 1975 – I worked in them. And the telephone was a pretty revolutionary form of communication that allowed instantaneous contact if you needed it. The change in the position of women over the last twenty-five years is nothing like as remarkable as the change in women's status since the turn of the century. Of all your points only the fall of the Soviet Union represents a true quantum leap; surely the foundations of all the rest were in place twenty-five years ago.

If I pushed myself on the question I would say that what is different is the sense that change is all-encompassing and carries a new inevitability; its momentum is a superior power to any other, even that of the state. There is an interlocking between the technological advances you've mentioned, a more aggressive capitalism prepared to drive change along globally and a political leadership that sees no alternative but to allow the process to continue. All three trends are intertwined, and whether one's broadly optimistic – like you – about the consequences, or a pessimist, like the French writer Vivienne Forrester who predicts mayhem and social dislocation, everybody seems to agree that the force of change is close to irresistible. For while states may once again regain control either by themselves or in collaboration with others, at the moment their power has never felt more qualified.

All borders are coming down – economic, political and social. There is a new conception of time, risk and opportunity. There is already a 24-hour financial market, which you have mentioned. But increasingly there is the 24-hour day – working, shopping, banking. There is no nook or cranny of the economy where change or the potential for change is not happening, driven by technology, markets and powerful corporations, with all the knock-on consequences for patterns of working which in turn refract into our personal lives and relationships.

But having said that, we have to sort out what is new, and what is unchanging. Inequality and power imbalances exist just as they have always done. There has been technological change since the Industrial Revolution. Both Churchill and Bismarck insisted in their time that their countries lived through unparalleled transformations. What do we believe is so different about this era of change we're going through that allows us to redefine our political ideas and beliefs? How did we arrive at the conclusion that something so fundamental is going on with economic and social structures that the old distinction between left and right is outmoded? It is much deeper than just talking about information technology, satellite communication and financial markets. The argument has to be that the changes are of such degree that there has been a fundamental challenge to the operation and our understanding of capitalism.

AG: There is an enormous controversy going on at the moment about just what all these changes amount to and how far there are either continuities with the past or parallels to be found in previous eras. There are two quite opposing views. On the one hand, there are some who say there is nothing new under the sun. The term 'globalisation' may be bandied about a lot, but all the talk doesn't amount to very much. For these people the continuities and parallels with the past are much greater than the differences. They argue, for example, that a hundred years ago there was just as much globalisation as there is now. At the opening of the twentieth century, they say, there was already a quite open international trading system, with a good deal of trade in currencies. Most countries didn't even require passports at that period and there was a great deal of international migration. At the other extreme are the 'Gee-whiz' types, who are so impressed with all the changes happening today, especially those to do with technology, that they see a world breaking quite radically with its past. For them, the

3

new communications technologies, the role of knowledge as a factor in production, and the new discoveries in the life sciences, signal a profound transition in human history.

As usual, the truth is probably somewhere in the middle. But on the whole I tend more to agree with the Gee-whizzers, because I do think our era is in some ways profoundly different from the past – a mixture of new opportunities and deep threats and difficulties.

New Opportunities or Continuities of Risk?

WH: I'm more in the middle than you, tending to your view that something revolutionary is going on, especially technologically with the interaction of the personal computer and the internet, but equally not being certain that everything that mankind thought hitherto has to be jettisoned! Globalisation is so powerful an idea because of the sense of there being no escape. It's coming down the tracks straight at you. There is no escape, for example, from the impact of digitalisation that is transforming industrial structures, and the rash of cross-border mega-mergers and deals that is following in its wake. The food and chemical industries are coalescing; so are banking and insurance; so are information technology and television. And the new coalitions and structures do not respect national frontiers. The human genome project is a good example. It would have been impossible without the computing power now available; it is transnational; and it will revolutionise everything from medicine to insurance. The decline of national sovereignty is certainly another way of highlighting the pace of change. Whatever the aim – military intervention in Kosovo, the regulation of tax havens, doing something about drugs or crime – any state, even the USA to a degree, has to collaborate internationally to prosecute that aim. It's a pretence to argue that there is any substantive national sovereignty in areas like these, even though states, of course, remain the principal actors on the global stage.

AG: We have to include ecological questions in the new range of risk situations. I do agree with you that most of the new risks we face don't come from within the boundaries of any state and cannot be effectively responded to on a national level. For thousands of years human beings worried about risks coming from external nature – from, for example, floods, bad harvests, plagues and other natural disasters. They worried

4

about what nature could do to them. Relatively recently – in the short period of recent history we are discussing here – we started worrying less about what nature can do to us and more about what we have done to nature. We have created risks that no previous generation had to face.

WH: Of course the environment has to be included in any list of dangers. But don't forget globalisation also means the globalisation of crime, drugs and the like. The Mafia now operates globally. Laundering drugs money is a global business. There are real fears that the laundering of Russian Mafia cash could pollute the entire Western banking system. And any police response has to be global, too.

AG: Most of the issues we've just been talking about are more serious than the globalisation of crime. The knowledge economy, for instance, is changing the very character of how we live and work. Only a generation ago, in the Western countries, more than half of the labour force was working in manufacturing occupations or in agriculture. In other words there was a very large working class. Now in most of these societies the proportion of the population working in these sectors is well under 20 per cent and still declining. The industrial working class is almost ceasing to exist. Technological change and, to a lesser extent, the globalisation of trade have brought about this departure.

Take another example: the impact of science and technology on the food we eat. In most countries, including many of the less developed ones, there is no such thing as a 'natural' diet any more. Most food that is consumed includes a large range of additives, some of these involuntary, such as traces coming from herbicides and pesticides. There is rather little that is pure 'nature' left in all this. The genetic modification of crops is one further stage in the process.

WH: You're getting carried away! The decline in manufacturing and the rise in the service sector as sources of employment have been happening since the 1930s if not before; to equate the rise in the service sector with the new knowledge economy and growth in world trade is just not right. You scramble up the trends so that you overstate the importance of knowledge as a driver of change – and that can lead to dubious analysis and even more dubious policy prescriptions.

The rise in services concerned with health and care in old age, for example, is closely associated with a richer, ageing society and has nothing to do with the knowledge economy; the growth in personal household services is the result of the emergence of two-earner households who have to buy in services because the woman is no longer at home; the explosion in financial services has been driven by the growth of home ownership and the decline of the welfare state; the rise in hotel and restaurant services by the increase in personal mobility to do with the new car economy. All these sectors use personal computers and information technology (IT), which sometimes change how they operate, but it is not the IT revolution that has created their growth – and that is the area of dispute between us. The service sector may be cleverer than it was, but it is not its cleverness or association with the knowledge economy that is propelling its underlying growth. However, I am coming round to the view that the web and e-commerce may be transformatory in the future, but it has not happened yet.

I also think it is a grave mistake to underestimate the importance of the growth of crime, corruption and tax evasion as features of globalisation. They are deforming the character of international capitalism and undermining the long-run financial viability of some taxes and thus some states, which the web will exacerbate. Environmental risk is important; but so is crime. But where we absolutely agree is over the emergence of major new risks. I would cite genetically modified food and its risks as a classic example of our new globalising times; just take the pace of its introduction. GM food techniques are only about five to ten years old.

AG: What you say isn't correct, in my view anyway. The big change that has been happening over the longer term isn't the decline of manufacture, but the shrinking proportion of the population working in agriculture. Less than 2 per cent of the workforce in most industrial countries are now in agriculture, itself a pretty amazing phenomenon. That 2 per cent produces far more than we can eat – or, to put it more accurately, than farmers can sell.

Current trends are not just an extension of the tendency of the service sector to expand. Information technology has revolutionised the nature of manufacture itself, as well as how goods are distributed, bought and sold. 'Wired workers' – people who work with computers in decentralised work settings – are all over the place, in services just as much as manufacturing. Communications, information processing, entertainment and other 'weightless industries' are everywhere the major growth areas. Personal services only make up a fairly small proportion.

The new risks go along with all of those changes. No nation, or even group of nations, will be able to stop the spread of GM food. The UK or the European Union may take a very strict line against the testing of genetically modified crops, but it doesn't follow that those crops are not going to be very prevalent. They are already grown very extensively in North America and China. Most of us have already eaten foods that contain some form of genetically modified material. So it is a very good example of how difficult it is to contain these innovations within any national or regional context.

WH: Sorry, but you misunderstand my point. Of course the growth in agricultural productivity is remarkable, but it is simply factually wrong to say that it is now being matched in manufacturing and services to the extent you claim. Yes, computers are everywhere; in the USA, which is the leader in these trends, companies increased their investment in computers by fourteen times over the 1990s, and there has been stunning growth in the US IT sector – between 1995 and 1998 it represented a third of all US economic growth.

But while growth and productivity in the IT sector have been fantastic, they have not spread to manufacturing. Professor Robert Gordon, the leading US expert in productivity, says that outside the IT sector productivity in manufacturing has actually been falling recently – a trend that has been disguised by the growth in productivity in the IT sector. What is more, the 'roaring nineties' in the USA and the IT revolution have not yet begun to match the US productivity growth between 1950 and 1964, when chemicals, the internal combustion engine and terrestrial broadcast technology transformed the US economy. Economists at the Federal Reserve explain that IT technology tends to substitute for other ways of doing some things in a firm, but has not yet been transformatory. If that is true in the USA it is more true in Britain and the rest of the world. To argue that the growth of the service sector equals the growth of the knowledge economy and that all manufacturing is becoming a subset of the knowledge economy is a huge overstatement of what is happening. Although, as I say, I think there are signs that the next phase of growth could see IT drive into the warp and woof of the economy in a way it has not managed to do so far.

Take the arguments over genetically modified food, which must be the most extreme example of the trend you identify. Even in this area you can argue that genetic modification of food is just a more sophisticated technique of something that has always been practised. Human beings have been cross-breeding to improve animal stock and trying to improve the quality of seed by cross-pollination since agriculture began. When that was done by ancient peoples on the

Eurasian plain no one said, 'This is going to be the end of nature'; the manipulation of nature is as old as the human condition. On the other hand it is clear that GM food does raise new questions, but we have to be much more precise rather than just making sweeping statements that the old world is completely redundant and *passé*. So in your view what is the exact difference about GM food?

AG: But I should say 'Sorry, but you misunderstand my point' back to you. It isn't just a question of productivity, but the deep intrusion of IT into manufacturing processes themselves. This is true of almost any industry you care to look at, from the auto industry to oil production and distribution. One consequence is that quality of production is relatively easy to attain. What counts much more now in the success of a product is the market niche that is achieved. So far as GM foods go, there is absolutely no doubt that it is qualitatively different from the past. With the new genetic technologies, you can transplant or cross-breed across species. This was only possible in very marginal contexts with traditional forms of cross-breeding. It really is a quantum difference in terms of both its possible advantages and its risks. 'Nature' of course hasn't been entirely natural for a very long while. Some of the landscapes we love to admire in Greece were actually created by soil erosion produced by farming practices a long time ago. There are many other examples. We are talking of a quantum leap today, however, because of both the extent and the power of the changes we are making. They are on a completely different scale from the past.

WH: But we had the dust bowl in the 1930s. We had the elimination of the buffalo on the American plains at the end of the last century. There was the genocide of the native Indian population. There have been plenty of occasions in human history where human advance has been at the expense of the natural habitat, animal and even human population. After the Spanish colonised Latin America 90 per cent of the native population died from imported European diseases; GM food is a remarkable achievement, I agree, but it won't kill 90 per cent of the Latin American population.

We need to be much more precise about what is different today. You could argue that underneath the change there is a remarkable continuity of risk, along with the political and economic structures in which it is mediated. Inequality endures, for example, and is now more acute than it was a hundred years ago. There are immense imbalances in power. Extraordinary historical forms endure. Look at Buckingham Palace: the

Royal Family use modern communication skills to reinvent and so legitimise themselves, and at the beginning of the twenty-first century the Queen, the Prince of Wales and the other royals remain very influential and powerful.

AG: Yes, of course there are continuities with the past. This is true of all of the major transformations we are discussing. Science and technology, for example, have been deeply bound up with industrialism since its early origins in the eighteenth century. There have also been dramatic changes in communications technologies before. The invention of the Morse Code, in the early nineteenth century, had many social and economic consequences. With the electric telegraph, for the first time a message didn't have to be physically taken from one place to another in order to be transmitted. The invention of video, television and other mass media has also proved very consequential. The capitalist market-place, with its attendant inequalities, as you imply, is another source of continuity. People were already living in a capitalist economy two hundred years ago, as we are today.

But when we speak of capitalism, we can again see that the changes happening now are at least as impressive as the continuities. With the demise of communism, there is no longer any rival to capitalism as a mode of economic development. The global capitalist market-place, as we see it now, is marked by the qualities we discussed a little earlier: the massive influence of financial markets and the emergence of the weightless economy. Capitalism has had a continuity of existence for two centuries or beyond; but we are encountering a new form of capitalism in current times.

Capitalism Without Communism

WH: Here I emphatically agree with you; the collapse of the Soviet Union and the emergence of capitalism as having no world-wide rival is a remarkable change. Moreover it is a very particular kind of capitalism that has emerged victorious from its competition with communism. It's a capitalism that is much harder, more mobile, more ruthless and more certain about what it needs to make it tick. Edward Luttwak calls it turbo-capitalism, in contrast to the more controlled and regulated capitalism of the 1950s and 1960s. Its overriding objective is to serve the interests of property owners and shareholders, and it has a firm belief, effectively an ideological one, that all obstacles to its capacity to do that

– regulation, controls, trade unions, taxation, public ownership, etc. – are unjustified and should be removed. Its ideology is that shareholder value must be maximised, that labour markets should be 'flexible' and that capital should be free to invest and disinvest in industries and countries at will. It's the capitalism of both Wall Street and financial markets and of street trading and street markets: the capitalism at which the Anglo-Saxon community, and the Americans in particular, have been very good. It's a very febrile capitalism, but for all that and its short-termism it has been a very effective transmission agent for the new technologies and for creating the new global industries and markets. It is a tool both of job generation and of great inequality. One can't imagine a planned economy managing to be as creative or as destructive. The great Austrian economist Joseph Schumpeter described capitalism's genius as creative destruction. I think we are living through a classic orgy of creative self-destruction.

AG: I accept the last point, at least to some extent. Capitalism does thrive upon innovation and the capability to leave the past behind, sometimes very rapidly. The motto of Microsoft, after all, is 'Make your product obsolete'. On the other hand, it would be much too negative a view of capitalism to describe it only as destructive. Capitalism can be a very powerful constructive force as well. Think of the extraordinary interdependence which capitalist markets bring about. Its constructive qualities of course also involve systems of power. In previous times, the biggest and best buildings were always associated with religion. Now they are all in the financial centres of cities.

The new capitalism that is one of the driving forces of globalisation to some extent is a mystery. We don't fully know as yet just how it works. There has never been a globalised capitalist economy of this sort before. Moreover, capitalism without communism is a quite different animal from before. For me it isn't as wild and dangerous as you make it seem, and is more resonant with positive possibilities, materially as well as socially. Some of the more scary changes happening in the world aren't much to do with capitalism unless – as Marxists used to do – you stretch the concept so much that it becomes meaningless. They are bound up with the advance of science and technology, as we've been discussing, or with the impact of industrial production. And it's daffy to blame the Americans for all the ills of the world, or to exaggerate the scope of American power. It's only a few years since lots of people were saying how weak the US economy was, and due to be overtaken by the Rhenish or Asian models. What you are talking about is more an ideology of some financial and business circles, rather than a reality.

That ideology seems to be now on the decline. We need new ideas, and forms of global regulation, to fill the gap that the fall of communism has left.

WH: Well, which is it to be – regulation because capitalism can be destructive now that communism has left a gap or starry-eyed faith in capitalism's boundless creativity? Don't traduce Schumpeter. Your argument and his are essentially the same: capitalism may be ruthlessly destructive but it is also creative. At one moment you want to celebrate capitalism, at another you're wary of it, but without – unlike Schumpeter – offering an integrated view of how both propositions could be true.

But I want to return to how you think capitalism is developing now that communism has collapsed. I would say that communism, although it failed, did have one good impact; it kept capitalism on its guard – in a sense it kept it aware that it had to have a human face. Would you agree that now capitalism has no obstacles or alternatives, it can regress to its fundamentalist origins?

AG: No, I think you try to explain too much. There are many other changes going on. So many of our institutions, for example, were shaped by the Cold War. I think we are only just beginning to recognise fully how important this was. For instance, social democracy and the Keynesian welfare state perhaps were only able to develop as they did because of being in between American liberal capitalism and Soviet communism. Capitalism, at least for the moment, has hardly any critics. After all, in the past, it wasn't only the left that was critical of capitalist society and wished either to do away with it, or radically modify it. Many on the right had the same objective. Especially in Europe, the roots of the right lie in a hostility to capitalism, because of its very transformative character, its brashness and its promotion of vulgar commercial values.

More or less everyone has learned to accept, if not necessarily love, capitalism – in much the same way as they have democracy. In spite of the virulent criticism which it received, Francis Fukuyama's *End of History and the Last Man* was essentially correct. At least for the present time, no one can see any effective alternatives to the combination of a market economy and a democratic political system – even though each of these has great deficiencies and limitations. But perhaps at this point I should ask you exactly what does 'capitalism' mean in the global age?

Shareholder vs. Stakeholder Capitalism

WH: Capitalism has always had three fundamental properties. First, it is a system of the private ownership of property. Second, economic activity is guided by price signals set in markets. And third, it expects and depends upon the motivation for action to be the quest for profit. It is the combination of private property, the profit motive and commoditisation of all the inputs in the economic process in markets that defines capitalism.

But I do not regard these attributes of capitalism as absolutes; property, prices and profits are not independent of social mores and preferences, history and politics. Private property-holders can have complete autonomy and sovereignty over their property in some capitalist systems; in others they have to accept all manner of reciprocal obligations as part of the privilege of being a property owner. Equally what is considered a reasonable profit and over what period varies significantly between capitalist economies. And no society allows all the inputs into the economic process to be completely commoditised, so that nothing matters but the logic of supply and demand; labour, for example, is provided by human beings, and there are greater or lesser rules that determine the terms and conditions of their employment.

In fact the degree of deregulation of the labour market – one of the central institutions in a market economy – is a litmus test that shows how far any society allows capitalism to go. There has always been, ever since the Middle Ages, the idea of the just wage, which the Catholic Church supported – and which it continues to support as the recent papal encyclical makes clear. When Catholic societies embarked on capitalism in the nineteenth century they tried to retain the idea of the just wage for the worker, and with it notions of the just price, just profit and even the just enterprise. They still do, and it's the reason Christian democratic parties in mainland Europe are as attached as they are to a less raw, more stakeholder-oriented capitalism.

What the Americans say instead is that capitalism is opportunity for all and risk for all; if you win that game you get lucky. It is the alternative tradition of Catholic capitalism, social market capitalism, or stakeholder capitalism – call it what you like – that is retreating as globalisation spreads.

And it is this shareholder-driven capitalism that has been on the march, with its much harsher view that the purpose of capitalist endeavour is profit maximisation; essentially it says the interests of private property and shareholders are paramount. It is particularly powerful at a time of great technological change because not only does it encourage new entrants into markets, it also shakes up the sometimes powerful but sleepy companies who currently hold a lot of market power. Almost every business today is under severe technological and competitive threat; in the USA the change in the rankings of the top 500 companies is twice that of a generation ago; look what happened to IBM. One of the reasons for greater American dynamism is that the US system is better equipped for these moments of great technological change – although I think we shouldn't go overboard. The twenty or so great US IT companies like Microsoft and Intel – the so-called new titans – together employ only around 150,000 people, which is no more than one older company like Kodak or Boeing, and only a fraction of General Motors or Ford.

I think one of the temptations at the moment is to be so awestruck by the IT revolution and the potential impact of the internet that we forget the other reasons that have helped the long US boom – the international role of the dollar that has allowed the USA to finance astonishingly large trade deficits, low commodity prices, skilful monetary management and the place the USA plays in the world economy that nobody else can copy. Every other capitalism looks feebler and weaker; but there remain great strengths in the German and Japanese economies. I would not, for example, write off Daimler-Benz or Sony just yet, for all the current success of the US economy – and that success might look very different if Wall Street crashed or the dollar collapsed.

AG: Well, part of this very story is that one can only say that the American economy is doing well at the moment. As I said earlier, only a few years ago many astute economic observers were extolling the virtues of Japanese and German capitalism as holding the keys to the future in a way that American capitalism didn't. The American economy at that time looked vulnerable to the advance of different systems of capitalism elsewhere. What applies to IBM could happen to the US economy. No one knows how transitory or otherwise the current situation is, or whether the 'new paradigm' will hold. Rather than talking about the dynamism of American capitalism, we should perhaps be looking to the changes that lie behind it, and which apply much more generally – the harnessing of science and technology to production, plus the new role of electronic money markets.

WH: And the right, of course, add another element to all this. They lionise Reagan and Thatcher. Capitalism, they say, had become sclerotic in the 1970s because the state was too large; the regulatory and tax burden too heavy; trade unions too strong; inflation too embedded. In their view Reagan and Thatcher tackled those problems and so put the heart back into capitalism.

AG: The neo-liberal right certainly did introduce some policies that have had an impact world-wide, especially privatisation. But some of these changes would have happened anyway, because it wasn't only the right that saw there were basic transformations going on in the world economy. The right credits Reagan and Thatcher with too much influence and power. Moreover, I'm not sure the points you make apply to the USA in any case. The federal state was smaller than those in Europe, taxes were lower and the labour movement weaker. It wasn't only the right that was critical of the overextended state and of welfare systems. There were some on the left who were equally critical, although with different ends in view.

WH: The US federal state may be smaller, but when you include state-level and city government, public spending and taxation approach European levels. And the regulatory tradition in the USA has always been very fierce; think of the power of the Securities and Exchange Commission or the Internal Revenue Service. It is one of the reasons anti-state and anti-tax culture is so strong in the USA. But we mustn't get too impressed by capitalism's creativity or the right's view that Reagan and Thatcher were geniuses. Capitalism is a tough, hard, profit-seeking system and those two were lucky to preside over a period in which capitalism was fighting back – and would have fought back whoever was in power. The 1970s saw two great oil shocks that drove up energy prices at a time when organised labour was strong and Western governments were still anxious to prevent unemployment rising too strongly. As a result they tried to protect real wages largely through price controls, so the companies ended up with dramatically lower profits. The share of profits in GDP dropped to crisis proportions, reflected in stock market prices that sank to post-war lows. The profit share had to be rebuilt.

Over the last twenty years, especially in the USA, there has been a near doubling of the profit share and a stagnation, even a fall, in the real wages of blue-collar workers. This, interacting with the fall in interest rates, has been what has driven the rise in Wall Street, and also to an extent been one of the animating forces of globalisation as especially US companies seek to lower their cost base. The rise in Wall Street has then had a very stimulatory impact on the American economy. It has boosted personal consumption because individual consumers, who save by investing in Wall Street directly unlike their counterparts in Europe, have seen their wealth double and treble – and it has also boosted investment because companies can raise money more cheaply. And along the way huge personal fortunes have been made; Bill Gates's 100 billion dollars is only the most obvious example of many. There has been the re-emergence of the super-rich, conspicuous consumption and extraordinary wealth; annual membership of golf clubs that cost $200,000; $30,000 watches and all the rest. New industries have sprung up based on the provision of luxuries.

AG: I'm not certain exactly what you are saying the connection between Wall Street and Bill Gates actually is. Gates made his fortune by spotting the enormous potential of information technology and acting on his hunches. Gates's wealth is truly fabulous, but I'm not sure that he and other self-made individuals really go in for conspicuous consumption. He may have built himself an enormous house, but seems to be getting ready to give away large chunks of his fortune to charitable causes. In the USA, at the top there is a rising tide of affluence, rather than just the emergence of a few super rich. In his heyday, J. P. Morgan had enough money to meet the capital needs of the American economy for three months. With all his wealth, Bill Gates could do so now only for less than a day. Of course, all the things the traditional left says about the USA are still there, and even accentuated – the accumulation of fortunes, the vulgarity of new monied élites and so forth. Lots of people, one could say, have got far too much money for their own good or anyone else's. But I'm strongly against the knee-jerk anti-American-ism that so many of the European (and some of the American) left go in for. I don't see that the secretive, cosy world of old European big money is any more attractive than the brash American version. Economic inequality is much higher in the USA than in most EU countries, but some other forms of egalitarianism are more developed. The USA is much more of a multicultural country than the European societies. Europe hasn't a tradition of welcoming millions of immigrants – think of how difficult it is proving in Germany, France or Scandinavia at the moment. Minority groups, women, gays, the disabled – they've all been able to fight for their rights more effectively in the USA than in Europe.

I would also resist the idea that the expansion of the global economy is producing greater inequality everywhere. Even given their problems, the Asian tiger economies are a great success story. In a short period of time, millions of people have moved out of poverty.

WH: Well, again you make some fair points, but I don't think they are solid or general enough for you to attempt to draw the wider conclusions you want. I share your respect for the way the Americans integrate immigrant and minority groups, but civilisations like the US or Europe are much too complex to fall into simple Manichean categories in which one is largely 'good' and the other largely 'bad'. I doubt that Mexican guest-workers in Los Angeles fare better than Turkish guest-workers in Hamburg – and the waves of immigration the Germans have experienced are enormous.

For example, although there is more mobility in the USA along with wealth accruing to the genuinely entrepreneurial, there is also astonishing inequality that has little to do with the underlying worth of the rich. There is a whole superclass of company directors who have done well from executive share options, while salaries in professions like investment banking or the media are just extraordinary. There is little doubt that conspicuous consumption in the USA is widespread; upper middle-class people demolishing their homes and rebuilding them even more lavishly are commonplace, and some of the consumer spending patterns are simply baroque.

And you're right about Gates; he has given away a substantial part of his fortune, but then so did Rockefeller and Ford. There has been a long-standing tradition of charitable giving in the USA which takes the edge off the income inequalities and helps to legitimise wealth. But the mass of ordinary people in the USA have seen their wages stagnate or fall in real terms over the last twenty years – and they feel very exposed to job insecurity. The figures Jeff Faux and Larry Mishel provide in their chapter in this book are very telling in this respect, and Richard Sennett's account of modern work really strikes home. Susan Faludi's current best-seller about the crisis of the American male echoes Sennett's work – and these are not European but American critics.

We are also witnessing a wave of domestic and international mergers that presage some of the biggest concentrations of private corporate power the world has ever seen – think of the oil, car, or media business.

As for your last remark about globalisation aiding the development process for poor countries, I don't think any serious observer disputes that economic development is now very uneven and unequal. Asia is certainly better off than thirty years ago, but has just lived through two years of exceptional depression and turmoil. There are very few African countries not growing poorer with the collapse in commodity prices as are many parts of Latin America. The UN Development Report says that there is a rising number of countries in profound trouble. I think you have to be very careful that you don't paint a too Panglossian view of globalisation and America. The less developed countries were very critical of the way the rules on world trade favour the rich at the world trade talks in Seattle in 1999 – one of the reasons why the talks failed.

Beyond Left and Right: Were Capitalism's Critics Wrong?

AG: What about going back to the question of why capitalism has triumphed? Are all the problems that the critics of capitalism, from both the left and the right, once pointed to still there? Does capitalism inevitably mean large-scale economic fluctuation, the growth of inequality, tendencies towards monopoly and the general commercialisation of life? Or were the critics simply wrong?

WH: The socialists made some telling points in their critique of capitalism, but they were wrong to believe its defects would overwhelm it; and wrong to think that socialism was more economically creative, however fairer it might seem to be.

There is very little disagreement – even among capitalism's defenders – that it does produce growing inequality, dense concentrations of private power, monopoly and instability, as the socialists used to argue. And although commoditisation is an ugly word, I think it does capture the process by which capitalism tries to turn every relationship into a commercial exchange, which again the socialists were surely right to contest. For example, we continue to resist the extension of commercialisation in areas like medicine; you want to know that advice from your doctor is based on getting you well rather than increasing his or her income. But socialism was mistaken to insist that these deficiencies were so great that a planned economy would be an improvement. Scientific planners might have been satisfactory at planning an economy if technological change just stopped and all consumers' wants were frozen, although even that is doubtful; but planning at the political centre for uncertainty, change and myriads of wants was necessarily beyond them.

Capitalism is good at risk, change and modernisation, as I've argued. I don't think that any planned system would be so ruthless about introducing new technologies that so profoundly overturn so many vested interests.

AG: Well, who would have thought ten years ago that the Soviet Union would be no more? Nobody much.

WH: Nobody much.

AG: We have learned – or should have learned – a good deal over the past ten to twenty years about what makes a decent society possible. A good society, locally, nationally and globally, is one that balances the state and government, civil society and a market economy. There can be, and are, pathologies along the edges of all of these. A society where the state is too strong becomes oppressive. But where it is too weak, the society lacks steering mechanisms, including those necessary for stable economic development. Where civil society is inadequately developed, as in Russia today, there can be neither proper government nor stable economic growth. Yet where civil society is too strong, a society lapses into ethnic divisions and identity conflicts.

The same applies to the economy. A decent society can't be one where markets flood into everything and all values are commercialised. Yet without spaces for the market, freedom and prosperity are both threatened. So far as the market is concerned, wouldn't you have to concede that capitalism is both more rational and fairer than most socialists tended to assume? For Marx, and for many other socialists too, capitalism was simply an irrational way of running a modern economy. The economic theory of socialism was always based upon the idea that conscious regulation of the economy would make it both more efficient and fairer. Haven't we discovered that there is no effective substitute for the signalling mechanisms that capitalist markets provide, or for the innovative qualities that capitalism has?

WH: Well, I think we are going to have an argument about socialism as much as capitalism here. I've never really thought of socialism as even largely an economic doctrine. I've always thought of it as an ethical value system wanting to assert the worth of liberty, equality and fraternity; and that regulation, control and ownership of parts of the economy were no more than a means to that end. I also think it important to draw a distinction between socialism and communism;

communists believed that the socialisation of the means of production had a central role in overturning the capitalist economy, while socialists were readier to accept private ownership along with regulation – the kind of recommendation you made earlier about contemporary global capitalism needing some international rules!

The early arguments on the left were on the extent to which reformism or more wholehearted socialisation of ownership was necessary to deliver their ethical aims given capitalism's intrinsic irrationalities and systemic defects. But the fundamentalists were wrong. Liberty, equality and fraternity did not require scientific planning; and did not require the socialisation of production. Indeed planning and socialisation became the enemies of liberty, and paradoxically even of fraternity. I have always thought that, and always believed in the more effective signalling and innovative capacities of capitalism. So there is no concession for me to make. The question is to what extent we can modify capitalism so that it can live with other values like equality and social justice.

AG: I'm not sure how interested Marx was in liberty, equality or fraternity. He argued that socialism isn't an ethical doctrine and was extremely harsh with those who believed that it was. For Marx, and most of those influenced by him, socialism is about the effective organisation of industrial production. Socialists were simply wrong about that and it is a rather fundamental thing to have been wrong about. I'm not quite sure from your point of view where you think the rational capacities of capitalism lie.

WH: The rationality of capitalism doesn't lie in any supposed tendency to produce a stable equilibrium. Its rationality lies in its inherent capacity to accommodate risk, to experiment over investment for the future and to be creative about new forms of production and consumption; it is also very good at co-ordinating the millions of buying and selling decisions that characterise any economy.

AG: Surely you can't deny that there are equilibrium tendencies in capitalist markets? The rationality of capitalism can't just depend upon its relationship to the management of risk.

WH: Why not? One of the advances in modern economics is the incorporation of the new theories of chaos and non-linearity into its vision of how demand and supply interact. One of your own famous sociological theories is reflexivity which describes a continual and never-ending refashioning of social life; I take the same view of economic life. This notion that capitalism should be seen as a creative process rather than tending to unimprovable equilibria is one of the great strengths of the Austrian school of economists' championing of capitalism. Friedrich Hayek says that markets are brilliant means of capturing the collective judgements of individual intelligence because they allow decentralised decision-making, but we should not think of them as stable. I still believe Keynes's argument that the differential speed of adjustment and motives of the financial and real sectors of the economy – now at global level – means that the economy is in permanent tension. And there is Schumpeter's argument, which I mentioned, about creative destruction. The internet is one example; digitalisation and gene technology are others; the zest of property development another again.

A New Economic Paradigm? Technological Change and the Knowledge Economy

AG: I don't think those examples bear out the argument particularly well. None of them is simply created by markets. There is a difference between market capitalism and scientific innovation, no matter how closely they sometimes might become connected. The internet, digital technology and developments in the life sciences all have a strong input from scientific innovation, which is a creative process rather than a destructive one. I would tend to see the equilibrium tendencies in capitalism as in tension with scientific innovation and technological change. Both are essentially unpredictable and therefore have no particular connection to market-clearing qualities. It seems to me that these qualities, however, definitely do exist.

Technological change sometimes has the effect of producing a sort of quantum leap, forcing a sort of restructuring of the whole of the capitalist economy. A quantum leap of this kind is happening through the impact of the information revolution at the moment.

WH: Yes, but the pace of its introduction is much more ruthless under capitalism. Capitalists know that there is a fortune to be made by exploiting new technology, but nobody can know beforehand which technology will succeed. Think of the rivalry between VHS and Betacam in video technology twenty years ago, or at the moment whether digital television will be delivered by satellite or by cable. We just don't know; it's economic poker. But this is what capitalism is good at. As a Keynesian I am distrustful of the notion that capitalism has inevitable, ineluctable, market-clearing tendencies: I prefer to see the market as a permanent process rather than as tending to a moment of stability – the market clearing to produce a steady-state equilibrium. I don't think it's true in theory or in practice.

We are living through a time of great change at the moment. It hasn't always been like that. The period from 1950 to 1974, around the first oil shock, was a period of much broader economic stability. What helped the Asian miracle was that the economies were developing in a period when so much technology was relatively stable; cars, refrigerators, ships, steel and the like were changing only incrementally. And product development was incremental rather than qualitative.

AG: You now see the quantum leap more, don't you?

WH: That's just the point; we are now living through a quantum leap, although I think – like Manuel Castells in his chapter in our book – that it's as much to do with the spread, character and ambition of capitalism as the march of science. You can see similar moments in capitalist development over the last 250 years. The arrival of steam; then electricity; then oil: all represented quantum leaps in a core component of the economy, and each spawned a new generation of companies that rode to prominence on the new technology, but they interacted with developments in the structure of the financial and labour markets. The revolution brought by steam, for example, needed well-developed banks and the development of a labour market in order to drive that phase of the Industrial Revolution.

But I do think that these moments of technological turbulence are one of the ways new capitalists can make above-average profits and achieve market power; that was the story of the US rail and oil barons in the nineteenth century, and we're watching new barons emerge in information and biotechnology. The other way for a business to make above-average profits is to hold a franchise which gives the company a special market niche and a *de facto* monopoly, or to trade and deal well.

AG: But isn't consumer power central as a constraint to capitalism? See the point about Monsanto we made in our Preface.

WH: Of course. There are three broad constraints on capitalism: the consumer; social mores, moral codes and institutions; and governments.

Companies can exploit the quantum leaps in technology only if they can correctly anticipate how patterns of consumption will develop. That is why passing the market test is such an important component of capitalism. And I think we have been watching a new development over the last decade: consumers using their power collectively to get firms to behave more responsibly. The Monsanto example shows this; and there are a growing number of occasions when companies have changed their policies in response to campaigning consumer pressure groups. The second counterweight is that capitalism has to respect prevailing mores and social institutions; for example, at the moment multinationals find that they have to respect the growing green and human rights movements. Heineken had to pull out of Burma a couple of years ago because of objections to its supporting the military junta, while Unilever has said that by 2005 it will buy fish only from fishing companies who fish sustainably. Both have been at the receiving end of consumers prepared to be more ethical about how they spend their money. And lastly, capitalist markets do not spontaneously produce the best outcomes; they do not even produce the legal, transport and education systems – to name but three key areas – without which they would fail. That is where the state has a crucial and fundamental role.

AG: At one time I would have said unions as well.

WH: I would include unions under the second category. It's clear that unions are weaker than they were, but I would not write their obituary just yet. Workers feel very exposed to the harder, shareholder-value-driven capitalism with its demands for intensifying work effort, making jobs more insecure and laying people off. There are signs that workers are becoming readier to join unions; membership in Britain is stabilising for the first time in twenty years. They are still a constraint on capitalism, and may re-emerge.

AG: Let me try to sum up some of the changes going on in the economy. First, information and knowledge have now become media of production, displacing many kinds of manual work. Marx thought that the working class would bury capitalism, but as it has turned out, capitalism has buried the working class. The trading of information and knowledge is the very essence of the new global financial system, where money now consists solely of digits in computers. Financial markets tend to work incredibly rapidly. There are no long- or medium-term profit opportunities at all. Some strategies used by traders become obsolete almost at the time that they are invented, because of the speed with which others react to or displace them. It has aptly been said that whereas once upon a time the big tended to oust the small, now it is the fast that ousts the slow. The dematerialised economy is also a world of images. Products are defined according to the niche they have and the image they conjure up in the mind of the consumer. The knowledge economy seems to me already a reality: it isn't just a projection for the future.

These changes, as we would both agree, haven't done away with some of the more long-established features of the capitalist economy. Some have become more marked than before – I think, largely as a result of globalisation, with a dash of free market ideology; you emphasise as well the role of American economic power. Greater regulation is needed, especially on a global level, to stabilise some of the classic excesses of capitalism. But in my view we should also be working to build up a global civil society and a framework of law, and we should be thinking about possible forms of transnational democracy.

We're still quarrelling about just how much change there's been and about what the knowledge economy actually is.

WH: That is a fair summary: we agree that there is substantial change and there is a phenomenon called globalisation; we identify the same features and similar consequences; we both look for more global regulation and the creation of a global civil society. What is in dispute is what weight we attach to the possible drivers of this change. I put more weight on the character of contemporary capitalism; you put more weight on science and what you describe as the knowledge economy.

Of course I agree that there is a dynamic sector of the economy where knowledge is very important, and all firms can access and use the new processes to some degree. But over this discussion you have tended to use the weightless economy, knowledge economy and service economy as interchangeable ideas – and with that I disagree. I am also not sure that the inference we are meant to draw – that everything is cleverer and more knowledge-based and therefore that the fundamentals of capitalism have wholly changed – is right. The heart of the argument seems to be that an increasing amount of the value in a consumer good like a car or a microwave oven lies in its computer software which is lighter and more knowledge-based; less weight is synonymous with cleverness or knowledge. The production process is also cleverer, using more automation and robots. And even some of the materials are cleverer; a girder of steel, for example, is 'cleverer' than it was a hundred years ago because new alloys and techniques make it lighter and stronger. This cleverness spawns more services. So far I agree. Where we differ is that you then go on to make the generalisation that everything is transformed and that the rules of the capitalist game have changed.

But manufactured goods have been getting cleverer ever since the Industrial Revolution and the boundaries between manufacturing and services as a result have been getting cloudier – so what? There have been great inventions like digitalisation before – the petrol engine, the cathode tube, penicillin, etc – which have had a transformatory impact on the economy, but it has still been recognisably capitalist. And while I recognise the force of 'cleverness' driving change in parts of the economy, I hesitate to argue that the new economic paradigm of weightlessness and knowledge has changed the capitalist game. Rather weightlessness has been part of the capitalist process since it began.

AG: No, I don't think this is quite correct. It is a quantum leap because the essence of the economy has changed. What matters isn't how or where goods are manufactured, but the definition of the 'product' that is bought and sold. It is the idea that sells, not the material built into its construction. Human capital counts for far more than anything else in giving companies a competitive edge. Famously, the book value of the assets of Microsoft is tiny compared with the trading value of the company as a whole. But even if were talking about selling cars, a good deal of what is sold is in style and image. Moreover, the driving force of the new global market-place, the financial economy, is wholly demater-ialised. Gold and paper money have no relevance to electronic money at all now.

WH: There's obviously truth in that, and I don't begin to dispute it. What I think is disputable is to argue that the substantive character of capitalism has changed. Plainly there are no longer lots of factory and mining sites around the country where tens of thousands of men are working who feel solidarity with each other and can be organised into trade unions supporting a socialist party. They've gone, as we said earlier.

AG: Isn't that rather a big change?

WH: Yes, but on the other hand what have they been replaced by? Most people in contemporary Britain work for a living; they have tiny savings, little countervailing power against their employer and are thus two or three monthly pay cheques away from living on income support if they

24

lose their job. The men and women who live in those starter homes in the great big housing estates around our cities may not work in huge factories any more but they remain just as at risk to capitalism, employer power and loss of work as their forebears were. The working class remains; it is working in the service sector, wears suits and is harder to organise into trade unions. It may not be so solidaristic, but because it's harder to recognise we shouldn't dismiss its existence. Its relations to work and power are critically very similar to those of the old working class.

But while that is true, it is also true that what matters increasingly to contemporary capitalism is less where any given product is manufactured than who holds the patent. Intellectual property rights are increasingly what makes capitalism tick; control of the idea rather than production is what counts. In some respects distribution matters more than production. No self-respecting capitalist wants to be in a situation where his or her competitors have power and hold distribution channels that can keep him or her out of markets they could otherwise get into. Capitalism is becoming much more interested in distribution, wholesaling, retailing and intellectual property rights than the location and management of the production process. If you are a large player you can finance and manage successful manufacturing anywhere in the world frankly; you do it where it's most cost-efficient. But this 'weightlessness' does not transform the underlying tensions and motion of capitalism; rather it empowers knowledge-based workers over non-knowledge-based workers. The new commanding heights of the economy may be the so-called symbolic analysts who manipulate information rather than blue-collar workers making steel — but all the difficulties about exploitation, private ownership and instability remain remarkably the same

AG: You continually talk as though only capitalism creates risks and uncertainties! States have been far more dangerous and disturbing to their populations than business or markets ever have. Better to be 'at risk' to capitalism than at risk to communism or military government, surely.

Moreover, it is just wrong to say that the working class exists just as before, but is now transferred to the service sector. Manual work is far less common than it used to be. The economic circumstances as well as the political attitudes of wired workers are substantially different from those of the old working class. The project of the left for the incorporation of the working class within the wider society has lapsed.

25

Different forms of underprivilege and insecurity exist today. Social and economic life has become more individualised. The old working-class communities have more or less completely ceased to exist. Control of knowledge; control of image; control of branding: these matter far more than they ever did before. Production is easy – for the producers. . . .

WH: Easier, I would say, rather than easy; nor should you confuse the collapse of working-class communities – which is certainly true – with the collapse of the notion of people recognising that they are no more than workers.

But certainly what it means to manufacture is changing. The manufacture of the Model T Ford began in 1909 in Detroit and that approach to manufacture – breaking down all the constituent parts into tiny components that are performed on a permanently moving production line – has been the predominant form of economic activity most of the twentieth century. We have essentially been upgrading and refining Henry Ford's basic techniques. At least until now. Manufacturing output now represents just over 20 per cent of GDP in Britain and America and only around 30 per cent in Germany. But more importantly an increasing amount of that production is not performed on Fordist 'production lines'. The process is cleverer, less labour-intensive and more automated – even robotised.

AG: The intensity of competition is so much greater. When the first Model T Ford was built, there wasn't Toyota hovering in the wings prepared to improve on it immediately, was there? Most companies know pretty quickly what other companies are planning, because of the general profusion of information. Secrecy is much more difficult. Given the global nature of contemporary communications, there is no geographical isolation any longer.

WH: Talk to businessmen and you are astonished by how they perceive the intensity of competitive pressure. They see it as growing measurably even by the month.

AG: But I also feel very strongly that there is pressure on the inventiveness of ideas – much more than even a generation ago. When one talks to business people, one is struck by the intensity of the pressure of ideas on them. They are always thinking: what comes next, what should I be thinking about next? Where can I find a niche in this market for a while? They don't really any longer talk much about problems of production. You can't really do business these days without having a concept. No one opens a restaurant just to provide food. The issue is creating an image of food and eating that will attract customers.

WH: This is one of the aspects of the new knowledge economy where I agree with you. I am not always carping on about the dangers of capitalism; it is remarkably creative. In this respect we've all become converts, or at least part-converts.

Changing People's Lives

AG: Again, I would resist the idea that it is simply capitalism that produces these effects. The creativity of modern life comes not just from the driving force of markets, but also from the changes that ordinary people everywhere are making in their lives. One of the most important aspects of globalisation is the changing position of women. This is happening partly for economic reasons – the increasing involvement of women in the labour force – but also for a complex of other reasons too. It is directly related to democracy as well as to the impact of women's movements. Even in more traditional countries around the world, women are less and less prepared to put up with being treated as subordinates within the family and elsewhere. One of the main sources of the rise of fundamentalism, in my view, is the attempt to stall the gender revolution.

As a consequence of all these changes, particularly in the industrial countries, life has become more of a flux than it used to be. Sustaining a consistent identity and having an overall work career depend much more upon the individual than they did previously. In the more affluent parts of the world even poverty is less uniform than it used to be. Poverty has become individualised. People adapt in an active way to all the things they find around them including welfare provision and all sorts of other changes, such as moving in and out of poverty. Poverty probably used to be more of a condition than it is now. Just like marriage or old age.

WH: That's probably true, but again I find myself agreeing with you but having to qualify it because it is only part of the story – but you seem to want to claim a universal status for it. For example, I think you are right to say that poverty is much less uniform than it was, but don't forget that for a lot of people it remains just that: a desperate condition.

There are two and a half million men and women over fifty who are unemployed or economically inactive in Britain; they are not being very activist about their situation because they can't be. Think about what it's like to be over fifty and out of the labour market in Strathclyde, Liverpool, parts of Manchester, the north-east of England and parts of the West Midlands. Poverty does become a condition because for an over-50-year-old the odds of changing your situation are so hopeless. You tend to sit there squat because there is no alternative. Others who are younger or live closer to a more dynamic part of the economy, they may be more activist. So what you say is half but not completely true.

AG: Much of this is fairly new. Even for many working-class people, there used to be more stable employment up to and through one's fifties. I still don't think you should assume that people respond to these situations in a passive way. Some, of course, do, and they succumb to disillusionment and despair. There are big structural forces at work here and they certainly can't be simply thought away by those whom they affect. On the other hand, it is a great mistake to suppose that poorer people are always victims. Most take an active stance towards the world, especially as traditional ways of life become unfrozen. One won't get very far in social policy by treating the unemployed, or indeed the homeless, as if they formed homogeneous categories. All the studies of the homeless, for example, show what a differentiated group this is. Moreover for many there is a real mix of constraint and volition. For example, some of the teenagers on the streets today might earlier have been stuck within abusive families.

WH: Of course people don't sit there and write off their lives; they do try to change their circumstances – and may even be partially successful. But that doesn't mean that many others are not stuck in a condition of poverty. Look at the experience of the coal-mining communities. Unemployment is still very high in the neighbourhoods where the mines have closed. But what's also interesting is that two fifths of the people have migrated, trying to change their circumstances in the way you describe. But others just simply haven't been able to migrate, so for them poverty has become a condition. The two phenomena coexist.

AG: Yes, they normally coexist. Or rather, they don't so much coexist as interact with one another. The decline of coal-mining, for instance, is hardly a wholly bad thing, given the circumstances in which men had to work. Some who have been forced to look for a life outside the pit no doubt have come to very much the same conclusion. It isn't only capitalists who think, what opportunities are there for me here? What's going on in the wider world and how should I find ways of turning it to my advantage?

WH: But there's a very different power relationship between a middle-aged ex-coalminer trying to exploit the market with limited funds and any capitalist. That's why I insist that the intriguing aspect of our times is that great change is sitting side by side with enduring truths. You could have said at any time since the emergence of a national labour market in the nineteenth century that workers had to behave like mini-capitalists; if you like, trade unions are no more than workers' response to capitalism, trying to control the market like capitalists want to. But we can measure just how successful our worker-capitalists are about finding new work after they become unemployed. Re-entry jobs, as they are called in the jargon of labour market economists, on average offer an hourly wage rate some 20 per cent below the hourly wage that people earned in their previous job. As mini-capitalists they are forced into selling their services at a substantial discount to what they were earning previously. And on top the forms of employment they get tend to be more insecure. Classically an ex-coalminer will become a security guard on some sort of temporary contract.

AG: Something similar happened in the past, but with rather different dynamics. Many people working in working-class jobs got their peak earnings in their early twenties or even late teens. Their earnings then declined as they reached middle age. In the mining industry, wages went down as workers moved from the coalface to surface jobs. This was also the classic career pattern for most women. In the past, women rarely got back into the labour force at the same economic level as when they left it to have children. Research shows that even when they take several years off, women today tend to get back into the labour force at a higher level than they would have done in previous generations.

WH: You're right about the complexity. And you're right that for women the labour market has transformed; and you're right that jobs in coal-mining were less than perfect. I even agree about the existence of something we can call the weightless economy, though I think it coexists with the old rather than represents a wholly new paradigm, at least at the moment. But where we differ is your implied belief that being working class is a wholly sociological matter conditioned about the capacity to throw up solidaristic social institutions like trade unions. I have more of an economist's interpretation: that there is and was an economic base for working-class life. If you face the risk of unemployment with little capital and only income support to live on, and if on average the jobs after a period of unemployment pay 20 per cent less, then you remain as at risk as the old working class – arguably more so because trade unions are weaker. Your relation to capital or business or work – depending on how you want to characterise the relationship – remains the same.

AG: That's true, but no one any longer seriously disputes that the working class in industrial countries has contracted radically.

WH: The term 'working class' may get in the way, I think. I would agree that a 'true' working class in the old sense is disappearing. The whole picture is plainly fragmenting. But the relationship to economic power of the fragmented new working class is similar to that of the old, more solidaristic working class.

AG: There is certainly more than one side to technological change. Quite a few people died each year in the mining industry and others ended up chronically sick. On the whole, the advance of information technology is destroying a good deal of the harsher forms of manual work, at least in the developed societies.

WH: I never bought into the romance of being a coalminer; working in a pit miles underground which is inevitably dangerous and unhealthy is not a desirable way of making a living. That's not the issue. My point is that beneath the technological change some rough and tough old capitalist truths are being reasserted: that shareholder-driven capitalism is driving out the stakeholder variant of capitalism, and that beneath the glitz of modernity a lot of people are as exposed as ever to some hard brutalities.

Modernising the Stakeholder Capitalism: Lessons from Germany?

AG: What is your current view of stakeholder capitalism? The models that I take it you used to admire – German and Japanese capitalism – seem to be losing ground quite dramatically. I don't think there are many people at the moment who see these as a model for the future. On the other hand, we do need much firmer means of promoting corporate responsibility.

WH: Obviously globalisation favours shareholder-value-driven capitalism, and to an extent – as I was arguing earlier – is being driven by it, so it's hardly surprising that variants of capitalism that try to balance the other interests in the enterprise, like those of the workers, and to behave more ethically – stakeholder capitalisms – are under pressure. But that doesn't mean that the principle of stakeholder capitalism is wrong; it means rather that some of the means of achieving it have to be updated and modernised. And if you want to call that a third-way approach similar to stakeholding, then I'm with you.

I think that is what Gerhard Schröder in Germany is after; not the abandonment of the German social market, stakeholder model, but its modernisation. I also think that some of the almost joyful last rites that the British are delivering over German capitalism are vastly overdone. The German economy is twice the size of the British; its productivity is on average a fifth higher; and many of its recent difficulties are due to the overvaluation of the Mark and the burden of German reunification – East Germany is a disaster area. One of the consequences of the downward drift of the euro over 1999 has been to make German exports more competitive, and once the German export machine starts gearing up the German economy will start to pick up quite smartly. Over the 1990s German growth has averaged 2.4 per cent; British growth 1.9 per cent. It is true that German unemployment has been higher, on average about half as high again – but once you include the economically inactive labour force that in Britain doesn't count as formally unemployed because they aren't allowed to claim unemployment benefit, which they are in Germany, even that comparison is less flattering. So stakeholder capitalism is on the defensive, but it still has formidable strengths that are too often dismissed in this debate.

AG: I think that greatly underestimates the need for reform, not only of the German economy, but of the wider German society. Unemployment is a much more serious problem than you seem to suggest. The German economy has many strengths, but it needs quite substantial innovation if the enviable economic record Germany has had to date is to be continued. This will involve the structural reform of labour markets, business organisation and the welfare system. I'm quite surprised that you admire the German system so much, given its roots in conservatism and Catholicism. Germany has a heavy version of corporatism that makes it peculiarly resistant to change. The federal government and the regional states have to enter into frequent co-operation, while the largely independent federal bank and the federal constitutional court leave the central government with little room for creating reforms. The advantages of this set-up are fairly easy to see – it produces unforced collaboration that can be a valuable source of negotiation and consensus. But it is only poorly adapted to confront the transformations we've been discussing earlier. It doesn't follow that because Germany has done well in the past – in respect of prosperity as well as social justice – it will continue to do so in the future. Unemployment is a serious problem in what was West Germany, not only in the East – especially among younger people and immigrants. Nearly a million young people emigrated from Germany between 1989 and 1996, a much higher number than in the past. This goes back to an issue I mentioned before. The country is ill-equipped to handle its large influx of newcomers from other countries. Germany took more immigrants in the 1990s than the USA, but refuses to define itself as a multicultural society, because of its antiquated citizenship laws. Immigrants are foreigners. These laws are due to be modified now, though.

WH: I do respect Germany, and it has a lot of lessons for us; but my admiration is not unqualified – I think the German attitude to minorities and immigrants deplorable, for example, although the scale of immigration is not understood in Britain. And your history is a bit wobbly: the German social market economy was created after the war as a deliberate break with conservatism, and there is a powerful liberal tradition in German Catholicism. I also find a lot to admire in the USA even while I am critical of some parts of the US system.

But I would counsel you to be careful about calling for structural reform of labour markets and the welfare system as stand-alone recommendations for increasing German employment; what you really mean is that non-wage costs should be lowered, work made more insecure and the German system of social protection weakened. It may be true that the Germans have gone too far in some of this, but it is wrong to put the entire blame for German unemployment on these alleged structural weaknesses.

If you add formal and informal unemployment together (the people of working age who are economically inactive in the statistics), then unemployment is broadly the same in the old West Germany as in Britain. The unemployment problem in Germany is very much concentrated in East Germany, and that is largely because the exchange rate at reunification did not allow for much lower levels of productivity in the East, which have still not caught up with the West. What is holding back the rate of job generation in Germany is much more its less developed service sector, especially financial services. But British financial services have grown off the back of successive house-price booms and home ownership extending to 70 per cent of our households, and reforming Germany's welfare state is hardly the route to more home ownership even if that was thought desirable.

Britain also has a booming micro service sector providing household services ranging from tutoring to delivered meals, where Germany has been held back in part because fewer German women go to work and so the old division of labour in the household – where women care for the home – still stands. It is true that part-time work has been held back by regulations that make it less attractive, but the Germans are following the Dutch and putting part-time work on the same legal footing as full-time work – and that will bring about a progressive build-up of part-time work. The rules about shop-opening hours that hold back the spread of retailing are well known, and there are lots of what we consider silly regulations, but that is part of the German concern to promote social order. I'm not sure that 24-hour supermarkets are so wonderful, anyway; you just spread the same level of retail sales throughout the day while raising costs.

And you can't have it both ways. You admire the German education and training system, and strong public services like its health system. On any measure – incidence of breast cancer, heart disease, even obesity – the British score badly compared with Germany. High-quality education and high-quality health that are socially inclusive and promote genuine equality of opportunity cost money, and my view is that we should be levelling up to German standards rather than insisting on levelling down.

As for business organisation, the story is very complicated. If you are saying that the two-tier board system is cumbersome, then I think you are wrong. The system works extremely well and produces very well-managed German companies with clear strategic long-term goals. Are you saying that there should be more wheeler-dealing, takeovers and mergers? Is Britain's shareholder-value-driven capitalism with its insecure workforce really the model to be emulated? I am not saying that every aspect of the German system is perfect, heaven forbid. But you have to look at a system in the round.

And it always amuses me to hear British intellectuals and commentators like yourself saying how the Germans are hopeless and they have no future unless they reform. You gave an interview along those lines to a German newspaper the day Mannesmann made a £20 billion bid for Orange and which forced Vodaphone to respond with a counter-bid. The Germans own a large chunk of our investment banks, car and mobile phone industry, and our electronics industry; their share of world trade has risen over the last five years while ours has fallen. In ten years' time you will find that the German economy has restructured; that its social market economy has been modernised; and that its system of stakeholding will be updated. And its economic performance will have been superior to Britain's. I bet you £1,000 that I'm right, but we'll see in 2010!

AG: One needs to unpack the notion of stakeholder capitalism. There are some clear aspects in which American-style capitalism is more open, more transparent and even more regulated than German corporate capitalism. In the corporatist set-up, there is a great deal of cronyism. Many decisions are taken on the basis of who knows whom. Anti-trust regulations are stronger in the USA and are more strongly enforced than in most other industrial countries. There is a need to look for new models of corporate responsibility, backed by national and international regulation. I am sympathetic to those who say that Europe should resist Americanisation, but there are lessons to be learned from some aspects of American corporate practice. It isn't all the Great Evil. It wouldn't be true to say that the social market economy has failed – but if it can't adapt, and pretty quickly, it will fail. Some of the German Länder (state) governments have recognised this, and are pushing through reforms more effectively than the federal government has been able to do.

WH: Of course; I am glad you are qualifying some of your earlier criticism, and I agree that reform in Germany is urgent. But there is Wall Street cronyism as well as Milanese or Tokyo cronyism. It would be silly to think that American capitalism is as pure as the driven snow while stakeholding is rotten with corruption. The more serious criticism of stakeholding is its commitment to long-termism when the pace of technological change accelerates. It can be too slow-moving and sclerotic.

But I still think on balance the arguments for stakeholding stand. Every form of capitalism must possess a legal framework in which to do business. If you are competing for a deal, signing a major contract, hiring a new employee, or borrowing money, then there simply must be a robust system of law in which both sides of the bargain can have confidence. And that in turn means that firms must have legal standing; and to have a legal standing there needs to be a framework of corporate law, otherwise your capitalism descends into a dog-eat-dog, Mafia world of might being right. Thus the legal system, and in particular corporate law, is the indispensable bedrock upon which capitalism depends.

The neglect of this essential point was one of the reasons the transition from communism to capitalism has been so difficult. But obviously corporate, banking, pension fund, employment, trustee, contract and commercial law reflect conscious choices about what kind of capitalism any particular society wants – and my contention is that it can be biased significantly to favour interests other than property owners and private shareholders. For example, we could require company directors to do more than maximise profits; we could make share options more difficult to issue; we could require companies to set up remuneration committees with independent directors to assess executive pay. And we could require that a board of directors includes directors who represent the workforce.

Then there is pension fund law. Pension funds own nearly half the quoted shares in British companies. The question is what the law should insist should be the relationship and mutual responsibilities between those funds and the companies in which they invest. It is no longer adequate to say that they can turn up if they want once a year to an annual parliament of shareholders and sell their shares whenever they choose, especially if there is a hostile takeover bid. At the very least funds need to vote on key decisions, to play a part in setting commercial objectives and to ensure that executive pay is not excessive. As for bankruptcy and insolvency law, it is wrong that they should give such incentives to break up a company rather than keep it going; wrong that entrepreneurs should be treated as pariahs with a permanent mark of Cain if they fail; and wrong that shareholders should be so privileged over everybody else.

And there is employment law. Making anybody redundant is very serious, especially if they have worked for the firm for a long time. It should be expensive for companies to make people redundant rather than cheap.

AG: The comments you are making now bear out what I was saying. The examples you are giving here aren't taken from the German system as it exists at present. I strongly believe in the need to develop more effective legal frameworks for corporate responsibility – on an international as well as a national level. There should be standards of executive compensation that link salaries to productivity, and which limit ratios between the most poorly paid and the best paid. The theme 'no rights without responsibilities' should apply to executives as much as anyone else. I don't think you make the best case for these possibilities in the cases you mention. It might be possible to democratise pension funds, but for the core 'stakeholders' – those whose pensions are 'at stake' – the most important thing is effective, professional management. Such management should be encouraged by performance-related pay structures.

You wouldn't find many employers who wouldn't agree that long-standing employees are 'stakeholders in the enterprise'. I am the director of a publishing company. We want people to stay on as long as possible, because we have invested in them, and recognise their commitment to us. The last thing we wish for is people coming or going all the time. Yet companies have to have the capacity to fire people, or shed staff when things are going badly. It isn't in the overall social or economic interest to make it too expensive for firms to reduce their staff. When you became Editor of the *Observer* you fired people, didn't you?

WH: Yes, and it was the single most unpleasant episode in my working life – but it was a classic case, as you've just mentioned, of having to shed people because things were going badly. There was extreme pressure to cut costs at the *Observer* because we were losing millions, and the future of the paper and a lot of other jobs were at stake. But I only agreed to do it after the company had approved extremely generous redundancy terms; otherwise I would have resigned.

If you are going to lay people off you have got to pay them generously because being laid off is dreadful. They've got to rebuild their career and their life and they've got to have time in which to do both. The idea that you can just lay someone off, give them a week's money for every year they've worked and they should then hawk themselves round the labour market without any financial cushion is amazing. The objection is of course that if you make it expensive to sack people, then companies won't hire people, but I think that is greatly overstated. But you are in a comparable position at the London School of Economics. You can't run a world-class academic institution if you can never move anybody; but equally you have to be sensitive and ultra-generous if you do approach anybody to move on.

AG: In universities the stakeholder principle, one could say, is developed to an extreme. Most of the academic staff in universities have tenure. Along with judges, they are one of the last groups to have such a position. There is a trade-off, though. Academics exchange relatively low wages for the security they have. Yet there is also more of a global market-place in academic jobs these days. The leading scholars can get a job more or less where they wish. Academic staff are quite mobile, unlike universities themselves. Universities can't threaten to move elsewhere as transnational companies might do if they don't get the economic advantages they want.

WH: But how seriously should we take threats like that? Britain is the fifth biggest market in the world and corporations want to trade here. They need to have a distribution and production presence; you can't build a world market position and neglect Britain. The quid pro quo should be that corporations have to abide by British rules of the game; for example, if you trade here and make people redundant then you have to observe British rules. Pay British income tax rates. We should and could be braver about facing down threats to move if we pursue national policies we believe in.

Companies will huff and puff, but in the end they will not leave – or only a tiny handful will. Most big multinationals are very anxious to be seen as good corporate citizens, and as I argued earlier they are very responsive to consumer and public pressure. If they try to supply Britain off-shore then I think we should say to them – just as the Americans say to foreign companies trading in the USA – that it cuts no ice. If you've got a big trading presence here, it's no use trying to pretend you're off-shore. We will treat you as if you were resident in Britain. I agree that states have declining power, but we shouldn't write off our capacity to act.

AG: You seem to reverse yourself a bit here – usually you argue how powerful corporations are in this unfettered new world. They have more leverage here than you say. For example, not only countries, but regions and cities queue up to attract companies to set up plants, in the belief that new employment opportunities will follow. Government cultivation of the corporations isn't a negligible phenomenon. But the best companies are in any case interested in responsible policies and also want a stable sociopolitical environment with an educated labour force. So they will often come to, and stay in, an environment where there are quite strict regulative policies.

Tax havens are a problem. They distort the global economy, allow the rich to avoid taxation and also help authoritarian regimes. So many dire political leaders and oligarchies have bled their countries dry by siphoning off funds abroad. Tax havens, countries with anonymous bank accounts and so forth are deeply implicated in this. A tax haven should be treated a bit like a rogue state; it should be ostracised until it agrees to conform. I don't think it would be as difficult as many people imagine to close down most of the tax loopholes that exist on an international level. We could have a more effective world framework of corporate responsibility and we should push for this in my opinion. The leading countries should get together to develop a global framework of responsible business practice. Governments have sufficient motivation to do so, or should have: it will allow for greater tax revenue.

WH: Yes – I agree completely; the British have a particular responsibility for tax havens because so many are under our jurisdiction.

I'm not sure I have reversed myself over transnational corporations; they are very powerful in the way we both describe, but to an extent that is because we allow them to be powerful. States could be more determined in their dealings with them. I also think it important that there is quite a groundswell of opinion internationally that we need to do something to promote more responsible business practice. Some leading Democrat Senators in 1996 argued that Clinton should include in his campaign for re-election the idea of the Responsible or R Corporation. The idea was that the US government would provide a raft of tax breaks to encourage responsible corporate behaviour – on training, the environment, consultation of employees, to take a long-term view, and so on. The US Treasury and Federal Reserve killed the idea under pressure from Wall Street – and Clinton's own caution. But it was an intriguing proposal. I think it would be possible to build an international coalition to do something similar in this area.

Financial Markets and the Governance of the Global Economy

AG: It is actually happening, at least to some degree. There is much more of a groundswell of opinion, including among political leaders and the international financial community, in favour of greater governance of the global economy. This should include norms of corporate responsibility, but much else besides. Some of the Asian countries have rebounded very effectively, but they have made changes in order to do so. They haven't been most deeply affected by the 1998 crisis – that dubious honour falls to Russia, which is the most worrisome of all the major world states.

WH: I think that the markets are great democratic levellers in giving large numbers of corporations equivalent access to capital as long as they are sufficiently credit-worthy. And it's the same story at a national level. Countries, including less developed ones, can borrow and secure investment if they can again demonstrate that they are a credit-worthy investment. It is a valuable democratisation of finance. But there are immense problems. Money can enter countries more freely, but it can also, as we saw with the Asia crisis, exit more freely as well. The financial markets demand exacting standards of transparency and clarity, not so much when prices are climbing – they are often quite cynical then: who cares about honest accounts if there are fortunes to be made? – but when prices are falling. In general it's hard to attract and keep a lot of inward investment if international investors believe they are being duped by a network of domestic cronies.

And events over the last twelve months have proved again the power and resilience of the financial markets. In the autumn of 1998 the consequences of the Asia panic and the Russian crisis looked very serious; I was rather cautious at the time in saying there was a one-in-four chance of a world recession – many predicted much more difficulty. But once again the system has proved immensely robust. It's rolled with the punch. The markets that sank so low in Asia have come back quite strongly. There are the first signs of South Korea getting back on its two feet via a colossal increase in exports following the devaluation. Malaysia is prospering courtesy of its much decried capital controls.

But the experience underlines the hazards. A lot of pain has been encountered by these economies. They've been set back some years as a minimum, and there was a risk to Western banks that a large part of their capital had to be written off because of the losses they encountered. So the financial markets have been destructive, have risked imperilling a world recession, but now paradoxically they are helping the process of recovery; new investment is coming back.

AG: That surely bears out a point I made earlier, and which you resisted

– markets do display some self-correcting tendencies. But they have manifestly irrational features as well, especially in the instance of global financial markets. Panics and herd phenomena are most pronounced there because of the immediacy of most transactions – negative feedback can develop very quickly. While the markets can recover rapidly too, it doesn't follow that all countries affected by their fluctuations can do so – for some, there will be enduring hardship.

WH: I don't think I have described markets working to produce a self-correcting equilibrium; what you have watched is a wild process of experimentation and overshoot involving some crazy and avoidable risks and economic pain. Heaven knows what will happen next and to whom. I believe Wall Street, for example, is far too high with the Dow Jones over 11,000. Manuel Castells calls the financial markets the Automaton. They are not benign. They have their own ideology. And they are closely linked to the dollar and US financial interests.

I think you can trace the Asia crisis, for example, back to the late 1980s and early 1990s when economic policies in Asia were dictated by the need to meet the agenda of Western capitalism, and American capitalism in particular. The Americans said, if you want Wall Street money then you must peg your currencies to the dollar and open up your financial systems to our banks and financial institutions, and that was all done under this technocratic umbrella term – capital market liberalisation. I argue that the seeds of the financial crisis were sown not so much by crony capitalism but by the impact of this ill-judged capital market liberalisation interacting with the speculative international financial markets who had these pegged exchange rates to speculate against.

The USA wanted price stability and it wanted less exchange-rate risk for its overseas investments, and the dollar pegs seemed a good way of achieving both. But there could not have been a run on these currencies unless they had been pegged to the dollar; and the dollar peg was established in part to meet inflation targets, and in part to ensure that exchange-rate risk was borne by the host country so that the inward investors – mainly the Americans but also the Western Europeans – wouldn't have to insure themselves so heavily against so much risk. So it was more or less inevitable that the whole policy nexus would become unsustainable as soon as the financial deregulation caused asset price booms – bubble economies really – property booms and all the rest of it. Japan's economic collapse and China entering the world trade system did not help the declining growth in exports that were already uncompetitive; balance of payments deficits grew explosively.

So what really took place in the 1990s is a great power play: Asian capitalism versus American capitalism. US capitalism wins, with the Asia crisis of 97/98 actually being the flashpoint and the financial markets working in a way that furthers US interests. That's not the conventional view, and I think it puts an important question mark over globalisation. There is a dimension of globalisation that is about opening up the world to American interests in particular and Western capitalism in general. Unlike you I regard Fukuyama and the *End of History* as missing the point; underneath the glitz there remains the exercise of raw power.

AG: You've got too much of a conspiracy theory there. The USA isn't able to rig things quite as easily or completely as you say. I didn't see much sign that American governments of any complexion have wanted to overturn Asian capitalism, although at one point many thought it held the keys to the future – as you continue to think of Germany now.

Your position is still too close to old leftism. Its too easy to blame the ills of the world economy on US power. It's no good treating world financial markets as though they were part of some gigantic American scheme to control the world economy. Obviously the USA is by far the dominant economic power in the world and most of the big corporations are US-based. Yet the global market-place isn't just an extension of American power. The USA doesn't control financial markets any more than any other country or agency does.

WH: Not everything the old left believed is axiomatically wrong. I don't think Germany holds the key to the future; I think its system is more robust than you think, that's all. As for the USA, your use of the verb 'rig' overstates what I am arguing. As a matter of fact President Clinton did set up in 1993 the Economic Security Council, one of whose aims was expressly to open up ten countries to US trade and finance – and the Asian tigers were the principal target. It wasn't that the USA wanted to 'overturn' Asian capitalism; it wanted to open it up to US interests, much as it has been trying to do in Japan for the past thirty years. And it has been comparatively successful.

And don't underestimate US power now. I thought you were right earlier on to cite the collapse of the Soviet Union as being one of the chief events to change the world; but what it has also done is to leave the USA as unchallenged as the world's hegemonic power. The dollar is the world currency. It allows the USA to finance colossal trade deficits and extraordinary levels of domestic consumption. Whatever the issues, whether intellectual property rights or capital market liberalisation, they have been shaped by US power trying to increase its interests. This has been evident in all kinds of arenas, from not signing the Comprehensive Test Ban Treaty to unilaterally firing off cruise missiles at terrorist targets – and of course in the Sudan they proved not to be terrorist at all.

Equally the financial markets must not be seen just as sources of economic instability, although they are that. They are also transmission mechanisms of very particular economic ideas – like the belief in ultra-free markets – and of very particular economic interests which are overwhelmingly if not exclusively American.

AG: I don't see that, because you haven't specified any alternatives. Economic globalisation today is the medium of economic development, whatever its downsides might be, and I agree they are many. But no country that opts out of the new world economy has any chance of sustaining effective economic prosperity. The countries that have opted out most completely, such as North Korea or Burma, are among the poorest in the world. The Asian economies might have experienced setbacks, but they are nonetheless the most remarkable examples we have of countries that have achieved a breakthrough in economic development. I don't think you could say the Asian crisis was in the American interest. Moreover the crisis period passed because most of the Asian countries reacted in a dynamic way.

WH: I don't for a minute think the Americans designed the crisis; but as a matter of fact they did benefit hugely. The result of the emergency IMF programmes was to cement the commitment to liberalisation, opening up markets to US companies and forcing sales of assets to US investors – as especially in Korea. And the Federal Reserve cut interest rates aggressively. I'm not sure how dynamic the Asian response was in the sense of being driven from the top; it's very hard to avoid a sharp increase in your exports if your currency has halved, and I'm sure that all of them would have settled for no crisis in the first place!

You must not be naïve about the exercise of power, or the determined way the US Treasury and the IMF worked together to help US interests. And the reason I have not specified alternatives is that our conversation has not got that far yet; I think we share quite a lot of common ground over the need for more supranational and European level government and regulation – and our final chapter will address that.

AG: But I don't see why it's only the USA that gains. There isn't a zero sum game involved. When NAFTA was set up, many thought that the US economy would simply swamp the Mexican one. But, so far at least, the Mexican economy seems to be doing pretty well out of the deal. It doesn't make much sense to treat financial markets as the advance guard of American interests. After all, the financial markets are made up of many investors, looking for investment opportunities and assessing these against risk. They are also plainly subject to irrational fluctuations and panics. But there seems to me much more general will to regulate financial markets than there used to be. Neo-liberalism is pretty much dead.

WH: I don't recall any significant body of opinion saying that Mexico would be swamped by the USA when NAFTA was set up. The argument rather was that too many US companies would migrate to Mexico and take low-wage jobs with them, and that would be a problem in some of the older manufacturing areas in the USA – as it has been. As for the financial markets and Mexico, the country nearly went bust in 1981 and again in 1995, costing it years of lost growth. Dollarisation has come to Mexico with a vengeance, and it has become a regional economy of the USA without any accompanying rights.

As for the death of neo-liberalism, I'd like to believe that, but I'm not sure it's true. At the time of the crisis I thought neo-liberalism might be dead. There they were, the free market, University of Chicago, Nobel Prize-winning economists, who had designed complex computer-based, risk-assessment models, but whose basic economic assumption was that markets tend to clear and that prices tend to converge around some normal distribution. They were wrong, and hadn't factored the scale of price swings we saw during the Asia crisis into their models. I thought that would shock people into moving away from neo-liberalism but it has not. It may be true that in the intellectual economic and social science circles with which you and I are familiar, neo-liberalism is pretty much stone dead. But it lives on in politics. For example, the document that Schröder and Blair presented in June 1999 as their model of updated social democracy was an astonishing statement of neo-liberal principles. It continues to have a naïve trust in markets. It explicitly argues that the job of politicians is not to change, reform, or manage these markets; rather it is to attempt to improve the empowerment of our citizens to do better in these markets. Thus we can marry social justice and economic efficiency.

Both Schröder and Blair believe the neo-liberal doctrine that markets are essentially benevolent, a wealth-creating process that generates efficiencies. The argument is settled. You may think that it is dead, but it lives on in the mind of some of our leading politicians.

AG: I suppose this depends upon how one understands 'neo-liberalism'. The basic idea of neo-liberalism, as I would understand it, is that markets are in almost all respects superior to government. Markets not only provide for a rational allocation of products and labour power, they foreclose the need for any kind of programme of social justice. You don't need, and can't have, policies of social justice when – if the market is given full and free play – everything is bought and sold at its true value. The idea of minimal government flows directly from this. Government is needed only to provide a legal framework for contracts and for defence, law and order. As developed in Thatcherism and Reaganism, neo-liberalism also involved strongly conservative influences. Traditional symbols, the traditional family and the traditional nation were to be preserved.

Taken as this package, I don't think many people are neo-liberals any more. I don't just mean intellectuals. The voters aren't either. Most don't want to be told that 'you are on your own' in the face of the insecurities of the global market-place. Even some of the biggest fans of a neo-liberal perspective have now abandoned it. The major world organisations, for example, like the World Bank, are mostly talking of the need for better and more transparent government. They are also emphasising much more strongly than before the crucial importance of tackling world inequalities. I would certainly see this as a general shift in political consciousness. It goes along with the rise of third-way politics. No one much thinks that one can go back to top-down, bureaucratic government. If neo-liberalism is also in decline, we have to look for something different – a third way.

Reforming the Global Economy

AG: Even though one of its themes was globalisation, I was astounded by the global response to my book *The Third Way*. Third-way politics is being discussed in most countries, and all sorts of politicians – some of doubtful provenance – are laying claim to being 'third-way politicians'.

The idea of the third way has also sparked a barrage of critical responses from the more traditional left. To some extent our discussion is following the same divide – between the more traditional leftist views and the modernising left.

The values of the left – solidarity, social justice, protection of the vulnerable and the belief that active government is needed to achieve these – are still crucially important in the contemporary world. But the old strategies and institutions, including existing structures of the welfare state, are no longer able to deliver upon them. Most of our institutions need modernisation, where this means reforming them in response to the changes we've been analysing.

Third-way politics for me is about the rebirth of social democracy. It is definitively a left-of-centre project, but one that is unafraid to shed old leftist dogmas and prejudices. It is quite mistaken to identify third-way politics, as you did earlier, with letting markets rip. We must take globalisation seriously, which means responding above the level of the nation as well as domestically. It is both possible and necessary to achieve more effective global economic governance, greater world equality and better ecological regulation.

WH: I think you're being a bit naughty here. You know very well that I am not 'old left', but if the tag sticks that will delegitimise some of my arguments and legitimise yours. You have made some sweeping judgements about the reach of the knowledge economy, the systemic crisis of contemporary Germany and the improbability of the Americans directing globalisation that I have disputed and that I think are not supported by the facts. And there have been a number of occasions – such as your argument that poverty is no longer a condition and that any condemnation of inequality should be leavened by recognition that in America at least there is an inclusive attitude towards minorities – where I have felt that your argument is full of insight, but incomplete. And I feel very strongly that you can't have it both ways; the injustices you want to correct are not independent of the capitalism you admire – they result directly from its operation. Sometimes you have found yourself wanting both more regulation and more capitalism.

But to say this does not mean that I am 'old left' or want 'old left' responses. I have argued that capitalism is creative as well as destructive; globalisation presents new risks as well as new opportunities; capitalism's vitality can be turned to collective advantage; the effective response can only be global. When you get to specific points and examples, you find yourself in agreement with positions that you tend to dismiss as traditional in general – but which remain true.

AG: There are two general questions which we need to answer. Is globalisation, in sum, the same as Americanisation? More broadly put, is globalisation a set of processes dominated by Western countries to their own advantage? I would answer a qualified 'no' to each of these questions.

Globalisation, as we discussed before, refers to a complex of changes rather than a single one. No single country, or group of countries, controls any one of them. Economic globalisation, of course, has been and is shaped by US foreign and domestic policy. The health of the global economy at any one time is strongly influenced by the strength or otherwise of the US economy. During the Cold War period successive US governments were propagating a distinct 'way of life' around the world in a self-conscious struggle with communism. American economic power was backed by a global network of military alliances, by numerous forms of interventionism and by the propagating of 'proxy wars' in various places. Old habits die hard, but the USA doesn't have these strategic interests any more. The battle within the USA these days is between those who favour free trade and a global role for the country and those (a mixture of old left and republican right) who favour protectionism and disengagement.

WH: I would redefine that battle – you equate the old Democrat left and the Republican right in true third-way style but they are not equivalent. It is a battle between Americans who want to sustain a liberal international order in all its guises, for which there is a substantial majority on the left notwithstanding some protectionist tendencies; and others who want to assert US sovereignty, self-interest and long-standing isolationist proclivities – a set of propositions to which the Republican Party, with some honourable exceptions, is now passionately committed. You have just got the numbers wrong. Fifty-two Republican Senators voted against the Comprehensive Test Ban Treaty in October 1999 – and only four for it. Every Democrat Senator voted for it. It's the same story on land-mines, the International Criminal Court, contributions to the UN, reform of the IMF and committing to international agreements on the environment. American conservatives, with their allies in Fortune 500 and Wall Street, are against all these things. The liberals are broadly for them.

My point throughout this conversation is that liberal America has its back against the wall; that the conservatives are in the ascendant; and that they have been ruthless in pursuit of their interests, compromising the Clinton Presidency and shaping globalisation in US interests.

AG: The USA and the West are easily the dominant powers in 'globalisation from above' – financial markets, trade and technological innovation. But there are also fundamental processes of 'globalisation from below' which to some extent counterbalance the other set of forces. One of the biggest changes over the past thirty or so years has been a vast growth of non-governmental organisations, interest groups and pressure groups operating on a world-wide level. There used to be only a few hundred of these; now there are over 10,000. They act as something of a check upon the activities both of governments and business corporations. Save in a few closed societies, it is almost impossible nowadays to carry on dubious activities in any one corner of the world without their becoming widely known. Consumers can also play a part in these movements and pressures. In the Brent Spar episode, it wasn't only the activities of Greenpeace that forced Shell to change its position and policies, but consumer power too. People in a number of key countries stopped buying Shell products.

WH: Good point, and I broadly accept it – as we discussed earlier, Heineken, Unilever and Monsanto are having to adjust their corporate strategies to consumer power. The difficulty is that while consumers clearly have the power to buy or not to buy, it is pretty crude – and only arises when there is a well-publicised flashpoint. Consumers do not have a systematic voice through the democratic process or in the ways companies take decisions, although as we have discussed we would both like to see a much more robust web of national and international regulation to enforce responsible corporate behaviour.

Consumer power is also easily manipulable, and sometimes the manipulators are unaccountable and too free and easy with facts. Greenpeace has admitted that in the Brent Spar case their facts were wrong and they misled public opinion and a gullible media; and there is now a consensus that Shell's original plan for the rig was broadly reasonable. And perhaps most important of all, I am not sure that sufficient consumers are internationalist in their thinking and represent the basis for the global civil society you seek; look how in the recent beef war between Britain and France consumers very quickly became jingoistic. The NGOs are certainly formidable and sometimes effective, but again I am not sure you can generalise from them to draw the optimistic conclusions that you do.

AG: The structure of power in the main international organisations is plainly imbalanced in favour of the developed societies. Countries like India or Brazil are not represented on the UN Security Council. The other organisations, G7 of course, plus the World Bank and the IMF are also more or less wholly dominated by the affluent countries. The less developed states should be brought much more fully into the picture as they are to some degree in the new GX. India's decision to test nuclear weapons was prompted largely by its feeling of being overlooked in the world community. The Indians looked to the example of China, which has nuclear weapons, and which gets courted much more by the Western nations than India does.

WH: Well, this is an argument we will be developing more in the final chapter, but I wonder why do you think reform has been so difficult? If we are to win support for the changes we both want to see, I think there has to be recognition that until the relationship between the USA and China can be rebased the prospect of any substantive reform is minimal. The Chinese remain a communist power run by a military oligarchy, and they give the USA the pretext to stand by its unilateralist position. Idealistic internationalism has to be backed by a cool appreciation of where power lies and the balance of national interests, and I think this is where your arguments are sometimes weak.

AG: One of the most difficult issues, of course, at least on the face of things, is the environmental one. The poorer countries don't think it is just that they should accept limitations on their own economic development because of environmental problems caused primarily by industrial development in the West. However, I believe that with a certain amount of goodwill, and of rational understanding from both sides, these issues could be resolved. Most environmental pollution may have been caused by Western industrial development, but it now affects everyone. The less developed countries are threatened more by global warming than are the developed ones, which are nearly all in the more temperate zones. All countries have a material interest in collaborating to help resolve or limit these problems. In addition, new technologies offer the chance of skipping some of the phases of industrial development which an emerging country used to have to go through. Manufacture can in principle be both much more efficient and cleaner when dominated by information technology. New forms of waste management are also very promising. According to new ecological thinking 'waste' should become a redundant concept. Everything that goes into production can be recycled, quite often adding to profitability rather than detracting from it.

WH: Personally I think the environmental arguments will only be advanced in the face of real perceived problems – not the possibility that problems might emerge at some unspecified time in the future. I think the emerging water shortage in parts of Africa, the Middle East and Asia may bring a collaborative response, and we can see how the argument is developing over the food chain – with Monsanto now agreeing that it will not produce the so-called 'terminator gene'. I also think transport, both nationally and internationally, is a major environmental challenge.

But the more long-run problems, like global warming, seem to me very difficult to get agreement on, and rightly; after all, the case is not proven yet as a watertight proposition although the facts are pretty suggestive. If we had believed the Club of Rome prognostications thirty years ago, we would not have allowed the degree of economic growth of which you boasted earlier on. One of the green movement's favourite arguments is that environmentalism is win/win: profitable and environmentally friendly. I am much more cautious over the proposition. If recycling waste was so profitable, capitalism would have moved in; that it hasn't suggests that there is a lot of wishful thinking on the matter. I am very sympathetic to green arguments, but I am not sure that building international coalitions in this territory is ever going to be that easy.

AG: Shall we move to a summing up? There are some basic points on which it seems to me we disagree. I probably have a somewhat more favourable view of markets than you do. I tend to think that the USA, and the large corporations, are more hemmed in, in terms of their options, than you would accept. I look on American society in a more favourable light, and would tend to be more critical of Continental-style social democracy than you would. I would say Europe can learn at least as much from the USA as would be true in reverse. Perhaps because of the difference in our backgrounds, I see globalisation less in economic terms than you do. To me, globalisation is social, political and cultural just as much as it is economic. I see a larger break with the past than you do.

Perhaps these differences also express a slightly different political stance. For me at any rate post-1989 it is no longer sensible to say that all major political problems can be crammed into a left–right dimension. I certainly don't think the division between left and right goes away. But there are many issues, including how to respond to globalisation and the knowledge economy, which only to some extent can be clarified by following a left–right opposition. 'Radicalism' now means breaking with that division, and the dogmas associated with it, as often as it means sticking with it. To accept this doesn't imply that in politics we shouldn't still have a passion for social justice. It does mean that we have to think in an innovative way if we are to sustain that value, given all the changes we've been discussing.

WH: I think the third way is a very interesting political proposition; I made a film proposing the third way for BBC2 in 1989, and for a period it was the working title for my book *The State We're In*. So don't be so quick to label me as a believer in traditional left–right arguments when so much of my intellectual and political life has been spent trying to help establish a new paradigm for the left.

But I would trace some of our differences to my gut feeling that despite your dislike of neo-liberalism I think you have made too many concessions to its basic precepts. I am not sure what left dogmas you think remain or to which I subscribe; the left has abandoned any pretence that the economy can be planned and publicly owned. The 'prejudices' and 'dogmas' that I share with other social democrats are that all human beings are morally equal; that we have an equal entitlement to self-determination; that all life-chances should be as equal as possible; and that social justice is a condition of liberty. I believe that capitalism does not exist independently of society, and that it is proper for the democratic will to be asserted over business and private power. And I repeat the point I made earlier: markets do not regulate themselves and best outcomes do not happen spontaneously.

So yes, I am more guarded about the US economic and social model and less willing to join the fashionable chorus against Europe. I am all for radicalism in modernising our position, but it should not be an intellectual nihilism that rejects all previous social democratic insights and truths. And I think we have to be very clear-eyed about what the political coalition will be that will support the aims we have in mind. But I would also stress what we have in common. We take globalisation seriously and think it marks a decisive moment of change; we see opportunities as well as risks in the new environment; we look for new forms of global governance; we are both disturbed by growing inequality; we want to encourage emergent forms of countervailing power to the new global corporations; we are uneasy about the operation of the global financial markets. We have differences; but there is also a lot of common ground – I would say basically we are on the same side.

AG: We are, and I hope the reader will have profited from our dialogue as much as I have. I am very strongly pro-European. The EU is the most important and promising experiment in transnational governance now going on. On an economic level, of course, there is no single European model, nor should there be. I'm less of an admirer of old-style corporatism than you seem to be, but we absolutely must try to preserve the best aspects of social protection developed in European welfare states. We will only be able to do so through social and economic reform, not by sticking with existing structures.

WH: Who said I was a defender of old-style corporatism and every aspect of the European welfare state? I certainly want to defend the principles of stakeholding and social insurance, but I can see the case for modernisation too. We could go on: I would emphasise your last point. We have differences, but we are on the same side.

MANUEL CASTELLS

Information Technology and Global Capitalism

The Global, Networked Economy

In the last two decades of the twentieth century, a new economy has emerged around the world. It is certainly capitalist. Indeed, for the first time in history, the whole planet is either capitalist or highly dependent on capitalist economic processes. But it is a new brand of capitalism, characterised by three fundamental features.

Productivity and competitiveness are, by and large, a function of knowledge generation and information processing; firms and territories are organised in networks of production, management and distribution; the core economic activities are global – that is, they have the capacity to work as a unit in real time, or chosen time, on a planetary scale. Not everything is global. In fact, most employment is local or regional. Yet the strategically crucial activities and economic factors are networked around a globalised system of inputs and outputs, which conditions the fate of all economies and most jobs. By 'strategically crucial economic activities' I mean, primarily, capital markets, science and technology, information, specialised labour, affluent consumer markets, multi-national networks of production and management in manufacturing (including industrialised farming), and advanced services, media communication (including the internet), entertainment (including sports) and – not to forget – global crime.

New information and communication technologies, based on micro-electronics, telecommunications and network-oriented computer soft-ware, have provided the infrastructure for this new economy. While the internationalisation of economic activities is certainly not new, this technological infrastructure is. Network-oriented information and communication technologies allow for unprecedented speed and complexity in the management of the economy. Thus, economic transactions and production are able to increase their size dramatically without hampering their connectivity. They can operate in real time or in chosen time, and, furthermore, the flexibility of the new technological system makes it possible for this new economy to select its components around the planet, in an endlessly variable geometry of value searching. This implies bypassing economically valueless or devalued territories and people. So, the global economy is at the same time extraordinarily inclusive of what is valued in the networks of business interaction, and highly exclusive of what has little or no interest in a given time and space. There is no value judgement in the electronic networks, except for assessing value – which is increasingly measured in terms of prospective capital growth rather than profit rates. Indeed, short-term profit-making is not the correct indicator of value any longer, as shown by the high value of stocks for money-losing internet firms.

The versatility and dynamism of this networked, global/informational capitalism, powered by the most extraordinary technological revolution in history, seems to enable its expansion without limits, and without challenges. Or does it?

The Automaton: Global Financial Markets

If globalisation is widely acknowledged as a fundamental feature of our time, it is essentially because of the emergence of global financial markets. Indeed, to say that capital is globalised (or, more accurately, globally interconnected) in real time is not an incidental remark in a capitalist economy. While the process of financial globalisation has long historical roots and has gradually expanded over the past quarter of a century, its acceleration can be traced back to the late 1980s. To select, rather arbitrarily, a symbolic event, I would suggest the beginning of this new era was signalled by the City of London's 'Big Bang' on 27 October 1987, when the deregulation of capital and securities markets occurred. This is to emphasise that deregulation and liberalisation of financial trading were the crucial factors in spurring globalisation, allowing capital mobility between different segments of the financial industry and around the world, with fewer restrictions and a global view of investment opportunities. New technology was crucial both in allowing quasi-instantaneous trading world-wide, and in managing the new complexity brought in by deregulation and financial ingenuity.

Mutual funds, a household appliance these days in the homes of the rich world, were the direct result of new rules and new financial models, powered by computer technology. As another example, take derivatives, that catch-all word for all manner of new, synthetic securities.

Derivatives may combine underlying values of stocks, bonds, options, commodities, currencies or, for that matter, any other support of any monetary value, actual or potential. By recombining value across space (markets around the world) and through time (futures markets), derivatives extraordinarily increase the possibility of trading on value. In so doing, they create market capitalisation value out of market capitalisation value. How much? Some estimates put the market value of derivatives traded in 1997 at US $360 trillion. If this figure would stand scrutiny, it would represent something in the vicinity of twelve times the size of global gross domestic product (GDP) – not a very useful calculation, but a powerful image.

This extraordinary growth of tradable financial value is possible only because of the use of advanced mathematical models, made operational by powerful computer systems, fed with and constantly adjusted by information transmitted electronically from all over the world. Domestic deregulation, liberalisation of trans-border transactions, financial wizardry and new information technology have succeeded in mobilising potential sources for investment from everywhere to everywhere, and from whatever to whenever. In 1995, in the USA, investment by mutual funds, pension funds, and institutional investors in general, accounted for US $20 trillion, a tenfold increase since 1980 – and the trend has accelerated since then. In 1997, for the first time, a higher proportion of US households' assets were in securities than in real estate. As a result, the ratio between stock market capitalisation and GDP in the USA reached a record 140 per cent in 1998. Cross-border transactions of bonds and equities between 1970 and 1996, measured as a percentage of domestic GDP, increased by a factor of about 54 for the USA, of 55 for Japan, and of almost 60 for Germany. This financial investment frenzy went global, seizing in particular the opportunities offered by two different kinds of situation. One lay in the rapidly growing economies of the Asian Pacific, where investment appreciation could be anticipated. The other was generated by bargain prices in newly industrialising countries, particularly in Latin America (Argentina, Chile, Mexico, Peru, Brazil), but also in Russia in the mid-1990s, in spite of the economic uncertainty there. In the USA overseas investment by pension funds increased from less than 1 per cent of their assets in 1980 to 17 per cent in 1997. Between 1983 and 1995, calculating in average annual rates of change, while the world's real GDP grew by 3.4 per cent, and world exports volume increased by 6 per cent, total issues of loans and bonds grew by 8.2 per cent, and total stocks of outstanding bonds and loans increased by 9.8 per cent. As a result, in 1998, stocks of outstanding loans and bonds amounted to about $7.6 trillion, or about 5.5 times the GDP of the UK in 1998. Global investors took advantage of loose financial and banking regulations in the emerging markets, which enabled speculative manoeuvres. Investors also counted on the expected support from governments in case of financial crisis. The factors that are blamed for the 1997–8 financial crisis in emerging markets (government interference, lack of financial transparency) are thus among the key elements that attracted global financial investment in the first place. Under these conditions, acquisitions of overseas stocks by investors from industrialised countries increased by a factor of 197 between 1970 and 1997, inextricably linking financial markets around the planet. Currency markets exploded, becoming a critical element in the inability of any government to control economic policy, given that the value of the national currency, and thus interest rates, became largely determined by financial markets. In 1998, on average, global currency markets exchanged every day the equivalent of US $1.5 trillion – that is, about 110 per cent of the UK's GDP in 1998. This represented an increase in the value of global currency trading by a factor of 8 between 1986 and 1998. Financial markets have become interconnected in several ways. First of all, online transactions and computer-based information systems allow for very fast movements of capital between financial products, currencies and countries – often in a matter of seconds. Second, new financial products have appeared, mixing valuables from various countries to be traded in other countries. When one component of these products is affected by a sudden change in value in one market, it affects the product as a whole, in a range of markets. This was particularly the case of derivatives in Asian financial markets in 1997. Third, speculative investors looking for high financial rewards move swiftly from one market to another, trying to anticipate price movements of different products in different currencies, using forecasting models.

An important source of these speculative movements is hedge funds, another catch-all term covering non-conventional investment funds which don't rely on bonds, equities and money market funds. Hedge funds are, by and large, unregulated, and have extraordinarily increased in number and capital power in the 1990s: between 1990 and 1997 hedge funds assets increased by a factor of 12, and now there are about

3,500 hedge funds managing US $200 billion. To this sum must be added all they can borrow on the basis of these funds. Hedge funds manage the money of large investors, including banks, pension funds and institutional investors who circumvent their regulatory limits by the intermediation of hedge funds. To a large extent, we all are the speculators – willingly (through our pension funds), or unwillingly (through placing our savings, like most small investors, in mutual funds or retirement accounts). Besides hedge funds, investors of all kinds (large and small), equipped with networked computers, fed with information in real time, buy, sell and redistribute financial tradables of all kinds, of all origins and in most markets, inducing turbulences and reacting to them. A fourth major factor of interconnection must be emphasised: information-providers and opinion-makers. Market valuation firms, such as Standard&Poor or Moody's, business financial gurus and leading central bankers may induce market appreciation or depreciation for securities, currencies, or even whole national economies, by upgrading/downgrading their value (and thus the values of companies in the rated countries, according to the 'sovereign ceiling doctrine' which provides a benchmark for lenders, to give a range of key indicators of national financial distress). While it is debatable how objective these evaluations are, it is not the case that they are proved statements. If we add the impact of political events and of statements by influential decision-makers on financial markets, we can conclude that largely uncontrolled information turbulences are as important as supply and demand in setting prices and trends in global financial markets. Finally, international financial institutions, and particularly the International Monetary Fund (IMF), intervene as lenders of last resort in economies in crisis. The IMF's criteria, which are, by and large, uniformly applied as a standard recipe in its fundamentals, tend to unify the rules of the game in financial markets around the world. This is precisely the precondition for capital flows to move unfettered, thus further integrating global finance. The outcome of this process of financial globalisation may be that we have created an Automaton, at the core of our economies, decisively conditioning our lives. Humankind's nightmare of seeing our machines taking control of our world seems on the edge of becoming reality – not in the form of robots that eliminate jobs or government computers that police our lives, but as an electronically based system of financial transactions. The system overwhelms controls and regulations put in place by governments, international institutions and private financial firms, let alone the considerations of individual investors, consumers and citizens. Since income from all sources finds its way into financial markets, where the highest capital growth takes place, this network of electronic transactions, enacting global/local capital flows, has established itself as a collective capitalist. Its logic is not controlled by any individual capitalist or corporation – nor, for that matter, by any public institution. While capitalists, and capitalist managers, still exist, they are all determined by the Automaton. And this Automaton is not the market. It does not follow market rules – at least, not the kind of rules based on supply and demand which we learned from our economics primers. Movements in financial markets are induced by a mixture of market rules, business and political strategies, crowd psychology, rational expectations, irrational behaviour, speculative manoeuvres and information turbulences of all sorts. All these elements are recombined in increasingly unpredictable patterns whose frantic modelling occupies would-be Nobel Prize recipients and addicted financial gamblers (sometimes embodied in the same persons). Yet, how automatic is this Automaton? After all, new financial regulations were set in the New York Stock Exchange after automated trading by computer programs amplified market trends which helped to induce the crash of October 1987. There are few instances of fully automated transactions without the intervention of human decision-makers, apart from routine operations. Anthropologist Caitlin Zaloom, observing trading in the pits of the Chicago Board of Trade in 1998, reported that personal interaction, business savvy and company intermediation were alive and well in a critically important market. Technology backs up and implements human decision, but traditional securities trading does not disappear and regulations remain in place. However, there are major changes under way. Eurex, an electronic exchange system, controls now the major German bond futures market. MATIF, the French futures exchange, moved entirely to an electronic system in 1998, and London's LIFFE was planning to do so too.

In September 1998, New York's Cantor Fitzgerald Brokerage, the world's largest bond broker, started Cantor Exchange, an electronic exchange to trade future contracts on US Treasury bonds. The major change in stocks trading is related to the development of electronic communication networks (ECN) which grew as an offshoot of Nasdaq transactions. Nasdaq, a non-profit association like the New York Stock Exchange (however ironical that may sound), does not have a central trading floor. It is an electronic market-place built on computer networks. New rules designed to encourage electronic trading allowed ECNs to post orders from their clients on Nasdaq's system and receive a commission when the order was filled. Lured by potential profits, a number of firms, including some large Wall Street brokers, set up private electronic trading networks, the largest being Instinet, a subsidiary of Reuters Group plc. These networks are not subjected to the same strict regulations that hem in Nasdaq or the New York Stock Exchange. For instance, investors may trade anonymously. This could prompt the established trading markets to do the same, even further obscuring stocks transactions. Indeed, in 1999, the New York Stock Exchange was studying how it might set up its own electronic trading system, and with Nasdaq was exploring the possibility of their association, which would dramatically enhance the role of electronic trading in the future. Changes in financial trading have been accelerated by internet brokers since 1997. Day-traders, most of them individual investors, often investing in internet-related stocks, started the trend. In 1999, in the USA, electronic trading was used in about 25 per cent of transactions by individual investors. Major brokerage companies entered this trade, led by Charles Schwab & Co (with 27 per cent of the online trading market). In 1998, 14 per cent of all equity trades in the USA were online, a 50 per cent increase on 1997. The online brokerage industry in 1998, in the USA, doubled accounts to 7.3 million and doubled customers' assets to US $420 billion. It is important to retain this last figure, because US $420 billion represented the equivalent of 35 per cent of total value of German stocks in December 1998. Given the foreseeable rate of growth for online investment and the current value of its assets, this is clearly a formidable source of capital to reckon with in the near future.

What are the implications? Why does the technology of investment matter? First, it considerably reduces transaction costs associated with active trading (online trading commissions declined by 50 per cent in 1997 in the USA), thus attracting a much broader pull of individual investors. Second, it opens up investment opportunities to millions of individual investors, assessing value and opportunities on the basis of computerised information. It follows, on the one hand, that information turbulences, amplified by massive direct inputs from individual investors, may increase their role in affecting movements of capital. On the other hand, volatility of investments increases, since investment patterns become highly decentralised, investors go in and out of securities, and market trends trigger quasi-immediate reactions. More-over, the decline of central market-places, and the looser regulation of electronic trading, make it much more difficult to track capital movements. The growing secrecy of investment attracts large pools of capital but it also leaves small investors in the dark. There follows greater decentralisation of investment and broader participation of individual investors in stocks trading, but decreasing levels of information for them, because of the secrecy and anonymity allowed by looser regulations. These trends add uncertainty, on both grounds, to the overall investment pattern: more people invest, and more do so without having key information on their computer screens. The net result is greater complexity and greater volatility. Most electronic trading is taking place in the USA, for the time being, but it is rapidly expanding in Europe. Moreover, given the interdependence between US financial markets and global financial markets, movements in US markets (for instance, the irresistible ascension – and fall? – of internet stocks) deeply affect financial markets around the world. In sum, globally interdependent financial markets are not on automatic pilot – in fact, we have witnessed the opposite trend, as millions of investors, besides the competitive efforts of large institutional investors, and the guerrilla tactics of hedge funds and other speculative investors, jam market circuits with conflicting signals. This complex network of transactions, resulting from interactive, contradictory bets on market values in different space and time frames, is, as a whole, beyond the control of governments, financial institutions and specific business groups – regardless of their size and wealth.

Random movements rather than economic calculations seem to be the primary forces shaping market trends. So the random Automaton thrives, simultaneously inducing growth and wealth, and triggering disinvestment and crisis. However, financial markets are only one element, albeit extremely important, of the dynamics of global capitalism, which are reshaping our world.

Productivity, Technology and the New Economy

Volatility and the interdependence in global financial markets are at the roots of the crisis of emerging markets in 1997–9 – a crisis that, coming after the Mexican crisis of 1994, rocked the Asian Pacific (1997), Russia (1998) and Brazil (1999), and sent shock waves around the world. The global economy absorbed the shock. Most foreign banks that were in trouble because of their investments in emerging markets were bailed out by IMF-led policies. Capital flows simply reversed course, heading towards European and US markets: for instance, in 1996 private capital flows into Malaysia, the Philippines, South Korea, Thailand and

Indonesia amounted to US $93 billion. In 1997 there was an outflow of US $12 billion, and in 1998 an additional outflow of US $9 billion. This swing of US $114 billion in capital flows devalued the currencies of these countries and induced a severe recession in most of the Asian Pacific economies, as I have analysed elsewhere – yet capital investment world-wide has continued to grow, and stock market values in the USA reached a historic height in 1999, going over the 11,000 level on the Dow Jones index. European stock markets were also performing at a high level in mid-1999. The flexibility of the new techno-economic system allows for this geographic redistribution of investment so that, while economies suffer, most global investments do not. Some global investors may in fact benefit from devaluations, if they time their movements well, or simply get lucky. When crisis strikes in emerging markets or in advanced but shaky economies such as Japan, investment flows find new opportunities in the advanced Western economies. In 1997–8, while stock markets in Asian economies, including Japan, and in Russia and in Brazil were substantially devalued, the US stock market rose by 31 per cent and the German stock market by 54 per cent. While European Union economies performed well during the emerging markets' crisis, helped by the smooth transition to the euro, it is the performance of the US economy which keeps growth and dynamic stability in the global economy, by absorbing investment and exports from around the world. In a showcase of the bright side of the new economy, led by domestic consumption and stocks revaluation, the USA was able in 1998 to grow at 3.9 per cent (including a stunning 6.1 per cent in the last quarter of 1998), with low inflation, quasi-full employment (with the unemployment rate at 4.2 per cent in August 1999) and a surplus in the federal budget, albeit at the price of a significant increase in the current account trade deficit. This is why the rest of the world did not sink into global recession. Indeed, in 1999, most Asian economies were bouncing back, helped by their renewed exports competitiveness, and the return of foreign investment attracted by bargain prices of stocks and assets.

At the heart of the resilience of the global economy we find the performance of the US economy, which induces a virtuous circle by attracting foreign investment, both directly and in stocks acquisition.

European companies, which spent US $58.5 billion in acquiring US companies in 1996, and another US $48.4 billion in 1997, stepped up their cross-Atlantic investment, with a spending spree of US $280 billion in 1998 and the first two months of 1999, including the acquisition of Chrysler by Daimler-Benz, of Amoco by British

Petroleum, and of Airtouch Communications by Vodafone. Since American companies did their own business in Europe (Ford, for instance, bought Volvo's automobile business), a renewed Atlantic connection seems to have established itself as the axis of the global economy, as Lester Thurow predicted. However, the new system is somewhat more complex. On the one hand, geographical metaphors cannot account for the complexity and speed of global flows of capital and trade.

Networks, rather than countries or economic areas, are the true architectures of the new global economy. In this way recession in Asia offered tremendous investment opportunities to European and US companies. And they seized them, from Thailand, to South Korea, to Japan. The Japanese financial market is finally being cracked through the acquisition of, or participation in, Japanese banks and savings associations by US and European financial firms. This may represent global access to a gigantic and largely untapped savings market, in hundreds of billions of dollars – enough to refuel capital investment in the global economy, as long as there are investment opportunities. But are there? The answer lies, on the one hand, in how we assess the new US economy; on the other hand, it depends on the ability of the European Union to enter this 'new economy' on its own terms, preserving its social model. Without this, Europeans will simply resist the move. What is the secret behind the performance of the US economy? And what is this 'new economy'? How can it grow, as it did in 1998, adding 225,000 jobs per month (and 310,000 in July 1999), and increasing hourly wages by about an annual 4 per cent, with 1.6 per cent inflation? The usual suspect, in these cases, is productivity. With the exception of a few, if notorious, economists, such as Paul Krugman, many of us thought that new information technology and major organisational changes (networking in the first place) were about to induce a surge in productivity growth. I argued in my book *The Rise of the Network Society* (2000 [1996]) that the reasons we could not observe substantial productivity increases were twofold: the absolute inadequacy of our statistical categories to measure the new informational/global economy; and the necessary time-lag between technological innovation and organisational change for productivity potential to be realised. The first obstacle continues to exist, and it is a major hindrance in understanding our new world. But even with statistical measures that underestimate actual productivity growth, productivity is finally showing up, not only in the high-tech and advanced business services sectors, but in the US economy as a whole. In testimony before the US

Congress, on 23 February 1999, Alan Greenspan reported that productivity growth in non-financial corporations averaged 2.2 per cent in this business cycle, compared with 1.5 per cent in the late 1980s. Overall, productivity growth averaged 2 per cent in 1995–8, twice the growth rate between 1973 and 1995. Greenspan traced the origins of productivity increases back to 1993, when capital investment, particularly in information technology equipment, rose sharply.

Business spending on new equipment in the USA increased 60 per cent in 1994–8. Growth is led by information-based industries (such as software, communication and consulting) which add well-paying jobs at an annual rate of 3.7 per cent, twice the rate of the rest of the economy. These trends were not slowing down in 1998/9: overall work productivity growth in the fourth quarter of 1998 reached 4.6 per cent, the fastest growth in six years, and GDP growth for 1999 was projected to be around 3 per cent. In September 1999, Macroeconomic Advisers, a leading US economic forecasting firm, issued a report predicting productivity growth at annual rates around 2.3 per cent, as long as the investment boom in information technology would continue. Indeed, information technology is at the heart of this new economy in several ways. It provides the technology for business restructuring around networks. It reduces the prices of both equipment and consumer goods, from computers and VCRs to a whole range of household appliances. It is creating a whole new generation of products and processes by shifting from Operating System technologies, centred around the PC, to information-sharing technologies, decentred around electronic networks powered by co-operative servers. It is creating jobs and generating earnings at an unprecedented pace. And it is leading the growth of the stock market, as internet stocks skyrocket. This is partly because internet technology allows small investors to trade electronically following their own strategies, thus pushing up stock prices regardless of rational expectations based on previous trends. There is widespread belief that internet stocks will crash one day, and they may have crashed by the time you read this. But since investors continue to believe that it will be tomorrow, not today, they keep delaying the day of reckoning. Even when or if that day does happen, the huge amount of capital attracted to the internet industry in the meantime will have modified the realm of information technology and of business as a whole. Market capitalisation of internet companies, most of which still do not make profits, has reached extraordinary levels, as compared with giant companies of the industrial age. In January 1999, America OnLine, employing 10,000 people, was valued at US $66.4 billion. This can be contrasted to General Motors, employing 600,000 workers, whose market value was US $52.4 billion. In another telling example, Yahoo!, employing 673 people, was worth US $33.9 billion. Pure speculation? Unreal economy? In fact this is anticipation of trends. The S&P top five growth stocks for 1995–9 are Dell Computer (9,402 per cent increase in five years), Cisco Systems (2,356 per cent), Sun Microsystems (2,304 per cent), Qualcomm (1,646 per cent), and Charles Schwab (1,634 per cent), all firms making their business in/around the internet. Internet stock frenzy is in fact an indicator of the decisive shift of the economy to the new sources of value and growth.

Is Info-Growth Sustainable?

There is no scarcity of paradoxes in this brave new economic world. In early 1999, at the time the network economy was spurring growth in the USA, with stock markets' values rising on both sides of the Atlantic, there were widespread fears of a world-wide deflation that would crush the high hopes of information-based global capitalism at the very moment of take-off. According to calculations by *The Economist*, in 1998 producer prices fell in fourteen out of fifteen rich economies monitored. In February 1999, consumer price inflation was dropping to an average of 1 per cent in the rich economies. In the euro zone, in 1998, consumer prices increased by 0.8 per cent: French annual inflation rate was 0.3 per cent, German rate was 0.5 per cent. China's consumer prices fell by 1.2 per cent, and producer prices by 8 per cent, so that the Chinese government was establishing price controls to keep them up. In 1998, with most emerging economies stalled by austerity policies set up to defend their currencies, with investment down because of capital outflows, and with the Japanese economy in recession, over-capacity built up in standard chips, cars, steel, textiles, ships, chemicals and a long series of manufacturing industries. Even in the high-growth USA, 337,000 manufacturing jobs were lost between March 1998 and March 1999. The automobile industry, world-wide, had 30 per cent unused capacity. The extraordinary addition of manufacturing plants in the world during the 1990s, particularly in Asia, seemed to be leading to a glut of manufactured goods, thus lowering prices, sometimes below production costs. Furthermore, commodity prices fell by 30 per cent in 1997–8, according to *The Economist* index, which reached its lowest level in 150 years. Oil prices were down to their pre-1973 level. With emerging market economies reeling from the crisis, Japan politically paralysed in its economic restructuring and the European Central Bank still putting the brakes on European economies through interest rates, which, in early 1999, were not low in real terms (considering inflation rates were between 0.3 per cent and 1 per cent), global capitalism was dependent on the performance of the US economy. Deflation is like cholesterol in the human system: there are good and bad kinds. It is bad, very bad, when it reflects depressed demand, as a result of stagnant economy. It is good, very good, when it reflects gains in productivity (mainly because of technological innovation) and greater efficiency of economic management, both at the level of the firms (owing to networking and flexibility) and in macroeconomic terms (because of market integration and lower transactions costs, as with the advent of the euro).

All indications are that global capitalism at the end of the century features both kinds of deflationary trends – good and bad. But they do not cancel each other, because they are unevenly distributed across the regions of the global economy. By and large the US economy, fuelled by technology and networking, is sustaining a fast pace of info-growth. In contrast, many emerging economies, particularly in Latin America, plus the submerged economies of Africa, the ex-Soviet Union and many regions in other countries around the world, are stagnant, and suffering because of lower commodity prices, and austerity policies. However, in the summer of 1999, Japan seemed to be recovering from the recession, and the Asian Pacific economies, particularly in South Korea, resumed growth. The main European economies also started to grow again, after a period of stagnation in the first half of the year. They were helped by their exports performance, largely based on the weakness of the euro *vis-à-vis* the dollar. However, European and Asian recoveries seemed to be fragile, as they were partly induced by strong demand from the USA and, in Japan and South-East Asia, by new government spending. For this growth to be sustained the critical issue is if the sources of US productivity increase and economic growth can be adapted or adopted by Europe, and subsequently by Japan. In this case, the leading economies will become closely connected in a new pattern of info-growth. If this happens, global capitalism will thrive at its core and will reconnect again, in a much more selective and cautious way, the economies of emerging markets, articulating a self-expanding network of wealth creation and appropriation. However, it is not clear that Europe and Japan could join the info-growth model. If the institutional Automaton created by European countries (meaning Wim Duisenberg and his team of 'retro' inflation fighters in the European Central Bank) or the IMF's neo-classical globetrotters remain fixed on the terrors of the inflation age (actually a blip in economic history), they can wreck the capitalist ship simply out of bad management. It has happened before. Furthermore, if networking flexibility and technological innovation are perceived, in Japan and Europe, as being tantamount to dismantling the welfare state and curtailing workers' rights, there will be a backlash of social struggles and political reactions that will simply block reform and innovation. If this stalemate is long enough it will exhaust the growth capacity of the US economy, which is now interdependent on global performance. The USA cannot go on producing and consuming an increasing share of the world's output by itself (currently standing at over a quarter of the world's GDP) – mainly because domestic consumption remains the principal factor accounting for economic growth, and households' savings are reaching dangerously low levels. Productivity gains, after all, have to be realised by sale of output to someone with money to spend. Either Europe and Japan will join the expansion, or the US machine will stall and start spiralling downwards. Devaluation of stocks will erode the wealth accumulated on paper by both firms and households, and technology-led productivity potential will mutate into over-capacity, spilling into the morass of bad deflation on a global scale. Do not worry. Yet. It could still be worse.

A World of Silicon Valleys?

Let's imagine that Gerhard Schröder finds a way to seduce, convince, or blackmail Duisenberg, and the European Central Bank finally agrees in letting low-inflation growth happen in the European Union. By a stretch of imagination, let's consider the chance that British Labour's 'third way' approach to info-capitalism with a human face (which amounts to social democracy with an enhanced brain) succeeds in convincing European citizens that they can still live in a network society without becoming Yankees or, worse, Californians. Then, in the apotheosis of fictional political economics, let us hope the IMF/World Bank starts lending for growth instead of imposing retrenchment. Global capitalism will blossom, in a virtuous circle encompassing technologically led productivity, financially fuelled growth and socio-institutional engineering. We will be truly in the new Information Age – albeit, certainly, its capitalist incarnation. But all we have considered to this point still excludes a considerable proportion of humankind. The favourable hypothesis of weathering *fin-de-siècle* storms of global capitalism assumes a growing, dynamic integration between the USA–NAFTA bloc, the European Union and Japan. It further assumes a selective integration of emerging markets, though no longer with the carelessness that characterised global investment flows in the 1990s – not because governments will do much about it, but because investors will be more careful, knowing they cannot count on being bailed out by national governments and international institutions. While so-called speculative investments will continue to take place, because that is the nature of the beast, quick reaction systems will develop among the main financial players to minimise capital losses. Some regulatory procedures are already being put into place to limit destructive contagion into the core of global financial markets. This new and relatively cautious strategy by global investors (which is the fundamental lesson learned from the 1997–8 crisis) implies a much more limited penetration of emerging economies, creaming off the best opportunities in both stocks and direct investment, and letting the bulk of people and territories go about by themselves, until they find a way to make themselves valuable without being unreasonably risky for global investors. This leaves a substantial number of bodies out of the dynamic networks of global capitalism, for the time being. So-called emerging markets represented, in 1998, only about 7 per cent of global value in market capitalisation, but comprised about 85 per cent of humankind. Grant, generously, that 20 per cent of people in emerging economies will directly benefit from economic growth in these dynamic networks, and this will still leave over two thirds of humankind living under the influence of global capitalism but largely excluded from most of its benefits. If we add the considerable numbers of people who are socially excluded in advanced countries, the critical mass of disposable people – through the binary logic of being either in or out of the networks – expands significantly. In the USA, in the midst of this most extraordinary boom, other strata persist: about 15 per cent of the population living below poverty level (including 25 per cent of all children), and 5.5 million people in the criminal justice system (including almost 2 million in prisons). I have argued elsewhere that there is a systemic relationship between current features of global capitalism and the new technological system, because of the amplifying effects of information technologies on inequality and exclusion through disparities in education and networking capabilities. Nothing is wrong fundamentally with the technology – it could be the source of a symmetrically opposite effect, used (but by whom?) in a deliberate effort to create a more egalitarian society.

But educational possibilities are not the focus of my argument here. My question is this: is the trend sustainable? My answer is no. The illusion of a world made of Silicon Valley-like societies driven by technological ingenuity, financial adventurism and cultural individualism, high-tech archipelagos surrounded by areas of poverty and subsistence around most of the planet, is not only ethically questionable but, more important for our purpose, politically and socially unsustainable. The rise of fundamentalism, the spread of new epidemics, the expansion of the global criminal economy – with its corrosive effects on governments and societies around the world – the threat of biological/ nuclear terrorism (which obsesses Clinton, probably with some reason), the irreversible destruction of the environment (that is, of our natural capital, the most important legacy for our grandchildren), and the destruction of our own sense of humanity, all are potential consequences (many already under way) of this dynamic, yet exclusionary model of global capitalism.

In sum, there are three different, although inter-related, sources of unsustainability for info-capitalism:

- The dangers of implosion of global financial markets;
- The stagnation caused by relative shrinkage of solvent demand in proportion to the extraordinary productive capacity created by technological innovation, organisational networking, and mobilisation of capital resources;
- The social, cultural, and political rejection by large numbers of people around the world of an Automaton whose logic either ignores or devalues their humanity.

Taming the Automaton?

The Asian crisis of 1997 and its aftermath (Russia, Brazil, and beyond) has shaken the self-assurance of global capitalists, and their experts. The ugly sight of African massacres, of Aids epidemics, of global trade in children and women, of the fast-paced destruction of the planet's forests and of criminal networks taking over public institutions, prompted well-meaning philanthropists to imagine a less disruptive path to informational, global capitalism. The 1999 World Economic Forum meeting at Davos rang with discussions about various schemes to regulate and control global capital flows, and to avoid speculative movements that would disrupt markets. Proposals abounded, both there and in other forums closer to the decision-makers. There are major technical obstacles to their implementation. Given the global electronic connection between financial markets, it becomes extremely difficult to avoid the massive movement of capital, which can be achieved in seconds by a computer instruction. Financial firms have growing numbers of offshore bases in countries where there exist few regulations or none at all, and the internet enables investments to be moved around while obscuring their origin and destination, if desired. Because many financial products are synthetic combinations of values from different markets, the impact of their fluctuations affects markets around the world, independent of the actual movement of capital. Furthermore, unless regulations are internationally agreed upon and internationally enforced, countries imposing strict limits on capital movements on a continuing basis are or will be bypassed by capital flows. This is the main feature of the network economy, epitomised in its financial dimension: the ability to extend or retrench its geometry without excessive disruption, simply by reconforming the networks of investment and trade. This occurs in instants, in an endless flow of circulation. Recurrent examples of governments that have effectively implemented capital controls are proposed in every debate – a popular example is Chile's requirement for one year's deposit of 30 per cent of short-term capital invested in the country. It was successful and useful, as long as Chile had a considerable capital inflow, but it was eliminated in 1998 as soon as the foreign capital crunch started to be felt in Latin America. Another example commonly cited is Malaysia's effort to make inconvertible its unit of currency, the ringgit, and to impose strict controls on financial transaction by foreign capital, which it suspected of being a part of a Jewish global conspiracy. By mid-1999, thinking the worst of the crisis was over, Malaysia lifted most restrictions, while keeping the anti-Jewish and anti-Soros rhetoric, partly because the government was facing a serious domestic political challenge. China, the most important exception to the Asian crisis, at least until 1999, was showing the benefits of the non-convertibility of the People's Currency, the renminbi, and of the domestic insulation of its very troubled banking system. However, critics argue that this was China's good luck, simply as a consequence of its still limited integration into the global economy. Should China aim at becoming a full-fledged global player, it would need resumption of the extraordinary capital inflow it enjoyed in the

1990s, and this would be hardly compatible with strict government controls, particularly in matters of currency exchange and re-export of profits.

All in all, objections to capital controls derive from three main arguments. The first is a market fundamentalist argument about capital's fundamental right to unfettered freedom. This is losing ground in the face of widespread evidence about the damage caused by free-wheeling capitalism, something that our forebears understood in the 1930s and 1940s. That damage is now amplified by network technologies and global contagion. The second argument refers to the need for a concerted international action, at least among the G7 countries and their ancillary networks, to set up a new regulatory framework. Technical proposals are numerous, and some of them are discussed in this same volume, so I will not inflict upon the reader an additional diatribe. Third is the question of the technical feasibility of such controls in the age of electronic networks. My colleagues who are computer scientists voice the opinion that a global regulatory environment can be enforced technologically, precisely because of the extraordinary versatility and accuracy of new electronic technologies. For instance, if a financial tax (or mandatory deposit in the mode of Chile) were imposed on short-term transactions, all electronic financial networks could be programmed to include automatically such tax, rerouting the amount to a different account. In fact, you already have in your Windows 98 an individualised code that marks automatically all your computer documents in their trips around electronic networks (Microsoft just forgot to tell you). Book-keeping is now performed electronically, so a global financial inspection could have access to all accounts legally susceptible to inspection by using a virtually unbreakable password (it exists, and takes a code of a mere 4,096 bits). Speed and complexity can work both ways in the new technological environment. The Automaton could be dotted with electronic codes and instructions that would keep him (it's certainly not female) active but on a leash. All this discussion, and by extension the discussion about financial regulation in various forums, is entirely academic for the time being: it faces the opposition of the US government (represented lately by Robert Rubin and Larry Summers, but do not bet on the chances of a change of mind-set in the near future) and of its ancillary, the International Monetary Fund (officially presided over by a respectable French technocrat, as a guarantee of its independence, but actually managed by Stanley Fisher, a brilliant MIT product). Without US co-operation, there is no chance of global financial regulation, beyond what Rubin and his alma mater, Wall Street, propose – better global information systems and more transparency in accounting procedures and book-keeping, for governments, banks and corporations, plus more secure, and expeditious, bankruptcy laws. And more money for the IMF, so that, as lender of last resort (or financial rapid deployment force), it can intervene or lead pre-emptive strikes in countries in danger of financial turmoil – in exchange for assuming economic control in those countries until the conditions for safe global investment have been restored. Why has the USA so adamantly opposed global financial regulation, and why will it do so in the foreseeable future? Simple: the current system, at least in the short term, is working to the great advantage of the US economy and US firms, particularly those financial firms which are channelling a growing proportion of global investments. As for government officials, their mantra remains, 'It's the economy, stupid!' With its tremendous competitive advantage in technology, networking, information and management, the US economy is thriving. There is evidence that the US government, particularly during the Clinton administration, spearheaded the effort to expand global capitalism by opening up emerging markets, demanding the dismantling of regulations and government controls around the world.

And it worked, since the pain inflicted by the reversal of financial flows was suffered by other countries. Because such crises do not trigger immediate geopolitical dangers, given the military superiority of the USA and Nato, they can be contained within the economic sphere. The US economy cannot grow by itself in a globally interdependent economy, which is why the US government and the IMF are pressuring Japan and Europe for reflation, while trying to stabilise those emerging markets such as Brazil which could jeopardise global financial equilibrium. The belief is that with pragmatic attention to financial crises when and where they occur, everything will be all right and global capitalism will continue to blossom, with US capitalism as its renewed core – even if the core is now a node of a global network. As for the poor of the world, they ought to be taken care of by a combination of trickled-down economic benefits, targeted programmes led by the World Bank, grass-roots survival efforts helped by international charities, and a new round of family planning to stabilise population growth. Do not hold your breath as you wait for a serious attempt at global financial regulation. It will happen only if dramatic financial crisis or social upheaval hit info-capitalism.

The Great Disconnection?

The naive illusion of a comprehensive, integrated global economy, enacted by capital flows and computer networks, and reaching out to most people in the planet, was shattered on 2 July 1997 as economic crisis struck Asia. At the turn of the millennium, we find instead that most people, and most areas of the world, are suffering from, but not sharing in, the growth of global info-capitalism. Major economies, such as China and India (accounting for over one third of humankind), remain relatively autonomous in terms of global capital flows. Countries that suffered the shocks of financial volatility, such as Indonesia or Russia, are shrinking the market sector of their economies. Indonesia is witnessing a significant return to rural areas, as people fight for survival and leave crumbling megacities. The total value of Russian stocks in December 1998 was about half of the value of market capitalisation for the online book-trader Amazon (Russia's US $12 billion versus Amazon's US $25.4 billion). But life goes on, because about 50 per cent of the Russian economy works on a barter system, and because the inability to import foreign goods has stimulated Russian domestic production – an interesting revival of import substitution as a development strategy. In March 1999, Brazil yielded to the IMF's pressure to impose a state of austerity, in order to save its last currency reserves and avoid further devaluation and subsequent inflation. But the social and political cost was very high, threatening to destabilise society, with a consequently disruptive impact on the economy. Japan is stubbornly trying to rebuild its economy in its own terms, actually proposing an Asian zone and an Asian investment fund, dissociated from the IMF and the USA. Even the essential Atlantic integration between the European Union and the United States was clouded in March 1999 with threats of a trade war – over bananas, with the EU representing the interests of French Caribbean colonies and the USA representing the interests of its former colonial companies, harvesting bananas in Ecuador and Central America, in a new paradox of twisted globalisation. At the same time the European Commission came under suspicion of corruption, leading to the resignation of all the Commissioners. The fragility of this unevenly connected global system is such that a new round of financial instability, perhaps induced by the collapse of internet stocks or by a sudden panic around electronic trading networks, could trigger another stampede towards the exits. This time, there could be governments and whole societies, or significant segments

71

of societies, opting out of global capitalism – not necessarily to build an alternative system, but just to recover some degree of control over their lives, specific interests and values. For instance, in August 1999, Venezuela (the main oil supplier to the United States) engaged in a democratic process of nationalist reform, making clear it would not accept IMF-style imposition of austerity policies. The Great Disconnection is not mere political fiction. Its embryos are already planted in the social fabric of global capitalism. They may grow or not, depending upon the course of upcoming history. We know the probable response to such trends, from observing the currently dominant countries and firms. Networks of capital, technology, information and trade will be reconfigured, keeping what can be saved and discarding dead wood or spoiled human flesh. I am not sure it will work so easily next time.

And yet, the Information Age could be different. We do not have to choose between unfettered info-global capitalism and communal retrenchment. New information technologies (including ethically controlled genetic engineering) could yield their promise of a virtuous interaction between the power of mind and the well-being of society. No need to look into the future: just look around at courageous efforts such as those taking place in Finland. The Finns have quietly established themselves as the first true information society, with one website per person, internet access in 100 per cent of schools, a computer literacy campaign for adults, the largest diffusion of computer power and mobile telephony in the world, and a globally competitive information technology industry, spearheaded by Nokia. At the same time they have kept in place, with some fine-tuning, the welfare state. Finnish society fosters citizen participation and safeguards civility. It is probably not an accident that Linus Torvalds is a Finn. Torvalds is the software innovator who, as a 21-year-old student at the University of Helsinki, created Linux, a much better operating system than Microsoft's, and released it free on the internet. By so doing, he contributed to a growing open access software code movement, with thousands of Linux users contributing online to improve the code. Its users – currently about ten million – consider it far superior to any other Unix software, precisely because it is continuously improved by the work of their collective mind. Open information technology contributes to much better information technology, empowering minds around the world to use technology for living. That includes making money, without equating their lives to their stocks.

The catch is that Linus Torvalds now lives in Silicon Valley.

Notes

Data used in this chapter are in the public domain and have been reported by newspapers and business magazines, such as *The New York Times, Wall Street Journal, Financial Times, El Pais, Le Monde, Business Week, The Economist* and *Fortune*. Thus, I do not consider it necessary to burden the chapter with precise references to sources. The best synthesis of data and analyses on globalisation is Held *et al.* (1999). Global data on social exclusion and social inequality can be found in the United Nations' *Human Development Report* (1997, 1998 and 1999). This note should serve as generic reference to data sources.

I am citing a selected bibliography, limited to a few books that have been directly helpful in the analysis presented in this chapter. I refer the reader to these books for further elaboration on the issues discussed here. However, I consider it unnecessary to attach each reference to a specific paragraph in the text. This note should serve as generic reference to background sources.

Bibliography

Arthur, Brian (1998) *The New Economy*, Ann Arbor: University of Michigan Press.

Canals, Jordi (1997) *Universal Banking: International Comparisons and Theoretical Perspectives*, Oxford: Oxford University Press.

Carnoy, Martin (forthcoming) *Sustaining Flexibility: Work, Family, and Community in the Information Age*, New York: Russell Sage Foundation.

Castells, Manuel (2000 [1996]) *The Rise of the Network Society* (revised edition), Oxford: Blackwell.

Castells, Manuel (2000 [1998]) *End of Millennium* (revised edition), Oxford: Blackwell.

Castells, Manuel (1998) 'Globalization and Social Inequality', paper for United Nations Research Institute for Social Development's conference, Geneva, 22 June.

Eichengreen, Barry (1999) *Toward a New International Financial Architecture: A Practical Post-Asia Agenda*, Washington, DC: Institute for International Economics.

Held, David, McGrew, Anthony, Goldblatt, David, and Perraton, Jonathan (1999) *Global Transformations*, Stanford, CA: Stanford University Press.

Hoogvelt, Ankie (1997) *Globalisation and the Post-colonial World*, London: Macmillan.

Kelly, Kevin (1998) *New Rules for the New Economy*, New York: Viking/ Penguin.

Sachs, Jeffrey (1998a) 'International Economics: Unlocking the Mysteries of Globalization', *Foreign Affairs*, Spring: 97–111.

Sachs, Jeffrey (1998b) 'The IMF and the Asian Flu', *The American Prospect*, March–April: 16–21.

Scott, Allen (1998) *Regions and the World Economy*, Oxford: Oxford University Press.

Shapiro, Carl, and Varian, Hal R. (1998) *Information Rules: A Strategic Guide to the Network Economy*, Cambridge, MA: Harvard Business School Publishing.

Tapscott, Don (ed.) (1998) *Blueprint to the Digital Economy: Wealth Creation in the Era of E-business*, New York: McGraw Hill.

Touraine, Alain (1999) *Comment sortir du liberalisme?*, Paris: Fayard.

Zaloom, Caitlin, 'Information Technology and Global Finance: the View from the Pits', Berkeley: University of California, PHD Dissertation in Anthropology (in progress).

Acknowledgements

I wish to thank, for their insightful comments to this chapter, my students at two graduate seminars (CS 290, and CP 229) at the University of California, Berkeley, in the Spring Semester, 1999. I particularly thank Caitlin Zaloom. I also want to acknowledge comments from my colleagues Jerry Feldman, Martin Carnoy and Vilmar Faria.

PAUL A. VOLCKER

The Sea of Global Finance

What has been labelled the 'Asian financial crisis' caught the world by surprise in the middle of 1997. There had been concern for some months about the valuation of the Thai baht, leading to substantial outflows of capital. More generally, however, East Asia had maintained exceptionally rapid rates of economic growth for more than a decade; at the same time, the region had managed to contain inflation, and budgetary and monetary policies were considered responsible. All of that had been attested to in commentary by the World Bank and the International Monetary Fund (IMF) as late as the spring of the year, only weeks before speculative pressures forced (with IMF encouragement) devaluation of the baht.

In a matter of months, strong doubts about the value of currencies spread throughout the East Asian emerging economies. Domestic financial systems in Thailand, Indonesia and Korea collapsed in the face of savage currency depreciation and skyrocketing interest rates. Malaysia withstood the storm better than most only by retreating into exchange controls so comprehensive that they were hardly consistent with long-term growth and full participation in the world economy. By the summer of 1998, a further shock reverberated through the world financial system when Russia unilaterally announced a revaluation of its domestic government debt that amounted to *de facto* default. All of that shifted attention to Latin America, where Brazil, with enormous short-term public debt and a deteriorating external financial position, seemed vulnerable.

Economic prospects for the emerging world that seemed so bright only two years earlier have thus abruptly dimmed, certainly for the first year or two of the new century. All of this is particularly disturbing in light of the intellectual triumph and practical application of the ideas of

75

free and open markets for money and capital that swept the world after the end of the Cold War. We cannot now escape a conclusion that these dramatic events, the latest episode in a continuing saga of international financial crisis, raise basic questions about global finance and its implications for economic development.

Financial crises, national and international, have, of course, been a recurrent part of capitalism. But somehow they seem to be coming more frequently and with greater force these days, at least as they impact upon emerging economies. Not much more than a decade after the start of the severe Latin American debt crisis of the 1980s, Mexico in 1994 and 1995 found itself in renewed financial turmoil. There were reverberations throughout South America. The international community, led by the United States and the IMF, felt it necessary to respond with official credits that dwarfed amounts that had been lent, or even imagined, only a few years earlier.

Massive new IMF programmes did not stem the financial contagion that followed the Thai devaluation. It is now evident that South-East Asia and Korea – with their vaunted 'tiger' economies – are suffering a severe economic setback. China's plans for sustaining growth in the area of 7 to 8 per cent have been jeopardised even though its financial markets have, to a degree, been insulated by lack of full currency convertibility. The Russian economy and banking system, chronically unsettled and vulnerable to financial collapse, have broken down. And the outcome of the battle to maintain stability in Brazil – the largest and strongest Latin American economy – is not clear despite the availability of tens of billions of dollars from international and foreign institutions.

In searching for common ground in all this, one interesting point stands out. With the exception of Russia, the crisis countries had been characterised by exceptionally good economic growth and good progress towards price stability. Domestic savings were high, substantial progress had been made towards more open markets for both goods and capital, and investment had flourished – the kind of thing that attracts foreign capital. Virtually on the eve of the financial turmoil that engulfed some of those countries, no lesser authorities than the World Bank and the IMF had acknowledged the effectiveness of their macro-economic policies.

As the crisis spread, much attention centred on perceived structural defects in Asian emerging economies: weak banking systems, lack of adequate and timely information, governmental subsidies and favouritism, crony capitalism and widespread corruption. These are, of course, matters that have persisted over many years of remarkably rapid growth.

At best, change will be uneven and slow and will bring uncertainties of its own.

Quite obviously, something has been lacking in our analyses and in our response. Emerging nations making good progress towards liberal policies and reforms have been hit hard. The problem is not regional, but international. And there is every indication that it is systemic – systemic in the literal sense that it arises not from some *deus ex machina*, but from within the ordinary workings of the international financial system itself.

Conceptually and practically, open international capital markets should offer huge potential benefits in speeding and sustaining the economic growth of emerging and transitional economies. There are clear examples of those benefits in Asia and elsewhere. At the same time, the recurrent volatility of those global markets can impact with devastating force on inherently small and poorly developed national markets and institutions.

Clearly, a great deal is at stake in coming to some common understanding of that dilemma and how to deal with it. For that reason, I welcome the calls we are now hearing from both inside and outside official circles for a new look at the workings of the international financial system and its main institutions. But it is also my sense that we are a long way from achieving a good understanding of, much less implementing, new approaches that are convincing.

In emphasising so strongly the systemic nature of the financial problems, I do not want to be misunderstood. I abhor corruption, in finance or elsewhere. I believe, over time, that crony capitalism, state ownership and official industrial policies are all inherently less efficient than open competitive markets.

I have always favoured strong banks, well supervised and with experienced and prudent management. I have for many years fought against the indiscriminate mingling of banking with commerce in the USA. I believe it is generally bad policy, a conclusion reinforced by what has been happening in the emerging economies of Asia, in Russia, and in Japan.

I also agree that more – rather than less – information, widely disseminated, must almost always be better – and in any case will be required in a modern democracy.

In varying degrees, all the countries caught up in the present financial crisis – certainly those in Asia – have had marked weaknesses in these respects. Over time, basic reforms will be needed to support sustained growth. In some cases, a strong political commitment to basic reform –

reforms extending beyond the economic – has become necessary to restore confidence in government, and is surely helpful in restoring financial stability. In that respect, both Korea and Thailand are fortunate in having in place new governments eager to embrace reform.

What I do not believe is that the timing, nature and force of the Asian financial crisis (or, for instance, the crises in Mexico) can be explained in terms of those structural factors, important as they may be over time in reducing economic potential. None of them is new. None of them has been unknown. Nor, to the best of my knowledge, have they suddenly become worse.

There are, in fact, basic reasons why growth among the Asian tigers, old and new, has been sustained for decades at unprecedented rates. There is a good supply of energetic and intelligent workers. A strong entrepreneurial spirit appears to be alive and well. There is a willingness to adopt and adapt to new technology and to maintain high rates of saving. All that means low costs and rapidly rising productivity, even in the face of what appear, by Western standards, to be flawed and weak institutional structures. That potential remains intact today. But clearly something has abruptly happened to disrupt that process. It seems to me that this 'something' lies more in the financial arena than in the structural flaws that have been at the centre of so much attention.

Flows of funds and their valuation in free financial markets are influenced as much by perceptions as by objective reality – or, perhaps more precisely, the perception is the reality. The herd instinct is strong. Only in hindsight do episodes of strong 'overshooting' or 'undershooting' become evident, and the reversals are typically sudden.

All that has always been true. The resulting volatility can ordinarily be accepted as a small price to pay for the immense benefits that broad and active financial markets can bring. That is certainly true for large and well-diversified economies, with sturdy financial structures. They typically have the resilience to ride out the storm with limited and temporary damage.

The situation is more difficult for emerging economies. By definition, they and their financial institutions are tiny in relation to the size of international markets. To put that in perspective, the entire banking systems of Indonesia or Thailand or Malaysia are comparable to one good-sized regional bank in the USA. Their entire GNPs are smaller than the funds controlled by our largest financial institutions, including large mutual fund families and other investors caught up in intense competition to outperform their rivals.

I need not review in detail the enormous growth in the supply of financial capital nor the irreversible changes in technology that permit money to move around the world almost instantaneously with much smaller transaction costs. At the same time, the organisation of the markets – away from traditional commercial banking towards a variety of institutions more focused on transactions – has made the markets both more impersonal and more fluid. Competition to 'outperform' is intense.

One result has been a capacity and willingness to reach out for more exotic, potentially high-yielding investments. The private sectors of emerging economies, with their strong growth potential, have become prime targets.

Those countries have in recent years become converts to the basic philosophy that more open markets for capital, as well as for goods, will bolster growth. One manifestation is their greater willingness to accept direct investment. Its longer-term orientation and technological and managerial components have been mutually beneficial. But there have been strong incentives to accept and encourage portfolio capital as well, where the benefits to the economy are more indirect and the potential risks greater. And much of that investment can be moved on very short notice – at least until a crisis shuts down the market.

The process for a time is self-reinforcing. An inflow of foreign money helps to keep interest rates down and equity prices up. Investment is spurred, export capabilities enhanced, and high rates of economic growth sustained. The supporting of a strong exchange rate means that inflation is contained and a sense of stability reinforced. Profit opportunities blossom for local banks and other financial institutions as they intermediate the flow of funds. And the apparent success of the early investors encourages more to join, allocating amounts that from their individual perspectives may be marginal.

The difficulty is that what may be marginal to the increasing numbers of investment institutions with mobile money can, in its totality, be overpowering to the small receiving country. The possibility of simply sterilising the inflows is expensive and self-limiting. With money so freely available from abroad, banks will lend aggressively. Sooner or later investment is likely to run ahead of needs and be misallocated by governments or private investors. In the circumstances, a real estate boom will be almost inevitable and, whatever the particular exchange rate regime, the real exchange rate will appreciate, undercutting trade competitiveness and leading to growing current account deficits.

Sooner or later some event, internal or external, political or economic, will raise questions about the sustainability of it all. The capital inflows will slow or stop. Then the exchange rate will come under pressure, inducing capital flight. Reserves will be depleted, the exchange rate will sink way below what was thought to be reasonable, inflationary forces will rise, and interest rates will double and redouble. The crisis is at hand.

In one sense the pattern is all too familiar. But there is a large difference from most earlier experience when the source of the crisis could be traced to irresponsible macro-economic policies – loose budgets, excessive monetary expansion, an escalating wage/price spiral – the kind of thing towards which IMF rescue programmes have been typically and effectively directed in the past. The present situation is more complicated. It involves deep-seated questions about the operation of the global financial system, as well as macro-economic discipline. And it has become increasingly clear that simply supplying escalating amounts of short-term financial resources cannot provide a satisfactory approach – certainly not without providing creditors with a degree of assurance that would raise large questions of moral hazard.

The IMF and the official financial community have clearly been faced with difficult circumstances beyond the well-trodden approach of macro discipline and the provision of short-term credit. In the circumstances, one can empathise with the urge to deal aggressively with all those matters of internal reform to which I referred earlier. But there are limits and dangers to that approach as well, perceptual and political as well as economic.

One is the extreme difficulty of changing ingrained habits of governments and businesses, rooted in deep-seated cultural patterns. Ordinarily, it will be a slow process, and there can't be any assurance that radical change imposed in a crisis won't exacerbate uncertainty and dislocation; the contagious runs that followed the sudden closing of some Indonesian banks form one case in point. To the extent that 'reforms' are, or appear to be, imposed from abroad, the risk of a counterproductive backlash is increased.

The easy advice we give others about quick reform of their banking systems stands in stark contrast to the inability of the USA to pass legislation rationalising competition among its banks and competing financial institutions – an impasse that has lasted for more than fifteen years amid entrenched private interests. It is ironic that one of the matters at issue in Congress is the political pressure brought to bear in order to weaken traditional barriers to combinations of commerce and banking, precisely the practice in Asia and elsewhere that we rail against as a major source of institutional weakness.

More importantly in the present context, we have to deal with the simple fact that countries with strong banks, honest and democratic governments, relatively transparent accounting systems, and experienced regulators have not been immune to banking crises. The list is long, and it includes the USA.

Others have aptly pointed to the situation in Texas to make the point. Once an independent country, Texas has economic mass – its output approximately matches Korea's GNP. At the start of the 1980s it had some of the most strongly capitalised and profitable banks in the USA. They were fiercely resistant to permitting any 'foreign' ownership – 'foreign' being defined as New York or other out-of-state banks. No doubt there was a certain amount of cronyism among Texans, and we later learned there was a good deal of corruption in poorly supervised thrifts. But as one of the commercial bank regulators responsible at the time, I'd like to think that supervision was state-of-the-art. Certainly the bankers were experienced, accounting was in the hands of the Big Six applying GAAP standards, and SEC 10K reports and financial prospectuses were reviewed by the highest-paid analysis talent in the world. But none of that institutional strength insulated Texan financial institutions and the Texan economy from the excesses that accompanied the energy and real estate booms of the early 1980s.

By the middle of that decade, all the big Texan banks were bankrupt, *de jure* or *de facto*, and the remnants were acquired by out-of-state institutions. The savings and loan industry was decimated. The real economy was certainly affected. But the interesting fact is that the effects were limited and the recovery rapid, certainly relative to what we see in Asia.

Texas did and does have enormous advantages relative to a small emerging economy. It was part of the world's largest common currency area – the USA. As such, there could be no loss of confidence in its currency and no inflationary impetus from depreciation. Its interest rates were those of the USA – and they tended to fall rather than rise. Large companies were typically part of dispersed national and international operations. There was an effective lender of last resort and credible deposit insurance – and I might add a certain amount of regulatory forbearance.

Well, Indonesia, Thailand, Mexico, Korea and Russia are not Texas. But I think there are lessons to be learned from all this experience.

The first and most important is that small and open economies are inherently vulnerable to the volatility of global capital markets. The visual image of a vast sea of liquid capital strikes me as apt – the big and inevitable storms through which a great liner like the USA can safely sail will surely capsize even the sturdiest South Pacific canoe.

The natural defence is to seek the shelter of larger, inherently more diversified and stable ships. Texas is a case in point; by the end of the 1980s, every major bank in Texas, with the encouragement and support of the Federal Government, had become part of a much larger national banking organisation. With heroic effort, Argentina has effectively adopted the dollar as a parallel currency and only one sizeable private bank remains without substantial foreign ownership and interest. In Mexico, where resistance to foreign ownership of banks was a major issue only a few years ago in the NAFTA negotiations, four of the five largest banks today have important foreign capital. Thailand, strongly protective of its banks and finance companies before the crisis broke, now eagerly seeks foreign participation. On the other side of the world, in Eastern Europe, foreign ownership of banks is becoming commonplace.

In the non-financial world, there cannot be much doubt that similar forces are at work. Distressed industrial and commercial firms will naturally look more favourably on injections of capital from abroad, whether by means of joint ventures or outright sale. For large and diversified international companies faced with short-term difficulties in emerging markets, the depressed values in a financial crisis are also a buying opportunity.

To put the point more generally, the economic logic of living in a world of global capital markets is to have much more integration, with the crisis force-feeding the existing tendency. The obvious counterpoint is a growing lack of autonomy in economic management, easily perceived as an affront to sovereignty. That potential for political resistance will be all the greater if the changes seem to be forced not by economic logic and national decision but by external forces with their own agenda.

One thing is sure. If a country wants to participate in open markets for goods and other services, it can't feasibly opt out of world financial markets. That is the course that Malaysia has chosen, at least for the time being. The fact is that finance is intertwined with trade and investment. There are so many ways for funds to flow, and so many incentives to circumvent controls, that effective insulation cannot be achieved without stifling growth.

So what can we do to balance better the opportunities and risks of global financial markets?

For one thing, justified scepticism about the efficacy of controls doesn't mean we need to frown on more limited efforts to restrain inflows of potentially 'hot money'. Some countries, with Chile the leading case in point, have developed techniques to restrain those flows that are broadly consistent with the basic desirability of encouraging prudence in banking practices. The leading officials of the IMF have expressed some sympathy for that approach. I trust that in its zeal to incorporate freedom of capital movement into its basic charter, the Fund visualises the prospect of maintaining surveillance over such measures rather than assuming they are, *ipso facto*, objectionable. Ideological purity rigidly applied is hardly appropriate to present circumstances.

A much more fundamental and difficult matter is exchange rate management. It is, it seems to me, an area of intellectual confusion.

Not so long ago, there was considerable sympathy for the use of a stable exchange rate for smaller, inflation-prone countries as a key policy objective and an anchor for expectations. In the immediate aftermath of crises, criticism mounted that exchange rates had been managed too rigidly, and that something much closer to free-floating would have helped protect against volatile capital flows. The irony is that some of the fiercest critics of Thai and Indonesian exchange rate policy have also been among the most vociferous in urging that Hong Kong and emerging China, a tiny economic area, must, above all else, dedicate themselves to maintaining a strict peg against the dollar lest a new and devastating round of financial volatility break out in Asia.

The implication has been that a menu of exchange rate choices could be set out *à la carte*, without much sense of how those choices can meld. But now a different reality is beginning to sink in.

Left to the market, exchange rates of small and open economies are likely to be prone to wide and disturbing fluctuations. That is why the natural instinct is to seek shelter by maintaining a stable relationship with close trading partners or with one of the major world currencies. In the industrialised world, the ultimate expression of that instinct is the creation of a common currency in Europe. Another manifestation is the new interest in currency boards in emerging countries, accepting the loss of monetary sovereignty.

Much more common are compromise approaches, formally or informally setting a range of values around a reference currency or a basket of currencies. Quite a few countries have managed such arrangements for considerable periods. There will, of course, be strains in the face of volatile capital markets and all the pressures and uncertainties in real economies. That is all the more true in Asia, where trading and financial patterns are so widely dispersed among North America, Japan and Europe. There, the choice of an appropriate anchor currency is not obvious.

Those difficulties are compounded when the major world currencies are themselves highly volatile. One precipitating factor in Asia was the large depreciation of the yen. With its currency loosely linked to the dollar, Thailand's competitive position was sharply and unexpectedly undercut. But the solution is not so clear.

With fluctuations in the yen/dollar rate in a range of 50 per cent or more over the space of a year or two, Thailand, or any similarly situated country, faces an insoluble dilemma. Both Japan and the USA are important markets and sources of finance. But stability against one currency is volatility against the other. Attempts to split the difference, even if practically feasible, cannot escape competitive distortions.

I count it as one of the few constructive by-products of the Asian crisis that, finally, questions are again being asked about the design – or, more accurately, the absence of design – of the exchange rate system. For years, the Big Three (Germany, Japan and the USA) have been reassuring each other that the recurrent volatility among their exchange rates would settle down – or if not, it didn't really matter much anyway. Today, that air of insouciance is much harder to maintain.

It is a frustrating time, analytically as well as practically. The problems of Asia's emerging economies are unprecedented. Criticism and unhappiness about the role of the IMF and the other major players in international finance have been inevitable. What is encouraging is that the Fund itself appears to recognise the need for stepping back and assessing with a fresh mind the challenges posed by the new world of global finance. The fact is, new approaches are needed.

There should also be no doubt about what is at stake. If, a few years down the road as we get into the new millennium, market turbulence persistently undercuts strong and consistent growth in emerging markets, then temptations to reject the ideology of open markets and multilateralism will increase. The kind of open, benign regionalism characteristic of much of today's trading world could turn malignantly inwards, with all that implies for political conflict as well as economic tension.

Plainly, the USA is the single most influential actor in all of this. It is not a helpless giant. To the contrary, the danger lies in a certain arrogance – a tendency in Congress particularly to pull back from international economic leadership, under the illusion that the USA can be secure in its own strength, lulled by the performance of its economy and booming financial markets.

I do not need to emphasise that even the USA is not, and cannot be, an economic or political island. The simple fact is, it needs to work within and through international organisations – organisations that it largely created – if it wants its vision of open markets and political consensus to prevail. One need not agree with every policy and every decision of the IMF to realise that it is the only vehicle available – and the appropriate vehicle – to bring consensus and legitimacy to reform of the financial system on a global scale.

There is another imperative for all the major industrialised countries. In the insistence that the beleaguered states of Asia take tough steps to reform their own economies, the need to keep the big markets open cannot be neglected. Even apart from the immediate economic interest of encouraging recovery and strong competition in the emerging world, the economic powerhouses must not fail to demonstrate by their own actions that advocacy of open trade is a lasting commitment, for fair weather and foul.

The turbulence in world financial markets strikes me as a test – of cooperative economic leadership in a world rapidly integrating economically and with dispersed political power and decision-making. I do not underestimate the difficulty of the challenge. But, with the danger so clear, the crisis affords opportunities for monetary reforms that have for so long been neglected.

GEORGE SOROS

The New Global Financial Architecture

The global financial crisis is now officially over. Emerging markets in Asia and Latin America have come roaring back. The mature markets at the centre of the global capitalist system were never really hurt, except for a brief sinking spell in the autumn of 1998. The global economy did suffer a setback and some countries were devastated, but the US economy went from strength to strength and there are now clear signs of recovery in the rest of the world, particularly Asia. Even if financial markets were to collapse now, it would have to be called a new crisis, not an extension of the old one.

At the height of the crisis there was a lot of talk about the global financial architecture and the need for a new Bretton Woods, and I was very much in favour of those discussions. The urge for radical reform has now subsided and from now on we shall work on the details. To use a fashionable metaphor, we shall fix the plumbing rather than work on a radically new design.

I want to make it clear that I am in no way opposed to fixing the plumbing. Traditional design combined with modern plumbing can provide very attractive accommodation. But we should not forget about the architecture because the recent crisis has revealed some serious structural weaknesses and – continuing the metaphors – it is important to understand where the cracks in the wall are before we paper over them. This will put us in a better position to deal with the next crisis.

A number of reforms have already been introduced or are under active consideration. As a result, global financial markets will never be quite the same as they were before. Most of the reforms are desirable, although some, particularly those concerned with 'bailing in' the lenders, could turn out to be counterproductive. I contend that the various measures need to be linked together into a coherent concept in order to make them effective.

I shall focus on the role of the IMF because that is where the linkage needs to be made. There is widespread agreement that in the recent crisis the IMF became as much a part of the problem as part of the solution. No doubt the IMF made several specific policy mistakes. It insisted on cutting public expenditures when the cause of the trouble was in the private sector, it underestimated the severity of the contagion and, in the case of Indonesia, it precipitated a run on the banks by closing some of them without first putting a deposit insurance scheme in place. But that is not what I am interested in. My aim is to identify the structural deficiencies in the way the IMF was operating because they are the ones that require structural changes.

I can identify two such deficiencies. One is a disparity between crisis prevention and intervention; the other is a disparity in the treatment of lenders and borrowers. I want to emphasise that the management of the IMF cannot really be blamed for either because the deficiencies were built into the system.

The primary mission of the IMF is to preserve the international financial system. Its task is to ensure that a debtor country will be able to meet its international obligations – if not right away, then within the foreseeable future. The conditions it imposes on the debtor country include punitively high interest rates, which serve the dual purpose of stabilising exchange rates and creating a trade surplus by precipitating a recession. Both developments indirectly benefit lenders because they facilitate the repayment of debts.

This method of operation has given rise to what is now recognised as a moral hazard. In case of trouble, lenders could count on the IMF to bail them out; this has tended to encourage international lenders to lend more than they would have otherwise. Actually, the moral hazard is better described as an asymmetry in the treatment of lenders and borrowers.

There is another asymmetry in the way the IMF has been operating. It could intervene only in times of crisis; it had no authority to prevent a crisis from developing. Since experience has shown that busts are best prevented by moderating the booms that precede them, this has been an invitation for trouble. The IMF could see trouble brewing in Thailand and – as we now know – it warned the Thai authorities in no uncertain terms; but it had to wait until it was called upon to intervene.

These two asymmetries, taken together, explain why the IMF has become part of the problem. In the recent crisis, the IMF imposed punitive interest rates and the countries concerned were plunged into deep recession. But when the crisis threatened the USA, the Federal Reserve lowered interest rates and the US economy escaped unscathed.

Take a look at the three Asian countries: Thailand, Indonesia and Korea. All three suffered from a structural imbalance: the private sector had borrowed too much money in hard currency without hedging it, and it did not have enough equity. Devaluation, when it came, increased the ratio of foreign debt to equity. The high interest rates and the sudden collapse in domestic demand imposed by the IMF programmes increased the burden of debt even further, bringing the solvency of the debtors into question. What these countries needed was a way to convert debt into equity. But to impose a moratorium and allow for a debt to equity conversion scheme would have hurt the international banks and bondholders too much and the IMF could not even contemplate such a move. So it proceeded with the usual prescriptions and got the usual result of plunging the countries into recession. The recapitalisation of the debtor companies had to wait until after the crisis had run its course. It is taking place currently.

I am, of course, not the only one to identify these structural deficiencies. Moral hazard has become a big issue in the recent crisis. There has been a groundswell of political opposition to the idea that public funds should be used to bail out the private sector. The pressure is so great that it has become practically impossible for the IMF to put together a rescue package without bailing in the private sector in some way or another. Exactly what bailing in means remains unclear. It involves making some sacrifice by taking losses or making long-term commitments. The trouble is that the private sector does not make sacrifices without charging for it so in the end the costs will be passed on to the borrowers. This is the most hotly debated subject today. The IMF is now using the Ukraine as a guinea pig, requiring it to restructure its bonds before receiving IMF assistance.

At the same time the authorities have recognised the importance of crisis prevention. The various endeavours to establish standards and best practices, particularly in banking but also in corporate governance and macro and structural policies, aim at prevention; so do the Contingent Credit Lines recently introduced by the IMF. Then there are proposals for establishing better bankruptcy and voluntary reorganisation procedures and for changing the terms of bond contracts and introducing collective action clauses: these would help the bailing-in process. So it can be seen that the various initiatives to improve the functioning of the global financial system address one or the other of the disparities I have identified.

The recently introduced Contingent Credit Lines have even begun to link the two disparities together. Making the facility available to those countries which follow sound policies provides an incentive for them to do so. I have been advocating such a facility and I consider it the most significant advance in the global financial architecture to date. Unfortunately few countries have indicated an interest to avail themselves of the facility. This is not surprising in view of an inherent flaw in its construction. On the demand side, there is no general access limit when warranted by exceptional circumstances. The supply side is constrained by the lack of funds. Certain funds – the GAB and the NAB – are available only for countries that pose a systemic risk and this leaves smaller countries, which are also exposed to contagion, out in the cold. I think the Contingent Credit Lines to be meaningful need to be backed by an issue of Special Drawing Lines.

The main area of confusion remains the issue of bailing-in the private sector and the uncertainty can be very harmful. For instance, in the case of Brazil, there was a lot of pressure on the Brazilian government to force the commercial banks to maintain their credit lines as part of the rescue package. Brazil resisted the suggestion but the banks saw the handwriting on the wall and reduced their credit lines while they could. This served to deepen the crisis.

On the other hand, it has also made it easier to turn it around because by the time the package was put together, the international banks were severely underinvested in Brazil.

I contend that the uncertainty could be best removed by linking the measures aimed at correcting two disparities together. Taking them separately, the various reform efforts are of questionable value. For instance, we may establish standards, but how can we provide incentives that would induce countries to abide by those standards? We may introduce collective action clauses into bond contracts, but how can we avoid investors charging a hefty risk premium? We want to reward countries that abide by the newly established standards but through our changing the terms of bond contracts we are liable to penalise the borrowers who will then have to pay higher interest rates.

The contradiction could be resolved by linking the performance of individual countries to the kind of assistance they can expect from the IMF. This is how it would work. Under the recently proposed reforms, the IMF is already committed to issue Public Information Notices (PINs) subsequent to Article 4 consultations, giving its assessment of a country's macro-economic health and degree of conformity to established standards and codes of conduct. I propose that the IMF should go a step further and declare that in the case of those countries that meet the required standards, IMF programmes would not involve debt restructuring, so that bondholders need not fear that the collective action clauses would be invoked except in the case of individual companies failing. This would enable the countries concerned to borrow in the markets at cheaper rates. It would provide a powerful incentive to meet the required standards and it would enable the IMF to act in a preventive manner.

The IMF assurance would be confined to publicly issued bonds and it would exclude bank lines. Providing banks with implicit guarantees has been at the core of the trouble in the recent crisis. In the case of the banks, the leverage that the IMF needs in order to prevent crises from developing could be provided by varying the capital requirements under the Basle accord according to the grade awarded by the IMF. The Basle accord is under review; this could be incorporated in the revised regulations.

The two changes taken together would provide both the sticks and the carrots the IMF needs in order to become an effective institution for crisis prevention. Moreover, the carrots would encourage long-term lending and the sticks discourage short-term lending. This would be a healthy development. I believe this proposal makes eminent sense, yet it has run into heavy opposition, because it raises the spectre of moral hazard. Wouldn't an IMF guarantee encourage unsound lending? It would certainly lower the cost of borrowing but the guarantee would not be unconditional. A country could be downgraded if it slips from the standards or exceeds certain limits on its borrowing and it could not issue additional bonds with the assurance that the collective action clause would not be invoked. It has been suggested that the consequences of disqualification would be so dire that the IMF would not dare to follow through with it or, if it did, might precipitate the crisis it was supposed to prevent. But the IMF has an institutional interest in preventing crises, and to downgrade a country sooner rather than later would reduce the risk of a crisis. It has also been objected that a distinction between countries that qualify and those that do not would create too much of a discontinuity. But the discontinuity could be moderated by introducing gradations; for instance, by distinguishing between countries where debt reorganisation would be required, those where it would be tolerated but not required, and those where it would not be tolerated. Capital requirements would also be graduated. But the fact remains that a small element of moral hazard cannot be avoided. Moral hazard is implicit in the operation of any lender of last resort.

The measure I am proposing – linking the performance of individual countries to the kind of assistance they can expect from the IMF – is hardly revolutionary. This makes it all the more remarkable that it has run into such heavy opposition. Moral hazard of any kind has become unacceptable. But the current campaign against moral hazard is just an excuse for resisting any kind of interference with the market mechanism. This resistance is based on the false doctrine of our age, namely that financial markets automatically tend towards equilibrium – from which it follows that there is no need to interfere because markets will correct their own excesses. The global financial crisis should have given the lie to this point of view, which I regard as both false and dangerous, but in a funny way it can also be used to reinforce the doctrine. After all, the IMF has not done well but the markets have recovered.

I should like to juxtapose to the slogan of 'moral hazard' the slogan of 'a level playing field'. The playing field of global finance is anything but level when interest rates at the periphery are so much higher than they are at the centre. Perhaps under the perceived protection of the IMF too much money has flown from the centre to the periphery, precipitating the crisis from which we are just now beginning to recover. But we are now swinging to the opposite extreme.

Most of the reform measures currently contemplated are designed to discourage excessive capital flows. As a result the new danger is that there will be too little financial capital available to the periphery countries and interest rate differentials will remain much too high. The disparity in the cost of capital – both in the form of debt and equity – will encourage the acquisition of domestic companies by multinationals, both in industry and in financial services. The new architecture emerging after the crisis tends to make it more difficult for domestic companies in periphery countries to compete with multinationals.

Take a recent example: in the privatisation of the state-owned Argentine oil company YPF, the Spanish company Repsol could easily outbid Argentine buyers because it could borrow much more cheaply, and eventually it could take over the entire company.

At present, direct investment is considered the most virtuous form of international investment and it certainly has the merit of being more stable than either portfolio investment or short-term lending. But it has its drawbacks and it may well run into political resistance, especially if it takes place on an uneven playing field. In the global capitalist system as it is currently constituted the centre has already too many advantages over the periphery. Those who are responsible for the global architecture ought to exert themselves to reduce the disparity rather than to increase it. When the ground is naturally uneven, creating a level playing field does require official intervention. Moral hazard has become a code word for resisting it. I think it should not be allowed to dominate the discourse.

Creating a level playing field should rank much higher as a priority because the real systemic danger facing the global capitalist system is political in character. The rising tide of nationalism can be contained only by spreading the benefits of global capitalism more evenly. The proposal I have outlined here is a very modest step in the right direction. It is all the more regrettable that it is running into such heavy opposition.

I have focused on a very narrow problem area because I had a very practical suggestion to make. Taking a larger view I should like to leave you with the following thought. The reform measures currently undertaken will ensure that we shall not have a repetition of the crisis we have just endured – much as the Maginot Line protected France in the Second World War against the conditions that prevailed in the First World War. But the next crisis is bound to originate from a different direction. The recent crisis was unique in the sense that it was not precipitated by a rise in interest rates or a decline in Wall Street.

The next test is liable to come when one of those events occurs. The recent crisis has shown that we have a very efficient mechanism for injecting liquidity at the centre, namely the Federal Reserve, but a very inadequate one for injecting liquidity into the countries at the periphery. That is the problem which needs to be solved in order to make the global capitalist system more acceptable and more enduring.

(*May 1999*)

JEFF FAUX and LARRY MISHEL

Inequality and the Global Economy

Unrealised Promises

In the spring of 1999, World Bank President James Wolfensohn observed of global financial markets: 'At the level of people, the system isn't working.'

An odd phrase – 'at the level of people'. One is tempted to ask, 'What other level is there?' Yet we all know that he means the system isn't providing most of the world's citizens a better material life.

There is little doubt that deregulation of the world's product and financial markets has enriched a world class of investors, entrepreneurs and professionals. At the very top, the accumulation of wealth has been extraordinary; in 1996 the United Nations Development Programme (UNDP) reported that the assets of the world's 358 billionaires exceeded the combined incomes of 45 per cent of the world's population. Moreover, as one can observe in the world's crowded airports, shopping malls and upscale restaurants, prosperity has also reached somewhat further down the income scale. But not as far down as the supporters of globalisation would like us to believe.

Central to the moral argument for the rapid universal expansion of the unregulated market-place is the claim that, as a result, living standards will rise faster and incomes – along with prices, interest rates and the cost of doing business – will converge. The promise of higher and converging incomes is necessary to justify the pain of dislocation that inevitably accompanies fast-paced creative destruction.

So far the promises have not been realised. As trade and financial markets have been flung open, incomes have risen not faster, but slower. Equality among nations has not improved, with many of the poorest nations suffering an absolute decline in incomes. Within nations, inequality seems to have worsened. The data are rough, but it is noteworthy that where the measurements of income distribution are most reliable, the trend is towards more inequality.

For the promoters of rapid deregulation of the global economy – a policy pursued under such labels as 'neo-liberalism', 'the Anglo-American model', 'the Washington consensus' – persistent and rising inequality was until recently only a modestly embarrassing imperfection in an otherwise appealing picture of market-driven prosperity.

Inequality among nations was explained away by the insistence that the leaders of poorer nations had not been pursuing the right policy mix – deregulated markets, privatised governments and broken labour unions.

But by the last year of the twentieth century, this rationalisation was undercut by a string of disasters that had befallen governments whose leaders and policies were considered exemplary. Mexico, Thailand, Indonesia, Korea, Brazil and at times even Russia adorned the gallery of nations whose economies soured shortly after their leaders were lauded by the global policy elite for pursuing sound economic fundamentals. Such confidence was clearly misplaced. Rather than by economic fundamentals, most of the booming growth rates seemed to have been driven by speculative movements of short-term capital that inflated local assets, making large numbers of people feel rich – for a while. When their bubbles imploded, the same countries were denounced by the policy elites for something called 'crony capitalism' – a year earlier, the term had been 'business-friendly environment'. Whatever the precise reasons for these débâcles, the fact remained that neither market players nor the policy elite could make an a priori identification between good policy and bad. Even more troubling has been the apparent growth of inequality within nations – especially the most developed. Rising inequality within developing nations can be excused as the price of change from a stable rural society to a more dynamic urban one. But once a nation has reached an advanced level of development, worsening inequality raises at least two serious questions about the economic model being pursued.

First, there is the question of economic justice: is an economy in which the benefits of growth are distributed in an increasingly lopsided manner achieving its social purpose?

Within a range of income distributions, the answers are bound to be subjective – a distribution of income that strikes one person as unfair may strike another as justified by differences in the contributions which the recipients make to the generation of that income. But at some point, rising inequality will go beyond the bounds of efficiency rationalisations. Thus, in the mid-1960s, when growth was rising at about 6 per cent per year, the ratio between the income of the top chief executive officers (CEOs) of American corporations and the wage of the average production worker was 39 to 1. In 1997, after three decades of slower growth, the CEO/worker ratio was 254 to 1. At this level of inequality, rationalisations rest more on ideological than on economic grounds.

Second, there is the question of sustainability – economic and political. The economic question is this: given the importance of maintaining consumer demand in any market economy, will a continued unequal distribution of income ultimately undermine economic growth? Some theorists of course doubt that there is a problem – free markets will always 'clear'. But we have had enough experience to know that income and wealth distribution have macro-economic consequences. In poor nations, the propensity of the rich to spend on imports can destabilise growth in the short term, and their propensity to invest their capital elsewhere can undermine it in the long term. At the other end of the scale, the depressed earnings of working families in the USA have led to a massive increase in consumer borrowing, which has driven the personal savings rate into negative territory and is unsustainable by the proof of simple arithmetic. And in the global economy as a whole we see evidence in a number of industries – autos, textiles, machinery, computer components – of a sustained tendency for capacity to outpace customer demand.

The effect of inequality on political sustainability is not quite captured by the slow-moving 'Gini coefficients' that measure the upward redistribution of income and wealth over large periods of time. In stable times, societies adjust to gradually rising inequality. The political crisis is more likely to come when an economic downturn occurs. People at the top of the income distribution in all countries not only have deeper financial reserves; their income is also more likely to be generated from capital that is more mobile and therefore more able to avoid being trapped in a depressed economy. People at the bottom, however, whose income is generated by their labour, are tied much more tightly to their immediate economic surroundings. Slowly rising Gini coefficients do not inspire an Indonesian worker to revolt. But when the crisis comes, and that worker is suddenly out on the street with no income to buy food for the children or to pay the rent, while the man who employed him has safely sent his capital abroad and is still living in luxury, the social order begins to shake.

Today, from unemployed rioters in Jakarta to strikers in Michigan, from sullen unpaid miners in Russia to out-of-work skinheads in East Germany, one can see signs of a building resentment against a globalisation that leaves a large number of people behind. Even in prosperous America, the unequal distribution of benefits and costs from globalisation has in the past few years motivated successful opposition to the Clinton administration's efforts to further deregulate international trade and capital flows.

Those inspired by the vision of one global economy ignore the issue of income and wealth inequality at their peril.

Income Trends

Despite their widened global horizons, the overwhelming majority of the world's people live and work in the same nation. Their living standards are closely connected to the national trends in per capita income growth and the changes in the distribution of that growth.

The acceleration of external trade and investment began for most nations in the early to mid-1970s. Since then, trade has grown faster than production, foreign direct investment has grown faster than trade, and the growth in international financial flows has been explosive. By 1980, the world's nations were moving to distinctly higher levels of economic interaction – yet in the two decades that followed, overall income growth slowed dramatically.

Table 1 Per Capita Income Growth by Level of Human Development, 1965-95

	Annual Per Capita Income Growth	
	1965-80	1980-95
High human development	4.8 %	1.4 %
Medium human development	3.8	3.1
Excluding China	3.2	0.6
China	4.1	8.6
Low human development	1.4	2.0
Excluding India	1.2	0.1
India	1.5	3.2
All developing countries	3.0	2.1
Least developed countries	0.4	−0.4
World	n.a.	0.9

Source: United Nations' Human Development Report, 1998

Table 1 shows the per capita income growth for various countries, grouped according to the United Nations' standards for 'human development'. Several points stand out. First, income growth has been slower in the most recent period in all but one category. Second, if one excludes China and India, income growth has been abysmally low since 1980, with per capita incomes growing only 0.6 per cent and 0.1 per cent annually, in medium-development and low-development countries respectively. Income growth was actually negative among the least developed countries; it dropped 0.4 per cent a year between 1980 and 1995.

The UNDP Report for 1996 documented that, since 1980, 'economic decline or stagnation has affected 100 countries, reducing the incomes of 1.6 billion people. In 70 of these countries, average incomes are less than they were in 1980 and in 43 countries, less than they were in 1970.'

In the more advanced countries, for which better data are available, income growth was lower in the 1990s than in the 1980s. Over the entire post-1980 period, it was substantially below that of the 1960s and 1970s. From 1989 to 1996, growth was even more sluggish in the G7 countries, including the United States, the United Kingdom, Germany, France, Italy and Canada, as shown in Table 2.

Table 2 Per Capita Income Growth in Advanced Countries, 1960–96

	Annual Growth Rate Per Capita Income*		
	1960–79	1979–89	1989–96
United States	2.3 %	1.5 %	1.0 %
Japan	6.4	3.1	2.0
Germany**	3.3	1.9	1.3
France	3.7	1.6	0.8
Italy	4.1	2.3	1.0
United Kingdom	2.2	2.2	1.0
Canada	3.4	1.8	−0.1
Average, excluding USA***	3.9	2.3	1.3

*At 1990 price levels and exchange rates.
**Eastern and Western Germany.
***Includes Australia, Austria, Belgium, Denmark, Finland, Ireland, Netherlands, New Zealand, Norway, Portugal, Spain, Sweden and Switzerland.

Source: Mishel *et al.* (1998: Table 8.1, p. 35).

Tracking the parallel changes in income distribution is much more complicated. Income inequality is hard enough to measure in the developed nations, very difficult in the less developed, and virtually impossible in the poorest. Moreover, the data among countries are inconsistent in methodology and across time. On the basis of what is known, it appears that the distribution of income in most developed nations and in most nations of Latin America improved during the 1960s and 1970s.

After 1980, the evidence suggests that the distribution of income in the global economy has generally worsened. The best and most comprehensive effort at measuring this trend is the study by Ravallion and Chen (1997) that gathered all of the credible observations of the Gini coefficients around the world and sorted them into 'spells' or time periods in which the coefficients rose or fell.

Table 3 Regional Summary of Changes in the Distribution of Income or Consumption

Region	Number of spells (c)	Inequality (a) Number of spells for which it		Polarisation (b) Number of spells for which it	
		fell	rose	fell	rose
East Asia	9	3	6	3	6
Eastern Europe and Central Asia	21	3	18	3	18
Latin America and the Caribbean	14	10	4	8	6
Middle East and North Africa	3	1	2	1	2
South Asia	10	6	4	4	6
Sub-Saharan Africa	7	4	3	5	2
Total	64	27	37	24	40
Total excluding Eastern Europe and Central Asia	43	24	19	21	22

(a) Measured by the Gini index.
(b) Measured by the Wolfson (1994) polarisation index. Polarisation increasing reflects 'hollowing' of middle and growth of low and high end of distribution.
(c) Spells are where there are consistent measures for a country at two points in time and can cover periods that range from one to six years.

Source: Deininger and Squire (1996: Table 3).

They found that, overall, after 1981 there were more periods where inequality rose (37) than fell (27) (see Table 3). About half of the periods where inequality rose occurred in Eastern European and Central Asian economies in transition from socialist to capitalist economies. The study also presents a measure of the trends in polarisation – where the middle zone shrinks and the bottom and top expand. Polarisation shows the same trend as overall inequality, with periods of polarisation prevalent in about half of the non-transitional economies and pervasive among transitional economies.

Inequality trends in the advanced countries are easier to assess, since there are more data and more efforts to develop consistent measurement. In the 1980s, income inequality grew in most of the advanced countries, particularly in the USA, the United Kingdom, Australia, Sweden, Japan, and the Netherlands (see Table 4). Italy stands out as the one instance of falling inequality, at least through 1991.

The main driving force behind this growth in income inequality has been the growing inequality of earnings, which has occurred in most of the advanced countries in the 1980s and 1990s. In fact, the largest increases in wage inequality took place in the countries that experienced the largest increases in income inequality, such as the United Kingdom and the USA.

As Gottschalk and Smeeding (1997: p. 671) remark: 'With earnings more than 70 per cent of market income, it should not be surprising that increased individual earnings inequality and other changes in earnings within the household would be important factors in accounting for change in income inequality.'

Other factors, such as demographics, can also lead to increased inequality. For instance, a growth of single-mother households or aged households can increase the number and share of low-income households. Although demographics have had some effect on inequality, most studies find economic factors to be much more important.

In many countries, the shift to a more unequal distribution of market-based income (capital and labour incomes) was offset by changes in the tax and transfer system so that the distribution of 'disposable income' remained unchanged. This was the case for Canada, Israel and Finland. In only one country, the USA, did changes in the tax and transfer system exacerbate inequality.

Table 4 Change in Income Inequality after 1979

Country	Period	Annual Change in Gini Coefficient*	
		Relative (per cent)	Absolute (point-change)
United States	1979–95	0.79	0.35
Japan	1979–93	0.84	0.25
Germany**	1979–95	0.50	0.13
France	1979–89	0.40	0.12
Italy	1980–91	−0.64	−0.58
United Kingdom	1979–95	1.80	0.22
Canada	1979–95	−0.02	0.00
Australia	1981–89	1.16	0.34
Austria	.	.	.
Belgium	.	.	.
Denmark	1981–90	1.20	.
Finland	1979–94	−0.10	−0.02
Ireland	.	.	.
Netherlands	1979–94	1.07	0.25
New Zealand	.	.	.
Norway	1979–92	0.22	0.05
Portugal	.	.	.
Spain	.	.	.
Sweden	1979–94	1.68	0.38
Switzerland	.	.	.

*Measured as the relative change in the Gini coefficient, where growth reflects more inequality.

**Western Germany.

Source: Analysis in Mishel *et al.* (1998) based on Gottschalk and Smeeding (1997).

Because of the strong social safety-net, represented by these tax and transfer offsets, there has not been a sizeable increase in poverty in most advanced countries corresponding to the growth of market-income inequality. The exceptions are the USA and the United Kingdom, where poverty grew, respectively, by 2.4 and 5.4 percentage points between 1979 and 1991.

Two 'Best Case' Examples

Aggregate statistics, in addition to their technical limitations, do not capture the mechanisms through which market economies channel the distribution of the benefits and costs of globalisation. To gain insight into how these mechanisms work, we must take a closer look at trends in specific countries. For this purpose, the economics of the USA and Mexico make an informative comparison. The USA represents the neo-liberal mode in its most advanced form. Mexico represents an economy that has been in transition from an inward, regulated economy to an outward, deregulated one. Moreover, Mexico's proximity to the USA gives it clear advantages among the so-called emerging markets. First, it has access to an export market that is the envy of the world. Second, the long mutual border provides an immigration safety valve to alleviate the stress of excess unemployment. Third, as the bail-out of Mexico's creditors in 1995 demonstrated, markets know that the USA – and therefore the International Monetary Fund and similar institutions – will provide foreigners who invest in Mexico with special protection. Mexico's circumstances therefore give it the best chance of any emerging country to navigate through the waters of its neo-liberal transformation in a way that maintains at least a stable, if not an improving, distribution of the benefits and costs of that transition.

Growth and Inequality in the USA

Over the past two decades, the USA has pursued an increasingly *laissez-faire* policy domestically (by weakening social protections, collective bargaining and minimum wages) and has pushed for ever wider trade and investment liberalisation. Its strong job creation, low unemployment and stock market boom of the 1980s and 1990s have therefore been the most persuasive argument for neo-liberal policies.

In this context, increasing inequality is dismissed as a small price to pay for the benefits of overall growth. Therefore, before examining changes in the distribution of income, it is important to note that the recent expansion of the US economy is not a historically unique phenomenon. A comparison of per capita income growth in the current recovery or business cycle with earlier ones shows that the US economy is performing below par, even judged relative to the 1970s and 1980s, let alone to the booms of the 1950s and 1960s.

For instance, per capita income growth in the 1990s cycle, up to early 1998, was 1.4 per cent – no better than the 1.6 per cent annually over the 1970s (1973–80) and 1980s (1980–90) business cycles and about half the growth over the 1960–73 period. Likewise, per capita income growth in the 1990s recovery, 1.8 per cent annually, was far less than the growth in each of the preceding five recoveries dating back to 1958 (which ranged from 2.7 per cent to 3.8 per cent annual growth).

Nor has the USA achieved per capita income growth exceeding that of other advanced countries. As Table 2 shows, per capita income growth in the USA was below that of the other advanced countries in the 1980s, 1.5 per cent versus 2.3 per cent, and below that of the other G7 countries. In the 1990s, US income growth was only equivalent to that of the other G7 countries (except Canada, where income declined).

Measured by the metric of median family income, which takes into account changes in growth and distribution, the lustre of the US economic performance further diminishes. The 1980s were a time of slow growth, with median family income rising just 0.4 per cent annually. The growth over the 1990s cycle (up to 1997) was even less, just 0.1 per cent annually. In fact, it was not until 1997 that the median family's income exceeded that of 1989 (the prior business cycle peak). So, it took four years of growth to recover from the 1989–93 income downturn with no net improvement over the entire 1989–97 period.

Family income growth slowed despite a greater (paid) work effort by families. For instance, a middle-class family's annual work hours (for all family members) grew from 3,020 in 1979, to 3,206 in 1989, and to 3,335 by 1997, a growth of 10.4 per cent in 18 years.

The consequence of these trends is that the pre-1973 decline in inequality has been more than reversed, with the USA experiencing a dramatic surge in the upward redistribution of income, surpassed only by the United Kingdom. The beneficiaries of the shift have been the richest 5 per cent, but particularly the richest 1 per cent whose pre-tax incomes grew by 93 per cent from 1977 to 1995.

This growth in inequality is a result of a shift of income from wages to capital income (profits and interest) and a growing inequality among wage earners. Both trends are symptomatic of a *laissez-faire* policy regime where employers' power in the labour market was increased through deregulation of industries, a weakening of unions, an erosion of the minimum wage, and increased globalisation (trade, investment and immigration). The result is that the median workers' hourly wage (inflation-adjusted) was about 3 per cent less in 1998 than in 1979. The median hourly wage for men fell 13 per cent over that period. Meanwhile, productivity grew by 22 per cent. The combination of lower real wages (labour costs) and higher productivity produced the highest corporate profit rates in more than three decades, helping to fuel the stock market boom.

Promoters of policies to accelerate globalisation often assert that increased inequality is not a product of more open borders. This leads to some intellectual contradictions. The USA is a more open economy, at least in terms of imports from developing countries, than is Japan or Europe, and this openness is claimed to have made US citizens better off, at least on average, as the USA shifts to a more efficient deployment of resources. Surely this must imply that there are some losses, primarily of less skilled, lower-wage workers. Otherwise, there could not have been much resource reallocation, and therefore not much gain. Given the threadbare American social safety-net, if there are gains from globalisation, there have to be losses at the bottom range of income distribution.

The effect of globalisation on incomes does not just work through the market mechanisms of lower import prices. A difficult-to-measure but very real phenomenon is that workers, union and non-union, do not press for higher wages and/or accept lower wages for fear that their jobs will be moved abroad. The shift of direct investment abroad also has an impact as demand for labour weakens in vulnerable sectors. The persistently large trade deficits in the USA have also played a role in shrinking the number of well-paid manufacturing jobs for those without a college degree. Globalisation has not necessarily been the whole story of the rise in inequality in the USA, but in its full dimension it has played a much larger role than conventional wisdom has allowed.

Finally, there is little evidence that the neo-liberal policy mix which has generated this inequality has also generated a more efficient economy. In fact, throughout the period of opening markets, productivity growth in the USA has not improved, being a sluggish 1 per cent or so in the 1980s and 1990s as in the 1970s. Such productivity growth is slow both by historical standards and by comparative international standards. Productivity growth has been twice as fast in other advanced countries as in the USA. In the past, this has been explained by the process of others 'catching up' to the USA, which is the technological leader. However, according to recent analyses by the Organisation for Economic Co-operation and Development (OECD) and others, the USA is no longer the productivity leader in many industries, and Germany, Belgium, France, Italy and the Netherlands have achieved US levels of economy-wide productivity. So, whatever the USA is doing, it has not generated an efficiency gain relative to major competitors. Likewise, whatever these European countries have done has not impeded their ability to become as efficient as the USA.

To be sure, the past two years have seen an increase in productivity and wage growth with wages growing fastest at the bottom. In judging how sustainable this trend might be, it is important to note that there has been an extraordinary growth in demand generated by an inflated stock market and consumer debt. Productivity has grown as firms satisfied fast-growing demand in a labour-scarce environment. We will have to go through a full business and financial market cycle before concluding that the productivity and wage growth of the past two years is a permanent fixture of the US economy.

Growth and Inequality in Mexico

From the 1950s to the 1980s, Mexico went through a period of dramatic industrialisation and high economic growth, based on the development of its internal markets. The state sector, under the rule of one party, the Partido Revolucionario Institucional (PRI), since the 1930s, followed deliberate import-substitution industrial policies that nurtured Mexican-owned firms. During the 1970s, this policy was aided by high world prices for oil and the eagerness of American and other banks to lend money to Mexico's public and private enterprises.

During those years of internally oriented development, Mexico's economy grew steadily. Between 1960 and 1982, per capita income rose 3.6 per cent per year. New industries were created and public spending on education, health and rural development rose. Like most Latin American societies, Mexico has always had a very unequal distribution of income and wealth but, as it modernised throughout this period, a somewhat greater share of the increment to national income went to those at the bottom. Gini coefficients improved by roughly 10 per cent between 1957 and 1984.

The collapse of oil prices in the early 1980s led to a debt crisis for the country. Under pressure from its creditors, Mexico gradually abandoned its inward development focus. In 1983, the ruling party cut back government spending, raised the prices of basic necessities and devalued the currency to favour exports. In 1985, it joined the General Agreement on Tariffs and Trade (GATT). From 1983 to 1989, Mexico's per capita growth dropped to 0.6 per cent.

Mexico's labour markets, like those in most developing countries, are characterised by real wage flexibility. Therefore, the brunt of the decline in income came in a sharp reduction in wages. The incidence of poverty rose from 29 per cent in 1984 to 36 per cent in 1989. Over those same years, the share of income received by the bottom nine tenths of the population declined, while the share of income of the top tenth expanded by 18 per cent.

The political result was a stunning and unprecedented challenge to the ruling oligarchy. On election night 1988, the count showed the PRI's candidate, Carlos Salinas de Gotari, trailing Cuauhtemoc Cardenas of a newly formed left-populist party. The government promptly declared that the computers had suddenly malfunctioned, and suspended the election count for several days. When it resumed, the government announced that Salinas had narrowly won. Mexico was on the brink of a civil war until Cardenas accepted the verdict to avoid bloodshed.

In 1989 Salinas, desperate to spur growth, deregulated the financial system – freeing up interest rates, eliminating credit controls, reducing reserve requirements, and privatising previously nationalised banks. Shortly afterwards, he began negotiations with the USA and Canada for the North American Free Trade Agreement (NAFTA). Under aggressive US sponsorship, Mexico was admitted to the OECD, which automatically reduced the risk premium for Mexican bonds. All of these political initiatives made Mexico the hottest of the emerging markets. Money poured into the economy, stimulating its growth. The decline in per capita income was reversed, although it did not reach the levels of the pre-liberalisation era. Between 1989 and 1994, per capita income rose 1.8 per cent per year.

Despite the spurt in growth, overall poverty and inequality did not improve. Indeed, for small farmers and urban workers they worsened. In rural areas, Salinas's neo-liberal programme called for the destruction of the traditional *ejido* system of common land ownership. The policy included reduced access to credit, subsidised fertiliser and water, and technical assistance. As a result, the wealthiest farmers bought up the newly privatised land from the poorest, who in turn became marginal rural workers. Another factor was the elimination of the international coffee agreement from 1989 to 1994, which lowered prices for that product. The agreement was revived in 1994, but as part of NAFTA, Mexico pledged not to be part of any international effort to maintain the price of coffee.

Nevertheless, the Mexican government became the poster child for the international financial institution's concept of wise reformed governance. Carried on the wave of the financial boom, Salinas's hand-picked successor was elected in the summer of 1994, and Salinas himself was the favourite candidate to head the newly formed World Trade Organisation (WTO).

The bubble burst in late 1994. Mexican reserves had been run down in an ill-fated effort to prop up the increasingly overvalued peso, and in December a group of Mexican investors close to the PRI bailed out of Mexican securities, precipitating a flight from the peso. The currency dropped 40 per cent against the dollar, interest rates rose to 50 per cent, and the stock market melted down.

Salinas lost his bid for the WTO job and ended up in comfortable, if discredited, exile. But, it was the typical Mexican worker who was hit hard. Almost two million jobs were lost and real wages in manufacturing fell almost 40 per cent. Direct measures of income distribution after 1994 are yet not available but economists at the Inter-American Development Bank projected that the incidence of poverty had risen 15 per cent in 1995. Moreover, they projected that, even if the Mexican economy grew steadily at 5 per cent, and if the distribution of income returned to the pattern of 1994, it would take another eight years for the incidence of poverty to fall back to where it was in 1984, just after the liberalisation of trade and investment began.

The increase in inequality in Mexico over these years came at the same time that inequality was rising among American workers. Basic economic theory says this is not supposed to happen. The Stolper–Samuelson Theorem, which is the foundation for modern international trade theory, tells us that increased trade between an advanced nation and a less developed one will raise inequality in the former and reduce it in the latter. This is because the comparative advantage for developed nations is supposed to reside in their ability to make products that require more skilled inputs, while the comparative advantage for less developed countries lies in their abundance of less skilled and therefore cheaper labour. NAFTA was supposed to increase demand for, and the relative wages of, skilled labour in the USA and reduce it for unskilled labour. In Mexico, the relative wage for unskilled labourers was supposed to rise. In fact, those at the low-wage end of the labour force in both countries suffered, and inequality increased in Mexico as well as the USA. Other nations in Latin America that have opened up their economies to the world – Chile, Uruguay, Columbia – showed similar patterns of expanding inequality driven by lower wages at the bottom.

Conclusion

For a long time, many policy-makers and journalists denied the reality of the slowdown in per capita growth, the stubborn persistence of rising poverty or the maldistribution of incomes. When this reality became impossible to deny, they belittled its importance. In the wake of a crash of financial markets and the subsequent tumble into deep recession of approximately 40 per cent of the world's population, the question of inequality can no longer be shrugged off.

The policy elite has responded to this question with four answers.

The first is to assert that it is still too early to pass judgement. According to this view, we have had some bad luck and, now that the practitioners of crony capitalism have been shamed, we can expect the promised sustainable long-term global expansion to begin. Perhaps. But it is a reasonable bet that, even if the current financial crisis is over and growth picks up, it will be another decade before per capita incomes in most of the affected parts of the world return to where they were in the early 1980s. Given the dramatic evidence of increased volatility of financial markets, chances of high, steady growth for the next ten years have to be rated low – and the chances of such growth over a much longer period must be even lower. Moreover, since the promoters of radical integration were wrong in their projections of the past twenty years, on what basis should we believe that their forecasts of the next twenty will be any better?

For those nations at the bottom – many of whom are so burdened with debt, poverty and a crumbling infrastructure – given the present global policy regime, there is little hope for recovery in any reasonable time-frame.

A second line of defence is to protect the reputation of trade liberalisation by claiming that the failures of integration have been limited to the financial markets. Thus, some greater transparency and the encouragement of more prudent lending and borrowing practices should reduce the dangers of financial volatility and allow the fundamentals of free trade to work their magic. According to this argument, if we soften the financial boom-and-bust cycles, we will also reduce the unequal economic burden of adjustment that is borne by those who work for a living.

Aside from the question of how radical a re-regulation is necessary to reduce financial instability, this argument ignores two issues. One issue is the difficult fact that, contrary to the predictions of trade theory, trade liberalisation appears to have reduced the living standards of people on the bottom in many developed and developing nations. The other issue is the way in which trade and financial market deregulation have been two sides of the same policy coin. Indeed, the WTO and trade agreements like NAFTA have been explicitly linked to the liberalisation of capital markets. The political pressure for globalisation comes largely from multinational corporations and financial institutions whose primary interest is not in allowing developing nations' low-wage producers access to advanced world markets, but in allowing themselves, directly or indirectly, to become producers in low-wage countries. They therefore demand, and get, rights and protections for their investments as part of the process of liberalising trade.

The third answer of the policy elite is to acknowledge that integration creates losers as well as winners, and to propose stronger social safety-nets to cushion the impact on the former. There is much to say for this view, which has long been a staple tenet of post-war social democracy. But the experiences of the past twenty years have raised some major questions about its practicality in today's neo-liberal politics. In most instances, for example, opening up to the global market-place has been associated with a shredding of the social safety-net, not a strengthening of it. In fact, the claim that domestic systems of income maintenance, health, education, and so on, cannot be afforded in the environment of global competition is a theme heard in the capitals of poor and rich nations alike.

Even in the USA, globalisation has created pressure to reduce the safety-net of tax and transfer programmes that would counteract the unequal effects of globalisation on incomes. To some extent, this is a political phenomenon, rather than a necessary economic effect of globalisation. Certainly, the USA can afford a more generous social safety-net than it has. But globalisation has strengthened the bargaining position and, therefore, the political power of capital over labour. And because capital's interest is in maximising its share of after-tax income, domestic politics has shifted against a stronger safety-net.

The same is true in most other nations participating in the global economy. This shift in domestic political power in favour of the owners of capital is reinforced by the pressures from the International Monetary Fund (IMF) and other international financial institutions (IFIs) to reduce social spending and to undercut the political power of labour unions by insisting that countries adopt 'flexible' labour market policies. To be sure, there is lip-service given to programmes to help the poor – who are usually defined only as those on the very bottom rung of the income distribution ladder. But policies targeted only at those on the very bottom isolate the poor from their allies in the broad working class, and insure that they will have insufficient domestic political support.

A fourth response is to search for new economic development techniques that will empower the poor in market-place competition. One example is the stress laid by public and private agencies on 'micro-enterprises'. The UNDP's Human Development Report urges the support of export-oriented small and medium enterprises in order to enter the export markets. This is a laudable project – but, given the modest number of potentially successful entrepreneurs relative to the population, it is obviously inadequate as a means of making a serious dent in the lopsided distribution of income and opportunity in poor nations. Moreover, it ignores an important channel through which market liberalisation works – that is, to destroy small businesses in favour of larger concentrations of capital. The effect of new foreign capital in most nations typically is not to create new industries but to modernise and reorganise the old. In most poor countries, micro-enterprises already exist in the form of small peasant farmers and artisans. Rural Mexico is a good example. The effect of NAFTA has been to decimate the small maize farmers with lower-cost imports from US and Canadian agribusiness and, as a result, to increase the concentration of land in corporate hands.

Thus, what we have learned over the past two decades is that, in the real world, forced economic integration has led to greater inequality of market incomes and a declining ability to offset that inequality with safety-nets and other public policies. What then might be a strategy for dealing with the increasing disparities in income and wealth generated by trade and investment liberalisation?

To begin with, we must do no further harm. Given the evidence of how the current structure of globalisation works 'at the level of people', we should refrain from policies to accelerate economic integration until we have in place policies that protect and advance the interests of workers and the poor, policies equal in effectiveness to those that now protect the interests of investors. Specifically, the next round of WTO trade negotiations should be slowed, if not postponed. Instead, the WTO should devote itself to an honest assessment of the effect of liberalisation on all levels of society.

The natural expansion of the global trade in goods, services and finance, in response to changing technology, tastes and shifts in the comparative advantage of nations, is generally beneficial, although the benefits are often exaggerated and do not in every case exceed the costs. But over the past two decades, the process has been artificially accelerated in ways that have been generally harmful to the majority of people who work for a living both in the USA and abroad.

Indeed, while the promoters of globalisation have grudgingly acknowledged that there are costs to society, they have assumed in all cases that the costs, whatever they are, must be less than the overall benefits to society, an assumption reinforced by the ideological disposition of economists to glorify free markets. But an examination of the post-war economy cannot find empirical evidence to support these claims. As Harvard University economist Dani Rodrik, a self-proclaimed free trader, observes: 'Economics is notoriously bad at quantifying forces that most people believe are quite important. For example, no widely accepted model attributes to post-war trade liberalisation more than a very tiny fraction of the increased prosperity of the advanced industrial countries. Yet most economists do believe that expanding trade was very important to this progress.'

It is time to move away from policies founded on belief, no matter how fiercely held, to policies for which the empirical case is stronger. Specifically, world leaders need to turn their attention to building up the global institutions and policies aimed at counterbalancing the power of capital.

We need to apply the hard-earned lessons of national economic development to the global market-place. For example, when the USA was transformed from a series of regional markets to a continental economy, it had to create continental institutions to keep the economy in balance – for instance, a central bank, financial regulations, crop insurance, labour and environmental protections, social insurance, and so on. The result was a sustained, broadly shared prosperity. In different scales and historical contexts, the same institutional elements supported the development of the world's other successful economies.

The global market-place has no such institutions to keep it balanced. So-called 'free trade' agreements are really protectionist for global investors, while leaving workers, farmers and small-business people to the mercies of a rigged market. Neither is the IMF a central bank charged with nurturing global growth and stability. It is, rather, a shallow-pockets lender, dependent on loans from its member countries and partnerships with private banks. It conditions its loans to troubled nations with austerity policies aimed at giving debt repayment through exports priority over domestic growth. And, along with the US financial authorities, it has a tendency to rescue dictatorships, big banks, and others who are 'too big to fail'.

Suspending the rush towards further trade and capital liberalisation would provide the time – and the incentive – to put into place some countervailing institutions and policies. These would include:

1 Debt reduction and, in some cases, forgiveness, for the poorest nations, with conditions that enhance broad-based domestic development, even at the expense of market-opening policies.
2 The enforceable protection of core human and labour rights in trade and

investment agreements in order to enhance the bargaining power of those on the bottom. Among other things, this would mean the strengthening of the capacity of the International Labour Organisation to monitor labour conditions and the willingness of the WTO, the IMF and other IFIs to make adherence to such rights a condition of loans and liberalised economic relationships.

3 Reduction of financial volatility, including capital controls, a tax on international securities transfers and an ending to IFI bail-outs that pay off private creditors and leave poor nations saddled with debts they cannot pay back.

This is an ambitious agenda. But for those who dream of a stable, prosperous world economy, there is no alternative. The current international economic regime of unregulated global markets is economically and politically unstable. People who work for a living, both at home and abroad, increasingly resist being pushed out into the stormy seas of global competition in economies where only the investors in first class get the life-jackets.

Bibliography

Deininger, Klaus, and Squire, Lyn (1996) 'A New Data Set Measuring Income Inequality', *The World Bank Economic Review*, vol. 10, no. 3, The International Bank for Reconstruction/The World Bank.

Gottschalk, Peter, and Smeeding, Timothy M. (1997) 'Cross National Comparison of Earnings and Income Inequality', *The Journal of Economic Literature*, vol. xxxv, no. 2, p. 671.

Human Development Report (1996 and 1998), United Nations Development Programme (UNDP).

Lustig, Nora, and Szekely, Miguel (1998) *Economic Trends, Poverty and Inequality in Mexico*, Inter-American Development Bank, technical study.

Mishel, Lawrence, Bernstein, Jared, and Schmitt, John (1998) *The State of Working America, 1998–99*, an Economic Policy Institute book, Ithaca, N.Y.: Cornell University Press.

Ravallion, Martin, and Chen, Shaohua (1997) 'What Can New Survey Data Tell Us About Recent Changes in Distribution and Poverty?' *The World Bank Economic Review*, vol. ii, no. 2, The International Bank for Reconstruction and Development/The World Bank.

Rodrik, Dani (1997) *Has Globalization Gone Too Far?* Institute for International Economics.

Wolfensohn, James (1999) quoted in Jim Hoagland, 'Richer and Poorer', *Washington Post*, 25 April.

Wolfson, Michael (1994) 'Diverging Inequality', *American Economic Review*, no. 84, 2 May.

VANDANA SHIVA

The World on the Edge

The Production of Ignorance

In 1992 citizens and governments gathered in Rio to address the most serious ecological threats of our time – climate change, biodiversity erosion, the depletion and pollution of water resources, the build-up of toxic wastes.

Yet even before the international community could start taking the faltering steps to evolve the Rio agenda which emerged from the Earth Summit, another agenda of globalisation and free trade swept across the world like a hurricane, undoing environmental gains, increasing environmental stresses, and generating new ecological risks such as the release of genetically engineered organisms.

We enter the next millennium with a deliberate production of ignorance about ecological risks such as the deregulation of environmental protection and the destruction of ecologically sustainable lifestyles for peasant, tribal, pastoral and craft communities across the Third World. These people are becoming the new global environmental refugees.

For the poorer two thirds of humanity living in the South, nature's capital is their source of sustenance and livelihood. The destruction, diversion and takeover of their eco-systems in order to extract natural resources or dump waste generates a disproportionate burden for the poor. In a world of globalised, deregulated commerce in which everything is tradable and economic strength is the only determinant of power and control, resources move from the poor to the rich, and pollution moves from the rich to the poor. The result is a global environmental apartheid.

Globalisation as Environmental Apartheid

Global free trade has caused world-wide environmental destruction in an asymmetric pattern. The international economy is controlled by the corporations of the North, who are increasingly exploiting Third World resources for their global activities. It is the South that is disproportionately bearing the environmental burden of the globalised economy.

The current environmental and social crisis demands that the world economy adjust to ecological limits and the needs of human survival. Instead, global institutions like the World Bank and the International Monetary Fund (IMF) and the World Trade Organisation (WTO) are forcing the costs of adjustment onto nature and women and the Third World. Across what the World Bank calls LDC (less developed countries), structural adjustment and trade liberalisation measures are becoming the most serious threat to human lives.

While the past five decades have been characterised by the global spread of maldevelopment and the export of a non-sustainable Western industrial paradigm in the name of development, the recent trends are towards an environmental apartheid in which, through global policy set by the 'holy trinity', the Western transnational corporations supported by the governments of the economically powerful countries attempt to maintain the North's economic power and the wasteful life-styles of the rich.

They do this by exporting the environmental costs to the Third World. Resource-hungry and pollution-intensive industries are being relocated in the South through the economies of free trade.

Lawrence Summers, who was the World Bank's chief economist, was responsible for the 1992 World Development Report which was devoted to the economics of the environment. This actually suggested that it made economic sense to transfer high-pollution industries to Third World countries. In a memo dated 12 December 1991 to senior World Bank staff, the Chief Economist wrote: 'Just between you and me, shouldn't the World Bank be encouraging more migration of the dirty industries to the LDC?' Summers justified the economic logic of increasing pollution in the Third World on three grounds.

First, since wages are low in the Third World, the economic costs of pollution arising from increased illness and death are lowest in the poorest countries. According to Summers, 'the logic of relocation of pollutants in the lowest wage countries is impeccable and we should face up to that'.

Second, since in large parts of the Third World pollution is still low,

113

it made economic sense to Summers to introduce pollution. 'I've always thought', he wrote, 'that countries in Africa are vastly underpolluted; their air quality is probably vastly, inefficiently high compared to Los Angeles or Mexico City.'

Finally, since the poor are poor, they cannot possibly worry about environmental problems. 'The concern over an agent that causes a one-in-a-million chance of prostate cancer is obviously going to be much higher in a country where people survive to get prostate cancer, than in a country where under-five mortality is 200 per thousand.'

Lawrence Summers has recommended the relocation of hazardous and polluting industry to the Third World because, in narrow economic terms, life is cheaper in the poorer countries. The economists' logic values life differently in the rich north and the poor south, but all life is precious to all. It is equally precious to the rich and the poor, the white and the black, the men and the women.

In this context, recent attempts by the North to link terms of trade with the environment using platforms such as the WTO need to be viewed as an attempt to build on environmental and economic apartheid. No Western country has stopped the export of its hazards, wastes and polluting industries to the South.

The issue of export of domestically prohibited goods was never fully developed in GATT, the General Agreement on Tariffs and Trade. The destruction of eco-systems and livelihoods as a result of trade liberalisation is a major environmental and social subsidy to global trade and commerce, and to those who control it. The main mantra of globalisation is 'international competitiveness'. In the context of the environment this translates into the largest corporations competing for the natural resources that the poor people in the Third World need for their survival.

The competition is highly unequal not only because the corporations are powerful and the poor are not, but because the rules of free trade allow corporations to use the machinery of the nation-state to appropriate resources from the people, and prevent people from asserting and exercising their rights.

It is often argued that globalisation will create more trade, trade will create growth, and growth will remove poverty. What is overlooked in this myth is that globalisation and liberalised trade and investment create growth through the destruction of the environment and local, sustainable livelihoods. They therefore create poverty instead of removing it. Globalisation policies have accelerated and expanded environmental destruction and displaced millions of people from their homes and their sustenance bases.

If pollution and waste migrate to the South under 'free trade' and the knowledge, biological diversity and wealth created from it are travelling north through the regimes controlling intellectual property rights, such as those associated with 'free trade' treaties like GATT, the inevitable outcome of globalisation must be environmental apartheid.

Globalisation of Environmental Stress

Every year, climatic instability is increasing. The forest fires in South-East Asia, ice storms in Canada, Hurricane Mitch in Central America – these might appear to be local phenomena, but they are all connected to climate changes – the ecological burden of atmospheric pollution.

Economic globalisation is contributing to global climate instability by promoting an energy-intensive, export-oriented model of development. As local production is dismantled by rules surrounding free trade, and all communities and countries export what they produce and import what they need, energy intensity of transport, packaging and production increases. The average chicken travels 2,000 km before being eaten. Yoghurt and its ingredients make accumulated journeys totalling 3,500 km, and another 4,500 km could be added during distribution.

According to the Danish Minister of Environment, 1 kilo of food transported globally generates 10 kg of CO_2. Studies done by Kassel University in Germany show that non-local food production contributes between six and twelve times more CO_2 than local production. It is estimated that 90 per cent of CO_2 emissions have been contributed to the global atmospheric commons by the rich industrialised countries. In the former West Germany, primary energy consumption increased by 85 per cent between 1960 and 1980. A citizen of the USA produces twenty-five times the annual CO_2 emissions of someone living in India.

The man-made greenhouse effect is mainly caused by emission of CO_2, chlorofluorocarbons (CFCs), halogens, methane, nitrogen oxides and hydrocarbons. In addition to destabilising climate, CFCs and halogens also deplete the ozone layer – the protective mantle surrounding the earth and filtering ultraviolet radiation from the sun. Most CFC production has also taken place in the industrialised world. In 1991, Africa used only 12,000 tonnes of CFCs compared with 90,000 tonnes in the USA.

The impact of climate instability and ozone depletion is borne unequally by the South. Since most Third World countries depend on agriculture, slight changes in climate can totally destroy rural livelihoods. Climate change threatens the very existence of low-lying island states like the Maldives and Barbados. The developed countries also produce 90 per cent of the hazardous waste around the world every year.

The USA generates more than 275 million tonnes of toxic waste every year; it is the leading waste-exporting country of the world. Toxic waste such as cyanide, mercury and arsenic is being shipped as 'recyclable waste' – a deliberate attempt to mislead and one that disguises the true nature of the wastes. In reality, there is no such use or demand to recover such toxic chemicals. It is purely waste.

Developed countries are offering lucrative prices (in Third World terms) to Third World 'recycling' companies to take their material for 'processing'. India is being used as a dumping ground by the northern industrialised countries, because the cost of treating and disposing of waste in a sustainable manner in the North has become highly expensive. Costs have become so high because of the stringent laws banning the dumping, burning, or burying of waste. Dumping in the developing world therefore becomes justified on grounds of economic cost efficiency.

The cost of burying 1 tonne of hazardous waste in the USA rose from $15 in 1980, to $350 in 1992. In Germany it is cheaper by $2,500 to ship a tonne of waste to a developing country than to dispose of it in Europe. Because India does not bear any land-filling costs, the profits to be made trading in waste have made the industry even more attractive.

Greenpeace says that international waste traffickers are still sending their toxic trash to India – in total defiance of Indian and international laws. Rich countries such as Australia and the USA continue to export waste in full knowledge they are blatantly violating Indian law and the Basel Convention, which governs the international movement and the disposal of hazardous waste. Asia remains the largest dumping ground today for the West's waste.

The Piracy of Third World Biological and Intellectual Wealth

The poorer two thirds of humanity sustains itself through livelihoods based upon biodiversity and indigenous knowledge. Today, this resource base of the poor is under threat as their plants and seeds are patented and claimed as inventions of Western scientists and Western corporations, denying the collective innovation of centuries of Third World peasants, healers and crafts people who are the true protectors and utilisers of this biodiversity.

Western-style industrial systems of intellectual property rights (IPRs) to ways of life are being forced on the Third World through the Trade Related Intellectual Property Rights (TRIPs) agreement of the WTO which introduced patents and seed industry monopolies.

The TRIPs agreement recognises IPRs only as private, not common, rights. This excludes all kinds of knowledge, ideas and innovations that take place in the intellectual commons – in villages among farmers, in forests among tribespeople, and even in universities among scientists. Such IPR protection will stifle the pluralistic ways of knowing that have enriched our world.

IPRs are recognised only when knowledge and innovation generate profit, not when they meet social needs. Profits and capital accumulation are the only ends to which creativity is put; the social good is no longer recognised. The universalisation of the preferred priorities of a very small part of human society will destroy creativity, not encourage it. By reducing human knowledge to the status of private property, intellectual property rights shrink the human potential to innovate and create; they transform the free exchange of ideas into theft and piracy.

In reality, IPRs are the sophisticated name for modern piracy. With no regard or respect for other species and cultures, IPRs are a moral, ecological and cultural outrage. Moreover, IPR actions in the biodiversity domain are tainted with cultural, racial and species-centred prejudice and arrogance. GATT is the platform where the capitalistic, patriarchal notion of freedom as the unrestrained right of men with economic power to own, control and destroy life is articulated as free trade. But for the Third World, and particularly for women, freedom has different meanings. In the domain of international trade, these different meanings of freedom are a focus of contest and conflict. Free trade in food and agriculture is the concrete location of the most fundamental ethical and economic issues facing humans today.

The TRIPs agreement of GATT and the WTO is not the result of democratic negotiations between the larger public and commercial interests or between industrialised countries and the Third World. It is the imposition of values and interests by Western transnational corporations on the diverse societies and cultures of the world.

The framework for the TRIPs agreement was conceived and shaped by three organisations – the Intellectual Property Committee (IPC), Keidanren and the Union of Industrial and Employees Confederations (UNICE). IPC is a coalition of twelve major US corporations: Bristol Myers, DuPont, General Electric, General Motors, Hewlett Packard, IBM, Johnson & Johnson, Merck, Monsanto, Pfizer, Rockwell and Warner; Keidanren is a federation of economic organisations in Japan; and UNICE is recognised as the official spokesperson for European business and industry. The transnational corporations have a vested interest in the TRIPs agreement. For example, Pfizer, Bristol Myers and Merck already have patents on Third World bio-materials collected without payment of royalties. Together, these groups worked closely to introduce intellectual property protection into GATT. James Enyart of Monsanto, commenting on the IPC strategy, stated:

> What I have described to you is absolutely unprecedented in GATT. Industry has identified a major problem for international trade. It crafted a solution, reduced it to a concrete proposal and sold it to our own and other governments. The industries and traders of world commerce have played simultaneously the roles of patients, the diagnosticians and the prescribing physicians.
>
> Enyart, 1990: 54–6

Life Inc.

With globalisation, life itself has emerged as the ultimate commodity. Planet Earth is being replaced by Life Inc. in the world of free trade and deregulated commerce. Through patents and genetic engineering, new colonies are being carved out. The land, the forests, the rivers, the oceans and the atmosphere have all been colonised, eroded and polluted. Capital now has to look for new colonies to invade and exploit for its further accumulation. These new colonies are, in my view, the interior spaces of the bodies of women, plants and animals.

Global chemical corporations have restructured themselves as 'Life Sciences Corporations', and have bought up seed and biotechnology companies. They have then merged. Ciba-Geigy and Sandoz merged to become Novartis. Zeneca has joined with Astra, Hoechst and Rhone Poulenc have merged to form Aventis. Companies like Monsanto have started to buy major seed companies around the world. Monsanto now owns and controls Cargill Seeds, Dekalb, Asgrow, Holden, Delta and

Pine Land, Calgene, Agracetus, MAHYCO and Sementes Agrocerus. As corporations control seed, they also control the food chain. According to Robert Farley of Monsanto: 'What you're seeing is not just the consolidation of seed companies, it's really a consolidation of the food chain.'

Traditional boundaries between pharmaceutical, biotechnology, agribusiness, food, chemicals, cosmetics and energy sectors are breaking down. The Life Sciences banner is the symbol of this consolidation and concentration.

If the twentieth century was the petroleum century, the twenty-first will be the century of biology. The ten leading food companies – Nestlé, Philip Morris, Unilever, Con Agra, Cargill, Pepsico, Coca-Cola, Diageo Guinness, Mars and Danone – had revenues of $45.3 billion in 1992. These are setting up joint ventures with seed companies to control the crops grown and food eaten. According to a public interest group, the Rural Advancement Foundation International: 'In an era of bio-serfdom, farmers are systematically eliminated from farm-level management and decision-making. They become renters of property germplasm from the "gene giants" or their subsidiaries.'

The global corporations are using a mixture of technological and legal control on the very basis and processes of life. Since living resources renew and multiply, converting life itself into a commodity and source of profit requires them to prevent life's renewal. This is being done legally through patents, so that farmers are forced to buy seed each year or pay royalties. The saving of seed by farmers is being redefined, from a sacred duty to the earth and future generations, into a crime. Corporations like Monsanto have hired detectives to hunt for seed-saving by farmers. Monsanto is also rewarding farmers who inform on their neighbours. According to Hope Shand of RAFI: 'Our rural communities are being turned into corporate police states and farmers are being turned into criminals.'

Besides using legal instruments such as patents, Life Sciences companies are also using genetic engineering to establish monopolies on life. The first method is to breed proprietary seed which requires the companies' chemicals. For instance, 70 per cent of all genetic engineering applications are for crops tolerant of herbicide such as Monsanto's Round-Up Ready soy and corn. All Life Sciences corporations are also developing anti-life modifiers such as 'Terminator Technologies'.

On 3 March 1998, the US Department of Agriculture (USDA) and the Delta and Pine Land Company, a subsidiary of Monsanto and the largest cotton seed company in the world, announced that they had jointly developed and received a patent on a new agricultural biotechnology. Benignly titled 'Control of Plant Gene Expression', the new patent permitted its owners and licensees to create sterile seed by selectively programming a plant's DNA to kill its own embryos. The patent applies to plants and seeds of all species. The result? If farmers save pods, tomatoes, peppers, heads of wheat and ears of corn, they will essentially be stockpiling seed morgues. The system will force farmers to buy seed from seed companies each year. It has been dubbed 'terminator technology' by groups such as RAFI, which says it threatens farmers' independence and the food security of over a billion poor farmers in Third World countries.

There is another potential dark side to the Terminator. Molecular biologists are examining the risk that the Terminator function could escape from the genomes of the crops into which it has been intentionally incorporated, and move into surrounding, open-pollinated crops or wild, related plants in fields nearby. Given nature's incredible adaptability, and the fact that the technology has never been tested on a large scale, the possibility that the Terminator may spread to surrounding food crops or to the natural environment must be taken seriously. The gradual spread of sterility in seeding plants would result in a global catastrophe that could eventually wipe out higher life-forms, including humans.

In a recent communiqué, RAFI states: 'If the Terminator Technology is widely utilised, it will give the multinational seed and agrochemical industry an unprecedented and extremely dangerous capacity to control the world's food supply.' That fear may be realised much sooner than anyone could have imagined.

As Geri Guidetli has written:

Never before has man created such an insidiously dangerous, far-reaching and potentially 'perfect' plan to control the livelihoods, food supply and even survival of all humans on the planet. In one broad, brazen stroke of his hand, man will have irretrievably broken the seed-plant-seed-plant-seed cycle, the cycle that supports most life on the planet. No seed, no food, unless you buy more seed. The Terminator Technology is brilliant science and arguably 'good business', but it has crossed the line, the tenuous line between genius and insanity. It is a dangerous, bad idea that should be banned. Period.

The Ecological Threat to the Food Chain

Food and water make life possible for humans and all species on the planet. Through globalisation the biggest threat to life is coming from food and water – from their pollution and contamination, and from monopolistic control over these vital products and resources.

Industrialisation of the food system has gifted us the Mad Cow, cancers and endocrine disrupters. Genetic engineering is now introducing new ecological risks through the food chain. Genetic pollution is emerging as a new source of health risks from food. From 1986 to 1997, approximately 25,000 transgenic crop field trials were conducted by forty-five countries on more than sixty crops and ten traits. Almost 28 million hectares of genetically engineered crops were grown world-wide in 1998, with soy bean, maize, cotton, rape and potato as the five principal transgenic crops.

Monsanto's transgenic seeds account for 88 per cent of the total genetically engineered crops planted. The reduction of biodiversity and of cultural diversity of food has major ecological and health implications.

India used to have 200,000 varieties of rice. The USA had 7,000 apple varieties. The Andean peasants have grown 3,000 varieties of potatoes. Papua New Guinea had as many as 5,000 varieties of sweet potatoes. In China, 10,000 wheat varieties used to be cultivated.

In peasant societies, small farms still have as many as 200 species which provide food for the soil, for animals and for humans. These systems of diverse crops and foods are being displaced by a global monoculture pushing millions of species to extinction and creating new health problems in the midst of overproduction as manipulated foods and reduced diversity create nutritional insecurity.

The source of 70 per cent of the world's food is still small farms, and 70 per cent of the world's farmers are women. Yet the millions of providers of food are being eclipsed by a handful of corporations which claim that they feed the world and must have more freedom to trade so that they can feed larger numbers.

As Monsanto advertised during its $1.6 million advertising campaign in Europe:

Worrying about starving future generations won't feed them. Food biotechnology will. The world's population is growing rapidly, adding the equivalent of a China to the globe every 10 years. To feed these billion more mouths, we can try extending our farming land or squeezing greater harvests out of existing cultivation. With the planet set to double in numbers around 2030, this heavy dependency on land can only become heavier. Soil erosion and mineral depletion will exhaust the ground. Lands such as rainforests will be forced into cultivation. Fertiliser, insecticide and herbicide use will increase globally. At Monsanto, we now believe food biotechnology is a better way forward.

Quoted in: Research Foundation, 1998

Nature provides thousands of nutritious species for our food. Sustainable ecological agriculture is a viable way to produce healthy, safe and adequate food for all. Yet the harvest of safe food is being stolen from consumers world-wide and they are being force-fed genetically engineered foods they do not want. The right to trade freely on a global scale is being established as the highest right. People's right to safe and adequate food is being treated as a non-tariff trade barrier, to be dismantled and destroyed.

While genetic engineering is always presented as a solution to hunger and food insecurity, the Life Sciences corporations are generating food insecurity by denying consumers the right to food safety, the right to know and the right to choose.

My colleague Mae Wan Ho has identified the following hazards to human and animal health:

1 Toxic or allergenic effects due to transgene products or from the interaction of products with host genes.
2 Increased use of toxic pesticides with pesticide-resistant crops, leading to pesticide-related illnesses in farm workers, and contamination of food and drinking water.
3 Spread of antibiotic resistance marker genes to gut bacteria and to pathogens.
4 Spread of virulence among pathogens across species by horizontal gene transfer and recombination.
5 Potential for horizontal gene transfer and recombination to create new pathogenic bacteria and viruses.
6 Potential infection of cells after ingestion of food, when regeneration of viruses could occur or damage to the cell's genome might cause harmful or lethal effects including cancer.

Mae Wan Ho, 1997

All genetically engineered crops use antibiotic resistance markers which can exacerbate the spread of antibiotic resistance. This is the reason the UK has rejected Ciba-Geigy's transgenic maize which contains the weaker gene for ampicillin resistance.

Many transgenic plants are engineered for resistance to viral diseases by incorporating the gene for the virus's coat protein. These viral genes may cause new diseases. There is a distinct possibility of new and wide-ranging recombinant viruses arising, which could cause major epidemics.

DNA can also break down in the gut and enter the bloodstream. It has long been assumed that our gut is full of enzymes that can rapidly digest DNA. In a study designed to test the survival of viral DNA in the gut, mice were fed DNA from a bacterial virus, and large fragments were found to survive passage through the gut and to enter the bloodstream. This research group has now shown that ingested DNA ends up, not only in the gut cells of the mice, but also in spleen and liver cells as well as white blood cells. 'In some cases, as much as one cell in a thousand had viral DNA' (Cohen, 1997: p. 14). Within the gut, molecules carrying antibiotic resistance markers may also be taken up by the gut bacteria, which would then serve as a mobile reservoir of antibiotic resistance genes for pathogenic bacteria. Horizontal gene transfer between gut bacteria has already been demonstrated in mice and chickens and in human beings. (Mae Wan Ho, 1997).

When L-tryptophan, a nutritional supplement, was genetically engineered and first marketed, 37 people died and 1,500 people were severely affected by eosinophilia myalgia, a painful and debilitating circulatory disorder (Lappe and Bailey, 1998: p. 134). In another case of health hazards induced by transgenic foods, the methionne-rich gene from a Brazil nut was apparently introduced into soy beans to increase their protein levels. The transgenic soy beans were contaminated by the allergenic properties of the Brazil nut (Nordlee *et al.*, 1996).

While many cases of health risks from genetically engineered crops have been detected, leading to calls for rigorous safety tests before these foods are commercialised, a myth of 'substantial equivalence' has been created to deny citizens the right to safety and deny scientists the right to practise sound and honest science.

One of the greatest achievements of the Rio process was the articulation of the Precautionary Principle. Principle 15 of the Rio Declaration, June 1992 states: 'Where there are threats of serious or irreversible damage, lack of full scientific certainty shall not be used as a reason for postponing cost-effective measures to prevent environmental degradation.'

In the case of genetically modified organisms (GMOs), the Precautionary Principle calls for better knowledge of risks and strong biosafety regulations, and commercialisation of GM foods only after they are proven safe and without ecological and health risks. The Precautionary Principle has been picked out for attack by free trade promoters. In his opening speech at the high level symposium organised by WTO in March 1998, Sir Leon Brittan stated that the Principle posed 'dangers' and could be 'invoked in an abusive way'. He went out of his way to state that the Precautionary Principle was not recognised by WTO. WTO free trade rules were also used by the USA and its allies for billing an international agreement on biosafety to regulate the ecological risks of GMOs. This legally binding agreement negotiated under the Convention on Biological Diversity (CBD) was finalised in Cartagena, Columbia, in February 1999. The absence of biosafety rules implies that ecological risks of GMOs will be unknown and unregulated. False assumptions of 'substantial equivalence' are preventing the assessment of such risks, and a science under corporate control defined by WTO, a trade body, as 'sound science' is putting profits above health and ecological safety. The US/Europe beef hormone trade conflict is a precursor to trade wars around GMOs. At the heart of these conflicts are the rights of citizens to safety *vs.* the rights of corporations to profit. Safety itself is being treated as a trade barrier, and the monopoly on the 'soundness' of scientific assessment of risks is linked to those commercial interests that risk reduction of profits if safety concerns are democratically and independently articulated.

The introduction of new risks and the deliberate manufacture of ignorance are a threat to the integrity of our food chain and the integrity of scientific knowledge.

Pollution, Depletion and Privatisation of Water

Water is probably the resource that is being most over-used and abused. According to the World Bank, 'The wars of the next century will be about water'.

Use of water is doubling every twenty years. More than thirty countries are facing water stress and scarcity and over a billion people lack adequate access to clean drinking water. By the year 2025 two thirds of the people of the world will face severe water shortages.

In the Maquiladora zone of Mexico, drinking water is so scarce that babies and children drink Coca-Cola and Pepsi. Water scarcity is clearly a source of corporate profits. Coca-Cola's products sell in 195 countries, generating revenues of $16 billion.

As an annual report of Coca-Cola says: 'All of us in the Coca-Cola family wake up each morning knowing that every single one of the world's 5.6 billion people will get thirsty that day. If we make it impossible for these 5.6 billion people to escape Coca-Cola, then we assure our future success for many years to come. Doing anything else is not an option.'

Converting the crisis of water scarcity into an opportunity for perpetual growth is also the basis of water privatisation. The privatisation of water is another dimension of the privatisation of life. Two transnationals, Générale des Eaux and Suez Lyonnaise des Eaux, lead the water industry. They own water companies in 120 countries and more than 100 million people are supported by their water. Bechtel, the dam builder, has launched a joint venture with United Utilities of Britain. Thames Water and Biwater, two British companies, are acquiring water concessions in Asia and South Africa.

Energy companies are entering the water sector. General Electric has joined forces with the World Bank and George Soros to invest billions of dollars in a 'Global Power Fund' to privatise energy and water around the world. Enron has acquired Wessex Water in Britain and is bidding for the $800-billion global water market. Monsanto, the Life Sciences giant, is now leading the race to control water. During 1999, Monsanto plans to launch a new water business, starting with India and Mexico, since both these countries are facing water shortages.

Monsanto is seeing a new business opportunity in water because of the emerging water crisis and the funding available to make this vital resource available to people. As it states in its strategy paper:

First we believe that discontinuities (either major policy changes or major trendline breaks in resource quality or quantity) are likely, particularly in the area of water, and we will be well positioned via these businesses to profit even more significantly when these discontinuities occur. Secondly, we are exploring the potential of non-conventional financing (non-governmental organisations, World Bank, USDA etc.,) that may lower our investment or provide local country business-building resources.

Monsanto, 1991

Thus, the crisis of pollution and depletion of water resources is viewed by Monsanto as a business opportunity. For Monsanto 'sustainable development' means the conversion of an ecological crisis into a market of scarce resources.

> The business logic of sustainable development is that population growth and economic development will apply increasing pressure on natural resource markets. These pressures, and the world's desire to prevent the consequences of these pressures if unabated, will create vast economic opportunity – when we look at the world through the lens of sustainability we are in a position to see current – and foresee impending – resource market trends and imbalances that create market needs. We have further focused this lens on the resource market of water and land and there are markets in which there are predictable sustainability challenges and therefore opportunities to create business value.
>
> Monsanto, 1991

Monsanto plans to earn revenues of $420 million and net income of $63 million by 2008 from its water business in India and Mexico. By the year 2010 it is projected that about 2.5 billion people in the world will lack access to safe drinking water. At least 30 per cent of the population in China, India, Mexico and the USA are expected to face severe water stress. By the year 2025 the supply of water in India will be 700 cubic km per year, while the demand is expected to rise to 1,050 units. Control over this scarce resource will of course be a source of guaranteed profits.

As John Bastin of the European Bank of Reconstruction and Development has stated: 'Water is the last infrastructure frontier for private investors.' Monsanto estimates that providing safe water is a market worth several billion dollars. It is growing at 25–30 per cent in rural communities and is estimated to be worth $300 million by 2000 in India and Mexico. This is the amount currently spent by national government organisations (NGOs) for water development projects and local government water supply schemes, and Monsanto hopes to tap these public finances for providing water to rural communities. The Indian government spent over $1.2 billion between 1992 and 1997 on various water projects, while the World Bank spent $900 million. Monsanto would like to divert this public money from the public supply of water to establishing Monsanto's water monopoly. Since in rural areas the poor cannot pay, Monsanto's view is this: 'Capturing a piece of the value created for this segment will require the creation of a non-traditional mechanism, targeted at building relationships with local government and NGOs as well as through innovative financing mechanisms, such as microcredit.'

Monsanto also plans to penetrate the Indian market for safe water by establishing a joint venture with Eureka Forbes/TATA, which controls 70 per cent of UV Technologies. To enter the water business, Monsanto acquired an equity stake in Water Health International (WHI) with an option to buy the rest of the business.

Monsanto will also buy a Japanese company which has developed electrolysis technology. The joint venture with Eureka Forbes/TATA is supposed to provide market access, and fabricate, distribute and service water systems. Monsanto will use leverage to force their brand equity into the Indian market. The joint venture route has been chosen so that 'Monsanto can achieve management control over local operations but not have legal consequences due to local issues'.

Another new business that Monsanto is starting in 1999 in Asia is aquaculture. The aquaculture business will build on the foundation of Monsanto's agricultural biotechnology and capabilities for fish feed and fish breeding. By 2008 Monsanto expects to earn revenues of $1 billion and a net income of $266 million from its aquaculture business. While Monsanto's entry into aquaculture is through its sustainable development activity, industrial aquaculture has been established to be highly non-sustainable. The Supreme Court of India had banned industrial shrimp farming because of its catastrophic consequences. However, the government, under pressure from the aquaculture industry, is attempting to change the laws, to undo the Supreme Court order. At the same time, attempts are being made by the World Bank to privatise water resources and establish trade in water rights. These trends will suit Monsanto well in establishing its new water and aquaculture businesses. The World Bank has already offered to help. As the Monsanto strategy paper states:

> We are particularly enthusiastic about the potential of partnering with the International Finance Corporation (IFC) of the World Bank to joint venture projects in developing markets.
>
> The IFC is eager to work with Monsanto to commercialise sustainability opportunities and would bring both investment capital and on-the-ground capabilities to our efforts. Monsanto's Water and Aquaculture business, like its seed business, is aimed at controlling vital resources necessary for survival – converting them into a market and using public finances to underwrite the investments. A more efficient conversion of public goods

into private profit would be difficult to find. Water is, however, too basic for life and survival. The right to water is the right to life.

Everything for Sale

Globalisation is not merely a geographic phenomenon which is tearing down national barriers to capital. Globalisation is also tearing down ethical and ecological limits on commerce. As everything becomes tradable, everything is for sale – genes, cells, plants, seeds, knowledge, water and even pollution. Life has lost its sanctity as living systems become the new raw material, the new sites of investment, the new locations for manufacture. Pollution and waste have also become a source of multi-million dollar trade. Instead of getting rid of pollution, systems are being evolved which allow the rich to sell their pollution to the poor. The poor are thus being doubly denied their right to life – first when the resources that sustain them are taken away from them in a free trade world, and then when the pollution and waste of the global economy are unequally and unjustly piled on them.

As dollars replace life processes in the domain of life, life itself is extinguished. The proposal to give market values to all resources as a solution of the ecological crisis is like offering the disease as the cure. The reduction of all value to commercial value and the removal of all spiritual, ecological, cultural and social limits to exploitation is a process that is being brought to completion through globalisation, though it started with industrialisation.

This shift in economic value is central to the ecological crisis. It is reflected in the change in the meaning of the term 'resource'. Resource originally implied life. Its root is the Latin verb *surgere*, which evoked the image of a spring that continually rose from the ground. Like a spring, a resource rises again and again, even if it has repeatedly been used and consumed. The concept highlighted nature's power of self-regeneration and called attention to her prodigious creativity. Moreover, it implied an ancient idea about the relationship between humans and nature – that the earth bestows gifts on humans who, in turn, are well advised to show diligence in order not to suffocate her generosity. In early modern times, resources therefore suggested reciprocity along with regeneration.

With industrialisation, the meaning of resources was transformed into raw materials for industry. A similar change seems to be taking place in the meaning of 'life'. As living resources and processes become the new raw materials, as vital resources like food and water become commodities for commercial profits rather than for the maintenance of life, Life Inc grows at the cost of the planet's life in all its diversity, vitality and renewability. Diversity is replaced by monocultures, the ecological web of life is replaced by engineering of life, sanctity of life is replaced by marketability of life.

With no ethical, ecological, or social limits to commerce, life itself is being pushed to the edge.

Bibliography

Cohen, Philip (1997) 'Can DNA in Food Find its Way into Cells?', *New Scientist* (4 January).

Enyart, James (1990) 'A GATT Intellectual Property Code', *Les Nouvelles* (June): pp. 54–6.

Lappe, M., and Bailey, B. (1998) *Against the Grain*, London: Earth Scan.

Mae Wan Ho (1997) *Genetic Engineering: Dreams or Nightmares?*, New Delhi: Research Foundation for Science, Technology and Ecology.

Monsanto (1991) strategy paper on water.

Research Foundation for Science, Technology and Ecology (ed.) (1998) *Monsanto: Peddling 'Life Sciences' or 'Death Sciences'?* New Delhi.

Nordlee, J., *et al.*, (1996) 'Bush Identification of a Brazil Nut Allergen in Transonic Soy Beans', *New England Journal of Medicine* 334: pp. 688–92.

ARLIE RUSSELL HOCHSCHILD

Global Care Chains and Emotional Surplus Value

Vicky Diaz (a pseudonym) is a 34-year-old mother-of-five. A college-educated former schoolteacher and travel agent in the Philippines, she migrated to the United States to work as a housekeeper and as nanny to the two-year-old son of a wealthy family in Beverly Hills, Los Angeles. She explained to the researcher Rhacel Parrenas:

> Even until now my children are trying to convince me to go home. The children were not angry when I left because they were still very young when I left them. My husband could not get angry either because he knew that was the only way I could seriously help him raise our children, so that our children could be sent to school. I send them money every month.

In her forthcoming book *The Global Servants*, Rhacel Parrenas tells this disquieting story of the 'globalisation of mothering'. 'Vicky' is her name for the respondent whom she quotes here. Vicky's story as well as other case material in this chapter is drawn from Parrenas's University of California dissertation.

The Beverly Hills family pays Vicky $400 a week and Vicky, in turn, pays her own family's live-in domestic worker back in the Philippines $40 a week. But living in this 'global care chain' is not easy on Vicky and her family. As she told Parrenas:

> Even though it's paid well, you are sinking in the amount of your work. Even while you are ironing the clothes, they can still call you to the kitchen to wash the plates. It was also very depressing. The only thing you can do is give all your love to the child [the two-year-old American child]. In my absence from my children, the most I could do with my situation is give all my love to that child.

130

Paradoxically, Vicky got her job by telling her prospective employer that she had experience raising children. As she recounted: 'I found out about the job in a newspaper ad and I called them and they asked me to come in for an interview. I was accepted after that. They just asked me if I knew how to take care of a child and I told them that I did because I had five children of my own. But come to think of it, I was not the one watching after them because I had a maid to do that.'

Global capitalism affects whatever it touches, and it touches virtually everything including what I call global care chains – a series of personal links between people across the globe based on the paid or unpaid work of caring. Usually women make up these chains, though it's possible that some chains are made up of both women and men, or, in rare cases, made up of just men. Such care chains may be local, national, or global. Global chains – like Vicky Diaz's – usually start in a poor country and end in a rich one. But some such chains start in poor countries, and move from rural to urban areas within that same poor country. Or they start in one poor country and extend to another slightly less poor country and then link one place to another within the latter country. Chains also vary in the number of links – some have one, others two or three – and each link varies in its connective strength. One common form of such a chain is: (1) an older daughter from a poor family who cares for her siblings while (2) her mother works as a nanny caring for the children of a migrating nanny who, in turn, (3) cares for the child of a family in a rich country. Some care chains are based on the object of care (say, a child, or an elderly person for whom a carer feels responsible), others on the subjects of care (the carers themselves, as they too receive care). Each kind of chain expresses an invisible human ecology of care, one kind of care depending on another and so on. The head of the International Organisation for Migration estimates that, in 1994, 120 million people migrated – legally and illegally – from one country to another: 2 per cent of the world's population. According to Stephen Castles and Mark Miller, over the next twenty years this migration will continue to globalise and accelerate. An increasing proportion of those migrants, they say, will also be women. Already in 1996 over half of those who legally emigrated to the USA were women, and their median age was twenty-nine. It is hard to say how many of these women form links in a care chain. But most of Parrenas's young female care workers were young female legal immigrants too.

In this chapter, I would like to ask: how are we to understand the impact of globalisation on care? What do we know about it and how do we think and feel about it? If more global care chains form, will their motivation and effect be marked by kindness or unkindness? Given the harshness of poverty itself, these are by no means simple questions. But we haven't fully addressed them, I believe, because for most of us the world is globalising faster than our minds or hearts are. We live global but feel local.

However long the chain is, wherever it begins and ends, many of us focusing at one link or another in the chain see the carer's love of a child as private, individual, uncircumscribed by context. As the employer above might think to herself, 'Mothers know how to love children.' Love always appears unique, and the love of a carer for the child in her care – like that of Vicky for the child she cares for – seems unique and individual. It has no other context than itself. From time to time, Vicky herself may feel keenly the link between her love for the children she is paid to care for and love of her own children whom she pays another to nurture. But her American employers are far more likely to see this love as natural, individual, contextless, private. 'Vicky is a loving person,' they might say, and 'Vicky loves Tommy.'

There are many good studies of globalisation that can help us overcome our localism. But they focus on people in the aggregate and don't shed a strong light on individual human relationships. Some scholars, however – especially those exploring globalisation and gender – have very much helped us see links between global trends and individual lives. Building on the pioneering work of Sylvia Chant, Pierrette Hondagneu-Sotelo, Beneria Lourdes, Maria Mies, Saskia Sassan, Sau-ling Wong and, especially, Rhacel Parrenas, I propose to set down some thoughts on the globalisation of care. In doing so I am drawing on various areas of research that scarcely connect. Most writing on globalisation focuses on money, markets and labour flows, while giving scant attention to women, children and the care of one for the other. At the same time, research on women in the USA and Europe focuses on a detached, chainless, two-person picture of 'work–family balance' without considering the child-care worker and the emotional ecology of which these workers are a part. Meanwhile research on women and development traces crucial links from the International Monetary Fund or the World Bank, through the strings tying Third World loans, to the scarcity of food for women and children. But this research, important as it is, does not trace the global links between the children of service-providers and those of service-recipients. The new work on care workers thus addresses a blind spot in our knowledge and to it I add a thought about the global pattern on displaced feeling. The task, as I see it, is to draw threads from each area of research, with an eye to both the macro- and micro-side of the story.

The straight globalisation literature tends to focus on three issues – marketisation, mobility and distribution of resources. Each of these sheds light on Vicky Diaz's dilemma. Money provides a powerful incentive to work, and the yawning global wage gap provides a powerful incentive to move, as Vicky Diaz's story shows, from a place where one is paid relatively little even for professional work to a place where one is paid more. Before they migrated from the Philippines to the USA and Italy, the Filipina domestic workers in Parrenas's study had averaged $176 a month – often as teachers, nurses and administrative and clerical workers. But by doing less skilled (though not easier) work as nannies and maids and care service workers, they can earn $200 a month in Singapore, $410 a month in Hong Kong, $700 a month in Italy and $1,400 a month in Los Angeles.

People like Vicky Diaz want not just better pay but also more security. Having access to a variety of jobs, and even a variety of national economies, can become an insurance against the very instabilities globalisation creates. Migration is a ticket to a better life but also an insurance policy against currency devaluations and business failures at home. As the migration expert Douglas Massey notes, the more globalisation, the more insecurity, and the more people try to insure against insecurity by migrating. In short, the more globalisation, the more globalisation.

And it should be said that while these care providers move to get better pay, they do not become money-making machines. One Filipina caretaker interviewed by Charlene Tung cared for an elderly Alzheimer's patient and had this to say: 'We [her friend and she] took care of him for so many years we cannot leave him at this time because we care for him very much. We don't stay for the pay. We could get more elsewhere. He's a very nice man.'

In response to the marketisation of care, then, many women migrate. But in what sense do they leave home? Studies suggest that migrants such as Vicky Diaz remain attached to the homes and people they leave. Vicky Diaz remained poised to return home, though she did not get back there for five years at a stretch. Indeed, most of the migrant workers Parrenas interviewed talked of going back but, in the end, it was their wages that went home while they themselves stayed on in the USA and Italy. Many of the migrants Parrenas interviewed seemed to develop a 'hypothetical self' – the idea of the person they would be if only they were back home. They spoke of the birthdays, the school events they would attend, the comfort they would give if only they were there. Although families are separated, sometimes for decades at a time, they are not in the Western sense 'broken'. They become what Parrenas calls 'transnational families' for whom obligations do not end but bend.

Analysts of globalisation also focus on the maldistribution of resources between the First and Third Worlds. Globalisation has clearly lifted populations of some countries out of poverty – Malaysia, Korea and parts of China, for example – while it has also depressed economic conditions in others. According to a recent report published by the United Nations Development programme, sixty countries are worse off in 1999 than they were in 1980 and inequities in wealth are likely to grow in the future (*The New York Times*, 13 July 1999). But we need to ask exactly what resources are being unequally distributed. The obvious answer is 'money', but is care or love also being inequitably redistributed around the globe? Marx's idea of 'surplus value' may help us form a picture of what's happening. For Marx, surplus value is simply the difference between the value a labourer adds to the thing he makes (say, a car, a pair of blue jeans) and the money he receives for his work. Factory owners and shareholders profit from the value a worker adds to a product; they do not share that skimmed-off 'surplus' value with the worker. In the material realm, we can say that one person gets money which another deserves.

Marx was talking about exploitation of workers in the public realm and he left human relations in the private realm out of the picture. But if we look at connections between events in the public realm (the love Vicky Diaz feels for the small boy in Beverly Hills she is paid to care for) and events in the private realm (her love for her five children back in the Philippines) the picture is far more complex than that which Marx discussed. For one thing, caring work touches on one's emotions. It is emotional labour, and often far more than that. For another thing, we are talking about the relation of children to their care-givers, which is partly visible, partly invisible. For, globalisation separates the worlds of the actors in this care chain. In contrast to a nineteenth-century industrialist and worker, the employer may have no clue about the world the nanny has left behind and the child there may know little about its mother's First World surrogate child. In contrast to the nineteenth-century industrialist and worker, also, given their options each party in a care chain would seem to be a voluntary participant, except, we might presume, for the children left behind. But the one thing both examples share in common is that the people lower down the class/race/nation chain do not share the 'profits'.

How are we to understand a 'transfer' of feeling between those cared for? Feeling is not a 'resource' that can be crassly taken from one person and given to another. But nor is it entirely unlike a resource either. According to Freud, displacement involves a redirecting of feeling: one doesn't give up a feeling but finds a new object onto which to project that feeling. For Freud, displacement was neither right nor wrong, but simply a process to which our feelings are subject. The most important displacement for Freud was of sexual feelings: the original object is the mother (for a boy) or the father (for a girl) and the later displacement is towards a sexually appropriate adult partner. While Freud applied the idea of displacement mainly to relations within the nuclear family, we can apply it to relations extending far outside it. In the words of Sau-ling Wong, nannies and au pairs often divert towards their young charges feelings that were originally directed towards their own young. As Wong puts it, 'Time and energy available for mothers are diverted from those who, by kinship or communal ties, are their more rightful recipients.'

Can attention, solicitude and love be 'displaced' from, say, Vicky Diaz's son Alfredo, back in the Philippines, onto, say, Tommy, the son of her employers in Los Angeles? And is the direction of displacement upwards in privilege and power? How is the emotional need of Vicky Diaz's five children back in the Philippines 'related to' that of the two-year-old child in Beverly Hills for whom Vicky is the nanny? Can we think of 'distribution' and emotional caring in the same breath? Are First World countries such as the United States importing maternal love as they have imported copper, zinc, gold and other ores from Third World countries in the past?

Within our own families we easily think of 'distribution' and 'care' in the same breath. A parent might love all the children equally or might favour one over another. But globalisation forces us to broaden our perspective on this question of 'distribution'. We are not accustomed to thinking in such widely ranging terms but, again, the Marxist idea of 'fetishisation' and 'defetishisation' is extremely useful here. To fetishise a thing – like an SUV – is to see the thing simply as that and to disregard who harvested the rubber (and at what rate of pay) that went into the tyres. Just as we can mentally isolate a thing from the human scene in which it was made, so too we can do this with a service – like that between Vicky Diaz and the two-year-old child for whom she cares. Seen as a thing in itself, Vicky's love for the Beverly Hills toddler is unique, individual, private. But elements in this emotion might be borrowed, so to speak, from somewhere and someone else. Is time spent with the First World child in some sense 'taken from' a child further down the care chain? Is the Beverly Hills child getting 'surplus' love?

The idea is unwelcome, both to Vicky Diaz who very much wants a First World job and to her well-meaning employers who very much need someone to give loving care to their child. Each person along the chain feels he or she is doing the right thing for good reasons.

How do nannies feel about their decision to come abroad to work? In Pierrette Hondagneu-Sotelo and Ernestine Avila's 'I'm Here, But I'm There: The Meanings of Latina Transnational Motherhood', the authors described how Latina nannies in Los Angeles saw their work (hard), and their employers (rich and egotistical). But about their own motherhood they seemed to feel two ways: on one hand, being a 'good mother' was earning money for the family, and they were used to a culture of shared mothering with kith and kin at home; at the same time, they felt that being a good mother required them to be with their children and not away from them. Being in a care chain, the authors conclude, is 'a brave odyssey . . . with deep costs'.

The person these Latina nannies most preferred as care for their children was their own mother. But she was not always available. In Parrenas's sample, one domestic worker relies on a paid domestic worker to care for her children in the Philippines as she takes care of the household work of a professional woman in Italy; another hires a domestic worker for the care of her elderly mother while she works in Los Angeles as a teacher (but previously as an elder-care worker); and another woman cleans houses of dual wage-earning families in Rome while she depends on her sisters-in-law for the care of her elderly mother.

Such chains often connect three sets of care-takers – one cares for the migrant's children back home, a second cares for the children of the woman who cares for the migrant's children, and a third, the migrating mother herself, cares for the children of professionals in the First World. Poorer women raise children for wealthier women while still poorer – or older or more rural – women raise their children.

Some migrant care workers care not just for one person all day long, but for many children, or many elderly and sick people. Given many clients, it might seem that an 'original' love would be harder to 'displace'. As Deborah Stone has observed, care in public settings is now subject to pressures to reduce costs, and to follow bureaucratic rules. For example, medical workers have to monitor and limit their time with clients and document specific medical problems for a patient while ignoring other perhaps pressing problems if these aren't listed as a reason for needing home care. As Stone notes, 'the main strategy of keeping costs down in home health care is to limit care to medical needs and medically related tasks, and to eliminate any case that is merely social' (1999: p. 63).

But despite the prohibitions of a deadening bureaucracy, feelings of concern and love passed from carer to cared-for. Stone observed that one care worker dropped off milk to an elderly man on her way to work, though she wasn't paid to do so. Others kept in touch by telephone, visited and otherwise cared for clients above and beyond the call of duty. Since it wasn't in the rule book, they felt guilty and furtive for doing so. Given the growing power of the market-place and bureaucracy, carers are pressured to deliver care in a standardised time-limited way. It is often women of colour who are on the front lines of institutional care and who thus fight the system to stay human.

Paid care fits a racial pattern. In the American South, before and after the Civil War, African-American mammies cared for the children of their white masters while older siblings or kin took care of their own, as in a story told by Toni Morrison in her novel *The Bluest Eye* (1994). In the Southwest, Mexican-American nannies took care of children of their white employers. In the American West, Asian-American domestic workers have done the same. As mothering is passed down the race/class/nation hierarchy, each woman becomes a provider and hires a wife. But increasingly today, the pass-down of care crosses national borders. For example, Parrenas reported that Carmen Ronquillo had worked for $750 a month as project manager of food services at Clark Airforce base in the Philippines when the base closed. She could find no job that paid nearly as much. So, although she'd criticised her sister for leaving her family to migrate abroad, Carmen too left her husband and two teenagers to take a job as a maid for an architect and single mother-of-two in Rome. As she explained to Parrenas:

When coming here, I mentally surrendered myself and forced my pride away from me to prepare myself. But I lost a lot of weight. I was not used to the work. You see, I had maids in the Philippines. I have a maid in the Philippines that has worked for me since my daughter was born twenty-four years ago. She is still with me. I paid her 300 pesos before and now I pay her 1,000 pesos. [Speaking of her job in Rome] I am a little bit luckier than others because I run the entire household. My employer is a divorced woman who is an architect. She does not have time to run her household so I do all the shopping. I am the one budgeting, I am the one cooking [laughs] and I am the one cleaning too. She has a 24- and 26-year-old . . . they still

live with her. I stay with her because I feel at home with her. She never
commands. She never orders me to do this and to do that.

Transfer of care takes its toll both on the Filipina child and on the
mother. 'When I saw my children, I thought, "Oh children do grow up
even without their mother." I left my youngest when she was only five
years old. She was already nine when I saw her again but she still
wanted for me to carry her [weeps]. That hurt me because it showed me
that my children missed out on a lot.'

Sometimes the toll it takes on the domestic worker is overwhelming,
and suggests that the nanny has not displaced her love onto an
employer's child but simply continues to long intensely for her own
child. As one woman told Parrenas:

> The first two years I felt like I was going crazy. You have to believe me
> when I say that it was like I was having intense psychological problems. I
> would catch myself gazing at nothing, thinking about my child. Every
> moment, every second of the day, I felt like I was thinking about my baby.
> My youngest, you have to understand, I left when he was only two months
> old . . . You know, whenever I receive a letter from my children, I cannot
> sleep. I cry. It's good that my job is more demanding at night.

Given the depth of this unhappiness, one might imagine that care
chains are a minimal part of the whole global show. But it seems that
this is not the case, at least in the Philippines. Since the early 1990s, 55
per cent of migrants out of the Philippines have been women and, next
to electronic manufacturing, their remittances make up the major source
of foreign currency in the Philippines. Recent improvements in the
economy have not reduced female emigration, which continues to
increase. In addition, migrants are not drawn from the poorest class, but
often include college-educated teachers, small businesswomen, secret-
aries: in Parrenas's study, over half of the nannies she interviewed had
college degrees and most were married mothers in their thirties. In
Parrenas's words, 'it is a transnational division of labour that is shaped
simultaneously by the system of global capitalism, the patriarchal system
of the sending country and the patriarchal system of the receiving
country'.

Where are men in this picture? For the most part, men – and
especially men at the top of the class ladder – leave child-rearing to
women. Many of the husbands and fathers of Parrenas's domestic

workers had migrated to the Arabian Peninsula and other places in search of better wages, relieving other men of 'male work' while being replaced themselves at home. Others remained at home, responsible fathers caring or partly caring for their children. But other men were present in women's lives as the tyrannical or abandoning persons they needed to escape. Indeed, many of the women migrants Parrenas interviewed didn't just leave; they fled. As one migrant maid explained:

> You have to understand that my problems were very heavy before I left the Philippines. My husband was abusive. I couldn't even think about my children, the only thing I could think about was the opportunity to escape my situation. If my husband was not going to kill me, I was probably going to kill him . . . He always beat me up and my parents wanted me to leave him for a long time. I left my children with my sister. I asked my husband for permission to leave the country and I told him that I was only going to be gone for two years. I was just telling him that so I could leave the country peacefully. In the plane . . . I felt like a bird whose cage had been locked for many years . . . I felt free . . . Deep inside, I felt homesick for my children but I also felt free for being able to escape the most dire problem that was slowly killing me.

Or again, a former public school teacher back in the Philippines confided: 'After three years of marriage, my husband left me for another woman. My husband supported us for just a little over a year. Then the support was stopped . . . The letters stopped. I have not seen him since.' In the absence of government aid, then, migration becomes a way of coping with abandonment.

Sometimes the husband of a female migrant worker is himself a migrant worker who takes turns with his wife migrating, but this isn't always enough to meet the needs of the children. One man worked in Saudi Arabia for ten years, coming home for a month each year. When he finally returned home for good, his wife set off to work as a maid in America while he took care of the children. As she explained to Parrenas:

> My children were very sad when I left them. My husband told me that when they came back home from the airport, my children could not touch their food and they wanted to cry. My son, whenever he writes me, always draws the head of Fido the dog with tears on the eyes. Whenever he goes to Mass on Sundays, he tells me that he misses me more because he sees his

friends with their mothers. Then he comes home and cries. He says that he does not want his father to see him crying so he locks himself in his room.

Over the Ocean

Just as global capitalism helps create a Third World supply of mothering, so it creates a First World demand for it. At the First World end, there has been a huge rise in the number of women in paid work – from 15 per cent of mothers of children aged six and under in 1950, to 65 per cent today. Indeed, American women now make up 45 per cent of the American labour force, and three-quarters of mothers of children aged eighteen and under now work, as do 65 per cent of mothers of children of six and under. In addition, according to a recent report by the international labour organisation, the average number of hours of work have been rising in the United States.

Partly because a lot of American grandmothers and other female kin, who might otherwise have looked after a worker's children, now do paid work themselves, over the past thirty years a decreasing proportion of families have relied on relatives for their child-care, and more are looking for non-family care. Thus, at the First World end of care chains we find working parents who are grateful to find a good nanny or child-care provider and able to pay more than the nanny could earn in her native country.

In addition, many American families rely on out-of-home care for their elderly – a fact of which many nannies themselves paradoxically disapprove. As one of Parrenas's respondents, a Los Angeles elder-care worker, put it critically: 'Domestics here are able to make a living from the elderly that families abandon. When they are older, the families do not want to take care of them. Some put them in convalescence homes, some put them in retirement homes and some hire private domestic workers.' But at the same time, the elder-care chain, like the child-care chain, means that nannies cannot take care of their own ailing parents, and if their daughters also go abroad to work, they may do an 'elder-care' version of a child-care chain – caring for First World elderly persons while a paid worker cares for their aged mother back in the Philippines.

First World women who hire nannies are themselves caught in a male-career pattern that has proved surprisingly resistant to change. While Parrenas did not interview the Los Angeles employers of Filipina maids and nannies, my own research for *The Second Shift* and *The Time*

Bind sheds some light on the First World end of the chain. Women have joined the law, academia, medicine, business, but such professions are still organised for men with families who are free of family responsibilities. Most careers are based on a well-known pattern: doing professional work, competing with fellow professionals, getting credit for work, building a reputation, doing it while you are young, hoarding scarce time, and minimising family life by finding someone else to do it. In the past, the professional was a man and the 'someone else to do it' was a wife. The wife oversaw the family, which was itself a pre-industrial, flexible institution absorbing the human vicissitudes of birth, sickness, death, that the workplace discarded. Today, men take on much more of the child-care and housework at home, but they still base their identity on demanding careers in the light of which children are a beloved impediment. Hence, the resistance to sharing care at home, and the search for care further 'down' the global chain.

Among these First World mothers are those who give their emotional labour, in turn, to companies which hold themselves out to the worker as a 'family'. In my research on a multinational, Fortune 500 manufacturing company I call Amerco, I discovered a disproportionate number of women employed in the human side of the company: public relations, marketing, human resources. In all sectors of the company, women often helped others sort out problems – both personal and professional – at work. It was often the welcoming voice and 'soft touch' of women workers that made Amerco seem like a family to other workers. Among the ultimate beneficiaries of various care chains we thus find large, multinational companies with strong work cultures. At the end of some care chains are company managers.

Three Perspectives on Care Chains

Given Parrenas's portrait of this global care chain, and given the chain's growing scope, it is worth asking how we are to respond to it. It would be good to know more than we currently do about such care chains. Some children back in the Philippines amidst kin in their own community may be doing fine; we don't know. But once we know more, with what perspective are we to view it?

I can think of three ways to see care chains – through the eyes of the primordialist, the sunshine modernist and (my own) the critical modernist. To the primordialist, the right thing would be for each of us to take care of only our own family, our own community in our own nation. If we all take care of our own primordial plots, a person with such a perspective would argue, everybody will be fine. The concept of displacement itself rests on the premise that some original first object of love gets first dibs and that second and third comers don't share that right. And for the primordialist, those first objects are members of one's most immediate family. In the end, the primordialist is an isolationist, a non-mixer, an anti-globalist. To such a person, the existence and the global nature of such care chains seem wrong. Because such care is usually done by women, primordialists often also believe that women should stay home to provide this primordial care.

For the sunshine modernist, on the other hand, care chains are an inevitable part of globalisation, which is itself uncritically accepted as good. Perhaps most sunshine modernists are uncritical of globalisation because they don't know about the relation between the care provided in the First World and that provided in the Third World; a minority knows but is not concerned. The idea of displacement is hard for them to catch onto, for the primary focus of the nanny's love depends on what seems right in a context of *laissez-faire* marketisation. If a supply of labour meets the demand for it, the sunshine modernist is satisfied. If the primordialist thinks such care chains are bad because they're global, the sunshine modernist thinks they're good because they're global. Either way, the issue of inequality of access to care disappears.

The critical modernist has a global sense of ethics. If she goes out to buy a pair of Nike shoes, she is concerned to learn how low the wage and how long the hours were for the Third World factory worker making them. She applies the same moral concern to care. So she cares about the welfare of the Filipino child back home. Thus, for the critical modernist, globalisation is a very mixed blessing. It brings with it new opportunities – and the nanny's access to good wages is an opportunity – but also new problems, including costs we have hardly begun to understand.

From the critical modernist perspective, globalisation may be increasing inequities not simply in access to money, important as that is, but in access to care. Though it is by no means always the case, the poor maid's child may be getting less motherly care than the First World child. We needn't lapse into primordialism to sense that something may be amiss in the picture Parrenas offers us and to search for some solutions.

Although I don't have a solution, I suggest that one approach is to try to reduce incentives to migrate by addressing the causes of the migrant's economic desperation. Thus, the obvious goal is one of developing the Philippine economy. But even with such an obvious idea, we find the solution not so simple.

According to the migration specialist Douglas Massey, surprisingly underdevelopment isn't the cause of migration; development is. As Massey notes, 'international migration . . . does not stem from a lack of economic development, but from development itself'. As Massey's research shows, American policy towards Mexico has been to encourage the flow of capital, goods and information (through NAFTA) and to bar the flow of migrants (by reducing social services to illegal aliens and even legal resident aliens, and increasing border vigilance). But the more the economy of Mexico is stirred up, the more Mexicans want and need to migrate – not just to get higher wages, but to achieve greater security through alternative survival strategies. If members of a family are laid off at home, a migrant's monthly remittance can see them through, often by making a capital outlay in a small business, or paying for a child's education

Also, the more development at home, the more opportunities to make a productive investment of capital back home, and the more need to diversify sources of income as a way of managing the greater risk associated with economic turmoil. Massey concludes, 'International migration . . . does not stem from a lack of economic development but from development itself . . . the higher the waves (of migration) in a person's community and the higher the percentage of women employed in local manufacturing, the greater the probability of leaving on a first undocumented trip to the US.' If development creates migration, and if, as critical modernists, we favour some form of development, we need to figure out more humane forms for the migration it is likely to cause.

Other solutions focus on other aspects of the care chain. In so far as part of the motive for female migration is to flee abusive husbands, part of the solution would be to create local refuges. Another might be to alter migration policies so as to encourage migrating nannies to bring their children with them. Alternatively, employers, or even government subsidies, could help them make regular visits home.

Another more underlying part of the solution would be to raise the value of caring work, such that whoever did it got more credit as well as money for it and care wasn't such a 'pass on' job. And now here's the rub. The value of the labour of raising a child – always low relative to the value of other kinds of labour – has, under the impact of globalisation, sunk lower still. Children matter to their parents immeasurably, of course, but the labour of raising them does not earn much credit in the eyes of the world. When middle-class housewives raised children as an unpaid full-time role, the work was dignified by the aura of middle-classness: that was the one up-side to the otherwise confining middle-class nineteenth- and early twentieth-century American 'cult of true womanhood'. But when the unpaid work of raising a child became the paid work of child-care workers, the low market value of child-care work – less than that of dog-catchers or traffic meter collectors in the USA – not only reveals the abiding low value of caring work, but further lowers it.

The low value placed on caring work is not due to the absence of a need for it, or to the simplicity or ease of the work, but to the cultural politics underlying this global exchange. The declining value of child-care anywhere in the world can be compared with the declining value of basic food crops, relative to manufactured goods on the international market. Though clearly more necessary to life, crops such as wheat, rice, or cocoa fetch low and declining prices while the prices of manufactured goods (relative to primary goods) continue to soar on the world market. Just as the market price of primary produce keeps the Third World low in the community of nations, so the low market value of care keeps the status of the women who do it – and, by association, all women – low.

A final basic solution would be to involve fathers in caring for their children. If fathers shared the care of children, world-wide, care would spread laterally instead of being passed down a social class ladder. There is a cultural embrace of this idea in the USA but a lag in implementation.

In sum, according to the International Labour Organisation, half of the world's women between fifteen and sixty-four are in paid work. Between 1960 and 1980, sixty-nine out of eighty-eight countries for which data are available showed a growing proportion of women in paid work. Since 1950, the rate of increase has skyrocketed in the USA and has been high in Scandinavia and the UK, and moderate in France and Germany. If we want developed societies with women doctors, political leaders, teachers, bus drivers and computer programmers, we will need qualified people to help care for their children. And there is no reason why every society should not enjoy such loving paid child-care. It may even be true that Vicky Diaz is the person to provide it. At the same time, critical modernists would be wise to extend their concern to the possible hidden losers in the care chain. For these days, the personal is global.

Bibliography

Afshar, H., and Dennis, C. (eds) (1992) *Women and Adjustment Policies in the Third World*, London: Macmillan.

Bakan, Abigail, and Stasiulis, Daiva (eds) (1997) *Not One of the Family: Foreign Domestic Workers in Canada*, Toronto: University of Toronto Press.

Beneria, Lourdes, and Dudley, M. J. (eds) (1996) *Economic Restructuring in the Americas*, Ithaca, NY: Cornell University Press.

Castles, Stephen, and Miller, Mark (1998) *The Age of Migration: International Population Movements in the Modern World*, 2nd edition, New York and London: The Guildford Press.

Chant, Sylvia, and McIlwaine, Kathy (1995) *Women of a Lesser Cost: Female Labour, Foreign Exchange and Philippine Development*, London and East Haven, CT: Pluto Press.

Cornia, G., Jolly, R., and Stewart, F. (eds) (1987) *Adjustment with a Human Face*, Oxford and New York: Clarendon Press.

Elson, D. (1994) 'Micro, Meso and Macro: Gender and Economic Analysis in the Context of Policy Reform', in I. Bakker (ed.) *The Strategic Silence; Gender and Economic Policy*, London: Zed Books with North-South Institute.

Feber, M., and Nelson, J. (eds) (1993) *Beyond Economic Man: Feminist Theory and Economics*, Chicago: University of Chicago Press.

Gladwin, C. H. (ed.) (1991) *Structural Adjustment and African Women Farmers*, Gainesville, FL: University of Florida Press.

Glenn, Evelyn Nakano (1992) 'From Servitude to Service Work: The Historical Continuities of Women's Paid and Unpaid Reproductive Labour', *Signs* 18(1): pp. 1–44.

Hochschild, Arlie Russell (1997) *The Time Bind: When Home Becomes Work and Work Becomes Home*, New York: Metropolitan Books.

——*The Managed Heart: The Commercialisation of Human Feeling*, Berkeley and Los Angeles: University of California Press.

——(1989) *The Second Shift: Working Parents and the Revolution at Home*, New York: Avon Books.

Hondagneu-Sotelo, Pierrette, and Avila, Ernestine (1997) 'I'm Here, But I'm There: The Meanings of Latina Transnational Motherhood', *Gender and Society*, II (5) (October): pp. 548–71.

Massey, Douglas S. (1998) 'March of Folly: US Immigration Policy after NAFTA', *The American Prospect* (March–April): pp. 22–33.

Mies, Maria (1982) *The Lacemakers of Narsapur: Indian Housewives Produce for the World Market*, Westport, CT: Lawrence Hill.

Morrison, Toni (1994) *The Bluest Eye*, New York: Plume Books.

Panda, Pradeep Kumar (1997) 'Gender and Structural Adjustment: Exploring the Connections', Center for Development Studies, Thiruvananthapuram, Kerala, India (unpublished paper).

Parrenas, Rhacel Salazar (forthcoming) *The Global Servants: Migrant Filipina Domestic Workers in Rome and Los Angeles*, Palo Alto, CA: Stanford University Press.

——(1998) 'The Global Servants: (Im)Migrant Filipina Domestic Workers in Rome and Los Angeles', dissertation (filed Spring), Department of Ethnic Studies, University of California, Berkeley.

Rollins, Judith (1985) *Between Women: Domestics and their Employers*, Philadelphia, PA: Temple University Press.

Romero, Mary (1997) 'Life as the Maid's Daughter: An Exploration of the Everyday Boundaries of Race, Class, and Gender', in Mary Romero, P. Hondagneu-Sotelo and Vima Ortiz (eds) *Challenging Fronteras: Structuring Latina, and Latino Lives in the US*, New York: Routledge.

Sassan, Saskia (1988) *The Mobility of Labor and Capital: A Study in International Investment and Labor*, New York: Cambridge University Press.

Stone, Deborah (1999) 'Care and Trembling', *The American Prospect* 43 (March–April): 61–7.

Tucker, Robert (ed.) (1978) *The Marx–Engels Reader*, 2nd ed. New York: W. W. Norton.

Tung, Charlene (forthcoming) 'The Cost of Caring, Reproductive Labour of Filipina Live-In Home Health Caregivers', *Frontiers: A Journal of Women's Studies* 21(1) (Spring 2000).

United Nations Research Institute for Social Development (1996) *Working Towards a More Gender Equitable Macro-Economic Agenda*, report of conference held in Rajendrapur, Bangladesh, 26–8 November, Geneva, Switzerland.

Wong, Sau-ling (1997) 'Diverted Mothering: Representations of Caregivers of Color in the Age of Multiculturalism', in E. Glenn, G. Chang and L. Forcey (eds) *Mothering: Ideology, Experience and Agency*, London: Routledge, pp. 67–91.

Wrigley, Julia (1995) *Other People's Children: An Intimate Account of the Dilemmas Facing Middle Class Parents and the Women They Hire to Raise Their Children*, New York: Basic Books.

Acknowledgement

Thanks to Adam Hochschild for hearing out the ideas and to Tony Giddens for very helpful and incisive comments on this chapter.

ROBERT KUTTNER

The Role of Governments in the Global Economy

The world's top corporations are now engaged in a bout of unprecedented global merger, acquisition and concentration. They have become not only centres of concentrated economic and financial power; they have become bearers of the prevailing *laissez-faire*, globalist ideology. As their economic power grows, so does their political and intellectual reach, at the expense of nation-states that once balanced their private economic power with public purposes and national stabilisation policies. The very economic success of global corporations is taken as proof that their world-view has to be correct: that global *laissez-faire* is the optimal way to organise a modern economy.

Before examining that claim, it is worthwhile to consider the new context of corporate power. In the past, there were barriers of both law and custom against the current degree of corporate concentration. In the United States, the first period of intense industrial combination in the late nineteenth century gave rise to the world's toughest antitrust laws. Under the Sherman (1890) and Clayton (1914) Acts, and under state public utilities regulation, large monopoly corporations, such as the old AT&T, could operate only as strictly regulated monopolies. The theory was that these corporations were in industries with natural economies of scale, making competition inefficient and wasteful.

The regulatory regimes, therefore, protected such monopolies from competition, and they regulated rates and profit margins – but also prohibited the corporations from venturing off their own main lines of business. AT&T, for example, dominated the telephone business. Not only could no prospective competitor come in; AT&T could not use its economic power to venture out from its fortress, into other lines of business. While such public utilities in America were typically regulated private companies, in Europe they were often state enterprises. A side-effect of these regimes, of course, was that conglomeration across neither lines of business nor national boundaries was possible.

In Europe and Asia, competition policy was not as highly developed. Indeed, Germany and Japan explicitly permitted (and often encouraged) industrial and financial cartels. Because these cartels, conglomerates and state enterprises were instruments of neo-mercantilist national economic policy, merger among large corporations from different countries was almost unknown. Except for a brief period of acquisition and concentration among the oil companies, leading to such hybrids as Royal Dutch Shell, and direct foreign investment mainly by British and American multinational corporations, merger and acquisition across national borders was rare until the late 1980s. Books such as Richard Barnet's *Global Reach* (1972) were in a sense premature, if prescient, since they were dealing with multinational corporations venturing into export markets, producing overseas for foreign home markets and, later, outsourcing production – but not yet combining with each other into truly global behemoths.

The last decade of the twentieth century, by contrast, saw enormous mergers on a global scale, in industries where countries had previously guarded their 'national champions'. These mergers were partly facilitated by national policies of deregulation and privatisation. The mergers created, for the first time, genuinely transnational enterprises, in formerly fortress industries as diverse as banking, pharmaceuticals, telecommunications, aircraft and airlines, autos, insurance and, of course, information technology. Their existence changed the dynamics of assessing what was in the national economic interest, and seemed to mute earlier debates about industrial policy. It no longer seemed to matter whether Britain owned auto companies, as long as some auto production was located in the UK. In a famous article in the *Harvard Business Review* titled 'Who Is Us?' (January/February 1990) Robert Reich called on his fellow liberals to stop worrying about the national identity of firms and rather to concentrate on the location of production and, by extension, the quality of the national workforce. If Honda produced in Ohio, and even re-exported some American-made cars to the Japanese home market, what did it matter that its top management and most of its shareholders were Japanese? The British government, working with Japanese auto-makers, adopted this strategy even more explicitly. After all, truly stateless companies would eventually be owned by shareholders all over the world. If a nation wanted to pursue 'competitiveness', the trick was to have a workforce and a national regulatory climate congenial to multinational enterprise.

Thus did these giant corporations become bearers not just of goods and services, but of an ideology. And their commitment to this ideology was hardly armchair philosophy. They also worked politically to elect ideological confrères, to influence policy and to carry out global rules of engagement that made congenial habitats for themselves. They won allies in the financial press and in the economics profession. They invested large sums to promote compatible scholarship.

In 1999, the Clinton administration found itself caught up in a nasty scandal involving revelations that nuclear secrets had been stolen by the Beijing government from America's national laboratories. This did not deter American corporations from a furious lobbying campaign to extend 'most favoured nation' (MFN) trading status to China and to bring China into the World Trade Organisation. Other issues, such as China's human rights violations or its treatment of workers, as well as its flagrant espionage, fell by the wayside, and the Clinton administration faithfully embraced the corporate agenda. The large corporations were interested in their ability to outsource production freely to China and to sell in China's growing domestic market, eager to beat other corporations to deals. The corporate agenda became the national agenda. Indeed, in the run-up to the Seattle WTO ministerial meeting in November 1999, a 'host committee' chaired by the chief executives of Seattle's two largest companies, Microsoft and Boeing, became a quasi-official part of the American delegation, and seats at the host committee meetings were actually sold to corporate representatives; corporate goals for the session essentially drove out human rights and labour goals – and, remarkably enough, even national security goals.

Now, finally, corporations are becoming truly global and we are beginning to see mergers of former national champions yielding such improbable combinations as DaimlerChrysler and Upjohn+Pharmacia. In the 1980s and 1990s, publishing conglomerates based in Germany, the Netherlands and Australia owned the premier publishing houses in the UK and the USA. Such former fortresses as telecommunications, insurance and banking became fair game for mergers and acquisitions.

By the dawn of the new millennium, global corporations were both the carriers and beneficiaries of a hegemonic world-view whose essence went something like this:

There is one true path to the efficient allocation of goods and services. It includes, above all, the dismantling of barriers to free commerce and free flows of financial capital. To the extent that there is a remnant regulatory role, it is to protect property, both tangible and intellectual; to assure open, non-discriminatory access; to allow any

149

investor to purchase or sell any asset or repatriate any profit anywhere in the world; to remove and prevent subsidies and other distortions of the *laissez-faire* pricing system; to dismantle what remains of government –industry alliances.

Thus, the remaining role for government should be mainly to assist this *laissez-faire* agenda. In the aftermath of the Asian financial crisis of 1997–8, conventional wisdom acknowledged something of a herd instinct in short-term speculative investments, with destructive results – but the remedy called mainly for tougher regulatory measures to assure 'transparency'. In other words, all that was really necessary was for Third World countries to become more like advanced industrial countries in their systems of corporate accounting and reporting, and in their supervision of banks and stock exchanges. This greater transparency in turn would lead to better informed investors, and the market in transnational investments would logically become more rational and less unstable – more like textbook economics. By the same token, conventional reformers called for measures such as refinements in the accords (defined by the Basle Committee on Banking Supervision) which set standards for banks, and for agreements that would 'harmonise' the tax laws, competition policies, intellectual property regimes, reporting requirements and other conditions of doing business across national borders – for the greater convenience of private business. Such harmonisation was almost invariably in the direction of reduced interference with flows of goods, services and capital.

This emergent regulatory role, of course, was very different from the regulatory role that nation-states assumed throughout the twentieth century, in several distinct respects. It was supra-national rather than national. The nascent supra-national agencies were undemocratic or democratically accountable only at several removes. Some were explicitly creatures of business itself – rather more in the spirit of global trade associations than global regulatory bodies – with little if any role for national governments.

Domestically, central bankers operate at one remove from political accountability. Globally, the IMF and the World Bank operate at two removes. The World Trade Organisation addresses issues of fair play that concern investors, but not workers or citizens. Even worse, the WTO lacks evolved rules of evidence, due process, public hearings, or the strictures against conflicts of interest that characterise courts in mature democracies. Moreover, while the regulatory role of the nation-state in the twentieth century was based on an understanding of the instability of *laissez-faire* and a necessary set of countervailing interventions, these new regulators were the opposite – institutions intended to enable *laissez-faire* to operate at its pleasure.

The more centrist of corporate ideologues agreed that the state might still have a residual role to play in subsidising the education and training of workers; in cushioning periodic dislocations; in financing pre-competitive research, and in providing (reduced) forms of social income. But the corporate community insisted that these remaining state activities be consistent with private sector implementation wherever possible; that tax levels be low and relatively flat; that public sector deficits be minimal; and that state-led economic stabilisation policies be scrapped as archaic, except in the case of monetary policy, whose paramount goal was to assure price stability.

This set of convictions and policies, in turn, was reinforced by the romance of the new information economy. The emergent consensus view held that the structure of the new economy comported perfectly with *laissez-faire* theory. *Laissez-faire*, on this account, was finally vindicated because of the immediacy of information flow, the frictionless ease with which supply could rendezvous with demand, the decentralisation of labour (which makes labour markets less sticky and more like goods markets) and the fact that technology truly enables markets to be global. Because of the swiftness of innovation and information flows, government could not possibly improve on the inventiveness of entrepreneurship; government could only slow things down. Hence, government needed mainly to get out of the way. Entrepreneurs needed to be free to move capital and production and to seek markets anywhere in the world, without political intrusion.

In this view, it was something in the structure of the old industrial economy, and not the essence of capitalism itself, that had led to the instability and inefficiency of *laissez-faire*. Imperfect information led markets to overshoot. Long lead times and rigid production schedules led to periodic oversupply and mismatch with shifting consumer tastes. The national boundaries around markets kept producers in advanced countries from accessing willing labour supplies in the Third World, and led to inefficient forms of national protectionism among the advanced countries, such as the European Union's common agricultural policy and the competitive subsidy of aircraft and steel production. Trade unions and archaic customs that were centred around the permanent business firm kept the price of labour from efficiently reacting to the demand for it, leading to bouts of unemployment in weak periods and wage inflation in strong ones.

The idea that social bargaining and state stabilisation policies might lead to non-inflationary full employment was now considered an outmoded concept. The new economy solved the problem, by making labour markets more like product markets, with the price of labour more variable and the supply of labour more flexible. Thanks to mobility of both financial and production capital, workforces are becoming increasingly 'virtual' – subject to easier adjustment of both price and quantity in response to shifts in demand. Because workers are increasingly paid a spot-market price, the cost of labour adjusts itself more as do costs in product markets. Enthusiasts also contend that these shifts allow workers to be paid more nearly in line with their actual contribution to marginal product. This increases inequality but also efficiency. Loyalty between worker and firm is also an archaic idea, since in a spot market loyalty is a sentimental and inefficient notion, and each transaction must be justified anew.

This general story of how the new economy works and should work is fervently held by today's captains of industry, who see themselves as the vanguard of a new, stateless elite. It is the subject of countless books, both scholarly and popular. This account is mainly held by the right but, with minor differences having to do with the role of the state in training workers and cushioning shocks, it is also embraced by the neo-liberal centre. Even some on the left, such as Michael Piore and Charles Sabel (in *The New Industrial Divide*), have argued that structural changes in the economy allow 'flexible specialisation' and short-term, customised production, substantially solving the problem of macro-economic equilibrium.

But is this new story essentially true? Has globalisation, in combination with the new information technology, truly led to a capitalism that is at last self-regulating as every *laissez-faire* prophet from Adam Smith to Milton Friedman has insisted? Or is it that the forms of instability have simply changed with the technologies, requiring different forms of state intervention? Moreover, how does the new economy affect the balance of political forces, on which the presence or absence of appropriate stabilisation policies depends?

Among the great political achievements of the twentieth century was the domesticating of *laissez-faire* capitalism's brute power, under democratic auspices. The nation-state accomplished this task in multiple ways. It pursued economic stabilisation and steady growth through an active macro-economic policy. It regulated the more self-destructive tendencies of markets, especially banks and financial markets. It empowered trade unions and put a floor under labour, and later created environmental standards. It provided social income in various forms of social insurance. It financed the education and training of schoolchildren and workers. And it made direct public investments.

All of this made for a more socially bearable, as well as a more economically efficient, brand of capitalism. It tempered capitalism's extremes, both the volatility and the inequality. Increased stability also enhanced the political and economic bargaining power of ordinary people, which rooted the mixed economy in a majority politics. These political majorities then reciprocated by providing reliable constituencies for parties that believed in a mixed economy. So strong was this consensus during the post-war boom that even centre-right parties did not dare challenge the basic social entente or the conception of what was required to domesticate a market economy.

Despite new technology, what has changed is less the fundamental dynamics of markets than the venue of their regulation and with it the balance of political forces. If markets are global, their regulators must also be global. But we have no global government (nor, probably, should we) and only the very weakest of transnational institutions of governance. Corporations, it is said gleefully, have outrun the writ of nation-states.

In principle, the shift to global *laissez-faire* is an unmitigated good because of the efficiency of the price system. From this perspective, the regulations and stabilising policies are mere 'distortions', whose elimination will produce only better allocation of economic resources. But this view ignores the fact that the domestic policy interventions were necessitated in the first place by irremediable market failures, in sectors of the economy where market forces could not by themselves optimise outcomes.

For example, financial markets still are prone to overshoot, and their speculative tendencies still risk spilling over into the real economy. A *laissez-faire* global monetary system still has an overall bias to deflation and slower-than-available growth. Curiously, the new architects of *laissez-faire* are not recommending the dismantling of central banks; they are not proposing that the advanced countries turn their monetary policy over to some faceless global entity; they are not abandoning the supervision of securities exchanges and banks. And in the face of speculative mornings-after in Mexico and East Asia, they were quick to rely on central banks and international agencies for rescue operations. All of this is tribute to the fact that even the prophets of *laissez-faire* do not entirely believe in it. Indeed, even if all transactions were perfectly 'transparent', herd instincts and speculative binges would continue to characterise financial flows. Since information is ever more quickly capitalised, the smart money has ever more of an incentive to get a jump on the pack. The speculative impulse never subsides, and with it survives the tendency of financial markets to overshoot.

Further, there are still very major sectors of the economy, whether international or not, where market forces do not price things correctly. These include health care and education, which display substantial positive externalities beyond the purchasing power of individuals, as well as research, public infrastructure, and other public goods. These sectors, all alone, equal something like 30 per cent of gross domestic product in the advanced countries. In addition, there are other economic sectors with scale-economies and monopoly tendencies, such as airlines, railways, power companies and the telecom firms. If these are not substantially regulated, monopoly pricing results. Further, market forces misprice the emission of pollutants. And *laissez-faire* leads to degrees of inequality of wealth and income that begin to compromise democratic citizenship itself.

In the area of labour markets, there is a high road to productive efficiency, and a low road. Regulations that compel decent wages and working conditions are a stimulus to technical progress. The employer who has masses of desperate workers at his disposal has little incentive to innovate. The ability of industry to outsource production to areas of the world with little or no social or environmental regulation undercuts political decisions to foster a decent workplace that reflect a century of democratic struggle. These collective, democratic decisions put a social floor under wages and working conditions. They coexisted benignly with the period of the most rapid, sustained growth in the history of industrial capitalism – the boom after the Second World War. But with globalism, areas of the world that insist on retaining such standards find themselves priced out of the market, in a general race-to-the-bottom. This reality does not mean that the market is 'correct' and the social standards are 'wrong'. It means only that there are many possible roads, that the market is myopic, and that whether we have such standards must be a political decision.

When critics point to the destabilising tendencies of global capital flows, they are often disparaged as simple protectionists or allies of special interest groups. But there is something more fundamental at stake. The fact is that the mixed economy of the post-war era was a magnificent achievement, and global free markets undermine the project of maintaining a mixed, managed and regulated economy at home, in several ways. Global *laissez-faire* pulls capital into corners of the globe where there is less regulation, which in turn makes it harder for the advanced nations to police their banks, stock exchanges and capital markets, as well as their social standards. So it is an entire economic system – its institutions, its politics, as well as its economics – that is undermined by the resurrection of *laissez-faire*, with great costs to stability, security, opportunity, growth and democratic citizenship.

Globalism also influences the domestic political balance, in favour of the forces that want more globalism. The century-old project of making raw capitalism socially bearable is undermined in countless ways by globalism. Domestically, there are regulatory mechanisms, and political constituencies. These are neatly swept away by leaving everything to markets in the name of free trade. The global market trumps the domestic mixed economy.

Labour and social democratic parties seem unable to deliver the benefits they once did: secure jobs, high and rising earnings, good social insurance. Working people either stop voting, as they have in the USA, or they internalise the values of the new economy and conclude that the lower economic horizons are their own problem. Globalism depoliticises issues that are inherently political. The slogan of the new economy might as well be: 'Anyone can be Bill Gates, and if you're not Bill Gates it's your own fault.'

Investors, who are free to move money to locations of cheap wages and scant regulation, gain power at the expense of citizens whose incomes are mainly based on wages and salaries. That tilt, in turn, engenders more deregulation and more globalism. The global money market, not the democratic electorate, becomes the arbiter of what policies are 'sound'. In this climate, a Democratic President, a Labour Prime Minister or a Social-Democratic Chancellor can snub the unions, but he'd better not offend Wall Street or the City of London or Frankfurt. Even the nominally left party begins behaving like the right party.

For democratic electorates, there are three possible approaches. The first is simply to let market forces rule, as the proponents of *laissez-faire* globalism recommend. This path carries with it a high risk of periodic crises, slower and more uneven growth than the economy is capable of attaining, widening extremes of income inequality, the removal of many properly political questions from democratic deliberation, and the steady dismantling of social protections in the advanced countries.

The second path entails the attempt to combine the free flow of goods, services and capital with some form of social investment. This approach is seemingly attractive and efficient, but at the end of the day it is politically naïve and inconsistent with the dynamics of globalism. An exponent of this course is the *New York Times* columnist Thomas Friedman, author of the recent best-selling book *The Lexus and the Olive Tree*. Friedman constructs a four-way matrix to describe different views of globalism. According to Friedman, one can be a 'free-trader' or a 'protectionist' as well as a 'safety-netter' or a 'let-'em-eat-caker'. People like Margaret Thatcher and Ronald Reagan are in the free-trade, let-'em-eat-cake quadrant. Arch-conservative nationalists such as Patrick Buchanan are protectionist but anti-welfare state; old Labour and the Richard Gephardt wing of the US Democratic Party, as well as most French socialists, are what Friedman would call protectionist and pro-safety-net. For Friedman (and most neo-liberals from nominally centre-left parties) the preferred quadrant combines free trade with the safety-net.

Intuitively, this neo-liberal recipe seems attractive: let markets set prices; let free trade and free movements of global capital work their efficient magic. If voters don't like the social or distributive consequences, use the state to temper the extremes and give the displaced new opportunities and skills. But this view is naïve. Tempering the excesses of the market requires substantial public outlay and regulation. Yet if the world is one big free market, capital tends to avoid nations that impose burdens on it. Moreover, as the founders of the post-war financial system at Bretton Woods grasped, leaving currency values and capital movements to financial speculators leads to competitive devaluations and deflation.

The very existence of *laissez-faire* unravels the safety-net. Social programmes are expensive and require either high levels of taxation or public borrowing, both of which are anathema to *laissez-faire* capital. Moreover, it is rare in practice to see the political groups that champion *laissez-faire* commercial policies also supporting expensive safety-net programmes. The very term 'safety-net' is misleading, since it connotes a Beveridge-style set of policies for those who lose out to market forces – income transfers to widows, orphans, the unemployed and the disabled – rather than a proactive set of policies to operate a mixed economy. Contrary to Friedman, mixing *laissez-faire* commerce with costly social outlay and regulation is a contradiction in terms, politically and intellectually. Either markets always optimise outcomes, or they don't.

The third path, therefore, entails the reconstruction of a mixed economy amid new institutional circumstances and challenges. And there are only two fundamental ways of doing this. Either nation-states reclaim some of the power lately commandeered by market forces, or new transnational institutions of governance must be devised, directly or via international agreements.

This has been achieved before. At the Bretton Woods conference, the architects of the post-war financial and payments system had a profound understanding of the deflationary bias of private financial speculation. Countries subject to the workings of private money markets were under pressure to maintain sound currencies; they would respond with slower domestic growth, and try to export their unemployment through protection or competitive deflation. At best, this would lead to global slow growth. At worse, as in the early inter-war period, it would lead to depression and a backlash of desperation and dictatorship and, eventually, war.

The IMF was intended to remove the business of exchange rates from these private speculative pressures, and to create a bias towards expansion. It is ironic that an institution that was created as a bolster against the irrationality of speculative private capital flows has turned certain countries into havens for speculators, and yet become an agent of gratuitous austerity.

During the Bretton Woods era, there was not free trade in currencies; rather, there was the legacy of capital controls from the Second World War, and there were ubiquitous non-tariff barriers. While more free trade was emerging within Europe, there was little low-wage competition from outside Europe or North America. This was also a period of high growth and full employment. In the mixed economy of the post-war era, for the first time in the history of capitalism, ordinary working people had rising living standards coupled with social supports and economic security. Our task is to reinvent a mixed economy for a new era, and to figure out what kind of global economic context is compatible with a managed market economy at home, and what kind of politics is necessary to support that project.

The new globalised information economy neither solves the problem of market inefficiency nor does it address the issue of what sort of mixed economy we should have. This is ultimately a political question and not a technical one. It simply poses old questions in new settings, and tilts the political balance against coalitions that favour a more managed form of capitalism.

The core issues of political economy are still exactly the same ones for which advocates of a mixed economy have struggled for more than a century. Far from addressing these tendencies towards instability and misallocation of resources, globalisation simply makes the project of stabilisation and management more difficult, institutionally and politically.

We need, in short, a kind of global economic regime that allows the mixed economy to flourish at home. This means a global financial regime that slows down short-term, speculative movement of capital and currency trades. It means a trade regime that puts labour and environmental rights on a par with property rights. It means a financial regulatory regime with global standards, and an end to unregulated offshore havens. It means that the IMF and World Bank must be reclaimed as agents of growth and stabilisation rather than of austerity. It means conventions on taxation that prevent multinational corporations from playing national governments against each another for tax concessions. Some of this rebuilding of a mixed economy will entail the emergence of regional entities such as the EU. Some of it will involve the construction of much more robust institutions of global governance, which are not simply agents of *laissez-faire*, like the current WTO. It may require a new strategy of limiting *laissez-faire* trade to regions with roughly the same regulatory and social standards, but a retention of some barriers between this free trade area and areas that do not respect basic social standards – a shift from the principle of unconditional Most Favoured Nation treatment to a new form of conditional MFN intended to prevent that 'race-to-the-bottom'.

All of this, in turn, is based on democratic politics. Ironically, centre-left governments now simultaneously govern in every major European nation for the first time in history – London, Paris, Rome, and Berlin. Of the fifteen nations of the European Union, no fewer than thirteen are governed by democratic-left parties. Liberal democrats also occupy the executive branch in Washington and Ottawa.

This stunning convergence actually entails a double irony. Supposedly, this is the supreme capitalist moment. Yet in nation after nation, voters evidently don't like the effects of capitalism in the raw. At the same time, however, it is not at all clear that these very de-radicalised leftists can do much to temper the market. For the most part, their policies are slightly more benign versions of the same neo-liberal policies put forth by their centre-right predecessors. Indeed, many on the left have moved to the centre not so much out of choice or even political tactic, but because globalised capitalism seems to leave them little alternative. Left programmes can no longer deliver, in the absence of radical change in the rules of the global market economy. Those with a more venturesome view of taming global capital, such as Oskar

Lafontaine or Richard Gephardt, are largely marginalised within their own parties.

The question, then, is whether centre-left parties and governments can muster the imagination, the will and the strategy to change the current rules, to reclaim space for the mixed economy national policy. Europe still offers an alternative social model, but unless Europeans act in concert to challenge constraints of the global market, they do not have a viable economic model.

The collapse of the Bretton Woods system of managed exchange rates, in 1971–3, ushered in a period of slow growth. François Mitterrand learned painfully, as the first Socialist President of France during the early 1980s, that a nation that tries to grow faster than its neighbours is rewarded with a run on its currency. Since then, the market has grown only more powerful and the policy levers of nation-states more stunted. Even in a nation with fiscal discipline, tough regulatory strictures or generous social benefits (and the taxes required to pay for them) will frighten away investors. As a result, most centre-left governments are mainly reduced to accepting the discipline of the global market and tinkering around the edges. Their first priority is to reassure capital markets. In the USA, the Clinton administration is enjoying the effects of a somewhat uneven boom based on very orthodox fiscal policy designed to win the confidence of the Federal Reserve and Wall Street. Even so, new public outlay is still off the table and existing social programmes are in retrenchment.

On the Continent, where unemployment remains stuck at around 12 per cent, most left-of-centre governments are placing their bets on conservative fiscal policies combined with heroic measures to improve education and training. They hope to deregulate labour markets partially and to reform taxes that discourage job creation so that industry will take on more workers. However, they are somewhat more venturesome in their willingness to revise the rules of global capital flows.

In Japan, the ghost of Keynes hovers over, of all things, a liquidity trap. The Japanese government, pressured to revise its entire system along Western *laissez-faire* lines, is stuck in a 1930s-style depression. Rather than a serious programme of public spending, the government is offering modest increases in public works and handing out shopping vouchers. The risk-averse Japanese, as they do in hard times, are increasing their personal savings. Curiously enough, despite globalism, crises can still take different forms in different societies.

Globalism, as noted, undermines the capacity of the nation-state to regulate the conditions of labour and to pursue policies of high growth and full employment. Many centre-left parties, as a second-best, pursue their own brand of 'supply-side' programmes, intended to raise productivity and competitiveness by improving the quality of the workforce. This approach is fine as far as it goes, but it doesn't go terribly far. It is certainly sensible to invest public funds in better educated workers, lifetime learning policies and other measures to make the labour market work better. But these policies have their limits when macro-economic factors produce a climate of high unemployment.

Some centre-left parties are also promoting work-spreading measures such as a shorter working week. Yet as European employers emulate their American counterparts and turn to temporary workers and outsourcing, the assumption that the state can define what constitutes a 'normal' working week is unrealistic. With slow overall growth, mandating a 35-hour week with 40 hours of pay will produce inflation. But a mandatory cut in both hours and pay, while non-inflationary, will produce moonlighting, and defeat the whole purpose. Shorter working time is the fruit of higher growth, not the engine.

Labour market policies, by themselves, do not add up to higher growth rates. They can work as complements to a more expansionary macro-economic policy, but not as substitutes for it. The Swedish Keynesians figured this out more than four decades ago. The recipe is to run as hot a macro-economic policy as you dare without triggering inflation, and then complement it with active labour market policies to match well-trained workers with employers. When unemployment gets down to a level that runs the risk of wage inflation, you enlist the unions in voluntary wage restraint, and soak up the remaining joblessness with retraining sabbaticals and public employment.

But Swedish Keynesianism doesn't work very well any more. The culprit is the global economy. Global growth is held hostage to creditors and financial speculators. And countries with good wages and expensive social outlays find themselves priced out of the market. The prevailing, feeble form of social democracy is not likely to change this economic trajectory very much. And if tinkering is their only contribution, the current spate of moderately left governments will very likely be repudiated by the voters.

There is an alternative to simply accepting a downward convergence of wages and benefits as an inevitable price to be paid for the 'efficiency' of the global market. But this alternative will require a fundamental shift in how centre-left governments view global capital. For the most part, American liberals and European social democrats have not challenged the neo-liberal view that all prices are efficiently set by markets. Yet there is a surprisingly strong dissent being voiced by mainstream economists who hold that there is one major exception to this rule – the price of currencies and the flow of global capital.

In the past few years, such mainstream economists as Jeffrey Sachs of Harvard, Paul Krugman of MIT, Barry Eichengreen of the University of California at Berkeley, Joseph Stiglitz, formerly of Stanford and the Clinton White House and now chief economist of the World Bank, and Jagdish Bhagwati of Columbia, formerly economic adviser to the director-general of the GATT, have all challenged whether free flows of capital and *laissez-faire* setting of currency parities actually optimise outcomes.

In the May–June 1997 issue of *Foreign Affairs*, Bhagwati, one of the most eminent and passionate of free trade economists, wrote a startling article contrasting trade in goods with trade in capital and currencies. 'Only an untutored economist will argue', Bhagwati wrote, 'that free trade in widgets and life insurance policies is the same as free capital mobility.' The reason is simple. Trade in ordinary goods and services tends to reach equilibrium. But global capital markets often tend to overshoot, pricing currencies wrongly, pouring capital in and yanking it out, doing serious damage to the real economy.

A good case in point is the Asian crisis. Foreign capital seeking supernormal returns abruptly swamped these newly liberalised capital markets. When overbuilding ensued and returns began sagging, the capital rushed out, devastating the currencies and economies. Bhagwati wrote, 'When a crisis hits, the downside of free capital mobility arises. To ensure that capital returns, the country must do everything it can to restore the confidence of those who have taken the money out. This typically means raising interest rates.' But higher interest rates only deepen local recession. Investors are 'reassured' at a devastating cost to the real economy.

The IMF, which comes in to 'restore confidence' (and supervise a fire sale) often serves as a handy scapegoat. But the deeper problem is the neo-liberal regime and its encouragement of short-term speculative capital flows to fragile economies in the first place. And those same speculative capital movements constrain the policy options of advanced economies.

Systemically, the effect of free capital mobility is not just periodic crises but a deflationary bias for the system as a whole, as nations competitively manipulate interest rates and exchange rates to reassure investors. In a downturn, this can take the form of competitive devaluations, as in Europe in the 1930s and Asia in the late 1990s. In an inflationary period, it can take the form of high real interest rates, as in Europe and America in the 1980s. The common effect is needless instability, creditor hegemony, slow growth and pressure on nations to jettison high wages and decent social benefits.

This critique is also tacitly shared by the world's finance ministers and central bankers. For although global capital flows are more or less free and currency values are more or less set by market forces, governments and central bankers do recognise, if only through periodic *ad hoc* interventions, that the stakes are simply too high to let speculative capital and currency swings determine the fate of the real economy.

Five times in the past two decades, the great powers have intervened in very significant ways to counteract the impulses – and the damage – of speculative forces in capital markets. These included the concerted intervention in late June 1998 to prevent the yen from crashing and taking the Asian economy with it; the Mexican rescues of 1983 and 1995; the Louvre Accord of 1988 to stabilise the dollar against the yen; and the Plaza Accord of 1985 which produced a period of co-ordinated reductions in interest rates.

Note that three of these occurred during the Reagan/Thatcher era, under administrations that elsewhere were fiercely committed to free markets. Note also that the recent co-ordinated moves to shore up the yen were undertaken out of fear that a weakening yen would trigger a chain of devaluation throughout Asia and very serious recession – which would lead to more irrationality in the market. Western powers have pressed the Chinese to continue pegging the Hong Kong dollar to the US dollar and to continue defending the Chinese yuan – two more violations of the idea that currency values should be set by market forces.

But while Western governments are willing to engage in *ad hoc* interventions to contain crises, they are uneasy about returning to a more regulated regime for private capital flows and exchange rates. However, re-regulation of capital flows is precisely what is needed if left-of-centre governments are to reclaim the capacity to pursue policies of high growth and social justice.

Casual observers of the mid-century economy failed to appreciate the importance of the Bretton Woods system. Bretton Woods fixed exchange rates. But by committing central banks to collectively support the fixed rates, it also precluded speculative currency trade and capital movements. The latter was its more important achievement. Regulation of global capital thus created a shelter under which it was possible for national governments to build high-employment, high-growth welfare states, free from the downward competitive pressure of global money markets.

The question is whether the concert of centre-left governments will now take the next step and also pursue strategies to limit speculative global capital flows. For example, Professor James Tobin's proposed tax on financial transactions, long scorned by free-market economists, is getting a respectful second hearing, as analysts look for ways to rein in private global money markets. Another good idea was devised by Chile, certainly no enemy of free markets. The Chileans required any foreign investor to place 30 per cent of the amount of the investment on deposit with the Chilean central bank for a year, as insurance against capital flight. They suspended this requirement in 1998, because their more *laissez-faire* neighbours were successfully competing for capital. But a global regime that rewarded longer-term cross-border investments and punished purely speculative ones would be salutary. Such measures move the world back towards regulated capital markets. Removing currency values and capital movements from purely speculative swings and resulting recessions such as the current Asia panic would allow both higher growth and more managed national economies.

Corporations, who live and die in the real, as opposed to the financial, economy, ought to be receptive to such measures. They were, after the experience of the Great Depression. But today's corporations, whether financial or industrial, are caught up in the romance of *laissez-faire*.

So it falls to the world's democratically elected governments and their citizens to take these questions seriously – to save the market system from its self-cannibalising tendencies, to create more domestic room for policy and to allow the world a higher rate of growth. The ancient question of how market forces need to be tempered for the greater good of the economy and society is now a global one. Either the irrationality of global capital flows will be harnessed once again by democratically elected governments, or those governments and their democratic electorates will continue to be enfeebled by the world's money markets. It is depressing to end a chapter by musing that it will take a crisis to stimulate a fundamental change in conventional thinking. But with so much of the sheer political and economic power cutting in the opposite direction, it is hard to see how imagination and foresight alone can achieve a dramatic change of course.

ULRICH BECK

Living Your Own Life in a Runaway World: Individualisation, Globalisation and Politics

There is hardly a desire more widespread in the West today than to lead 'a life of your own'. If a traveller in France, Finland, Poland, Switzerland, Britain, Germany, Hungary, the USA or Canada asks what really moves people there, what they strive and struggle to achieve, the answer may be money, work, power, love, God or whatever, but it would also be, more and more, the promise of 'a life of your own'. Money means your own money, space means your own space, even in the elementary sense of a precondition for a life you can call your own. Love, marriage and parenthood are required to bind and hold together the individual's own, centrifugal life-story. It would be only a slight exaggeration to say that the daily struggle for a life of your own has become the collective experience of the Western world. It expresses the remnant of our communal feeling.

What drives people to reach for the stars in their lives? Why is this new direction emerging which, though seemingly meaningful only at the level of the individual, is really unfolding in accordance with a schematic pattern? What explains the zeal, the fear and enthusiasm, the cunning and determination, with which large numbers of people fret and fight for their 'own lives'? For many, the answer obviously lies within the people themselves – in their individual wills, their inflated expectations, their insatiable hunger for new experience, their decreasing prepared-ness to obey commands, to get into lane, to make sacrifices. Such hasty explanations, however, throw up a new series of questions. How are we to explain the fact that people in many countries suddenly and simultaneously want to take control of their lives? Everything is acted out in the personalised costumes of the individual – independently, in the world's most varied cultures, languages and cities. Is this a kind of epidemic of egoism, an ego fever, to be overcome through daily doses of

164

ethics and references to the public good? Or are individuals, despite all the glitter of the campaign for their own lives, perhaps also in the vanguard of a deeper change? Do they point to new shores, towards a struggle for a new relationship between the individual and society, which still has to be invented? This is what the present chapter will argue.

We live in an age in which the social order of the national state, class, ethnicity and the traditional family is in decline. The ethic of individual self-fulfilment and achievement is the most powerful current in modern society. The choosing, deciding, shaping human being who aspires to be the author of his or her own life, the creator of an individual identity, is the central character of our time. It is the fundamental cause behind changes in the family and the global gender revolution in relation to work and politics. Any attempt to create a new sense of social cohesion has to start from the recognition that individualism, diversity and scepticism are written into Western culture (Beck and Beck-Gernsheim, 2000). The importance of a life of your own in a runaway world may be outlined in the following fifteen points.

One: the compulsion to lead your own life, and the possibility of doing it, emerge when a society is highly differentiated. To the extent that society breaks down into separate functional spheres that are neither interchangeable nor graftable onto one another, people are integrated into society only in their partial aspects as taxpayers, car drivers, students, consumers, voters, patients, producers, fathers, mothers, sisters, pedestrians, and so on. Constantly changing between different, partly incompatible logics of action, they are forced to take into their hands that which is in danger of breaking into pieces: their own lives. Modern society does not integrate them as whole persons into its functional systems; rather, it relies on the fact that individuals are not integrated but only partly and temporarily involved as they wander between different functional worlds. The social form of your own life is initially an empty space which an ever more differentiated society has opened up. It becomes filled with incompatibilities, the ruins of traditions, the junk of side-effects. The space left behind as once dominant certainties lose their power becomes a junkyard for the wreckage of people's own lives. Many Westerners could say: 'My life is not a continuum. It is not merely broken by day and night into black and white pieces. It is different versions of me which go to the station, sit in the office and make bookings, stalk through groves, write; I am the thinker-of-all-trades, of broken-up trades, who runs, smokes, kills, listens to the radio, says "Yes, sir" to the chief officer.' Such a person

165

has been called 'a tray full of sparkling snapshots' (Arno Schmidt, *Aus dem Leben eines Fauns*).

Two: your own life is not a life peculiar to yourself. In fact the opposite is true; a standardised life is produced that combines both achievement and justice, and in which the interest of the individual and rationalised society are merged. The expansion of nation-state produced and affirmed individualisation, with doctrines of socialisation and institutions of education to match. This is what I call the paradox of 'institutional individualism'. The legal norms of the welfare state make individuals (not groups) the recipients of benefits, thereby enforcing the rule that people should organise more and more of their own lives. People used to be born into traditional societies, as they were into social classes or religions. Today even God himself has to be chosen. And the ubiquitous rule is that, in order to survive the rat-race, one has to become active, inventive and resourceful, to develop ideas of one's own, to be faster, nimbler and more creative – not just on one occasion, but constantly, day after day. Individuals become actors, builders, jugglers, stage-managers of their own biographies and identities, but also of their social links and networks.

Three: your own life is thus completely dependent on institutions. In the place of binding traditions, institutional guidelines appear on the scene to organise your own life. The qualitative difference between traditional and modern life-stories is not, as many assume, that in older corporate and agrarian societies various suffocating controls and guidelines restricted the individual's say in his or her own life to a minimum, whereas today hardly any such restrictions are left. It is, in fact, in the bureaucratic and institutional jungle of modernity that life is most securely bound into networks of guidelines and regulations. The crucial difference is that modern guidelines actually compel the self-organisation and self-thematisation of people's biographies. In earlier times in Europe very precise rules governed wedding ceremonies, for example, so that in some regions and periods nearly half the population of marriageable age remained single. Today, by contrast, many sets of guidelines – in the educational system, the labour market, or the welfare state – involve demands that individuals should run their own lives, on pain of economic sanction.

Four: living your own life therefore means that standard biographies become elective biographies, 'do-it-yourself biographies', risk biographies, broken or broken-down biographies. Even behind façades of security and prosperity, the possibilities of biographical slippage and collapse are ever present. Hence the clinging and the fear, even in the externally wealthy middle layers of society. So there is a big difference to be made between individualisation where there are institutional resources like human rights, education and the welfare state to cope with the contradiction of modern biographies and 'atomisation' where there are not. The neo-liberal market ideology enforces atomisation with all its political . . .

Five: despite, or because of, the institutional guidelines and the often incalculable insecurity, your own life is condemned to activity. Even in failure, it is an active life in its structuring of demands. The other side of this obligation to be active is that failure becomes personal failure, no longer perceived as class experience in a 'culture of poverty'. It goes hand in hand with forms of self-responsibility. Whereas illness, addiction, unemployment and other deviations from the norm used to count as blows of fate, the emphasis today is on individual blame and responsibility. Living your own life therefore entails taking responsibility for personal misfortunes and unanticipated events. Typically, this is not only an individual perception, but a culturally binding mode of attribution. It corresponds to an image of society in which individuals are not passive reflections of circumstances but active shapers of their own lives, within varying degrees of limitation.

Six: your own life – your own failure. Consequently, social crisis phenomena such as structural unemployment can be shifted as a burden of risk onto the shoulders of individuals. Social problems can be directly turned into psychological dispositions: into guilt feelings, anxieties, conflicts and neuroses. Paradoxically enough, a new immediacy develops in the relationship between the individual and society, an immediacy of disorder such that social crises appear as individual and are no longer – or are only very indirectly – perceived in their social dimension. This is even true of the darker side of still-integrated societies: the new collective positions of underclass and exclusion. These are collectively individualised. Here is certainly one of the sources, both present and future, for the outbreaks of violence for its own sake that are directed against shifting victims ('foreigners', the disabled, homosexuals, Jews). Researchers distinguish between 'life-story' as a chain of actual events and 'biography' as the narrative form of events – which by no means necessarily coincide with each other. Thus, if biographies spoke only of 'blows of fate', 'objective conditions' and 'outside forces' that 'overwhelmed', 'predetermined', or 'compelled', that would refute the theory formulated above. For it has been argued that individuals have to perceive themselves as at least partly shaping themselves and the conditions of their lives, even or above all in the language of failure. A rough pragmatic indicator for the 'living your own life' theory is thus the presence of elements of an individualistic and active narrative form in people's own biographies. Life's events are ascribed not mainly to 'alien' causes, but to aspects of the individual (decisions, non-decisions, omissions, capacities, incapacities, achievements, compromises, defeats). This does not, of course, rule out the possibility of false consciousness.

Seven: people struggle to live their own lives in a world that increasingly and more evidently escapes their grasp, one that is irrevocably and globally networked. Even the most natural action of all – the inhaling of clean air – ultimately presupposes a revolution in the industrial world order. This brings us to the concept of the globalisation of biography. In the global age, one's own life is no longer sedentary or tied to a particular place. It is a travelling life, both literally and metaphorically, a nomadic life, a life spent in cars, aeroplanes and trains, on the telephone or the internet, supported by the mass media, a transnational life stretching across frontiers. The multi-local transnationality of your own life is a further reason for the hollowing-out of national sovereignty and the obsolescence of nation-based sociology. The association of place and community or society is coming unstuck (Beck, 1999a). Whether voluntarily or compulsorily or both, people spread their lives out across separate worlds. Globalisation of biography means place polygamy; people are wedded to several places at once. Place-polygamous ways of living are translated biographies: they have to be constantly translated both for oneself and for others, so that they can continue as in-between lives. The transition from the first to the second modernity is also a transition from place monogamy to place polygamy. To understand the social figure of globalisation as it applies to your own life, it is necessary to keep in view the different conflicting places across which that life is spread out. In this sense, not only global players but also Indian taxi-drivers in Chicago or Russian Jews in Israel live transnational lives. Globalisation of biographies means a very complex, contradictory process that generates novel conflicts and forms of separation. Thus, the upsurge of local nationalisms and the new emphasis on local identity should be seen as an unmistakable consequence of globalisation, and not – as they may first appear – as a phenomenon that contradicts it. This seventh thesis therefore implies that your own life is a global life. The framework of the national state has become too big and too small. What happens within your own life has a lot to do with world-wide influences, challenges and fashions, or with protection against them.

Eight: the other side of globalisation is detraditionalisation. The life of your own life is also a detraditionalised life. This does not mean that tradition no longer plays any role – often the opposite is the case. But traditions must be chosen and often invented, and they have force only through the decisions and experience of individuals. The sources of collective and group identity and of meaning which are characteristic of industrial society (ethnic identity, class consciousness, faith in progress), whose life-styles and notions of security underpinned Western democracies and economies into the 1960s, here lose their mystique and break up, exhausted. Those who live in this post-national, global society are constantly engaged in discarding old classifications and formulating new ones. The hybrid identities and cultures that ensue are precisely the individuality which then determines social integration. In this way, identity emerges through intersection and combination, and thus through conflict with other identities.

How does this differ from the historical and theoretical analyses of Georg Simmel, Emile Durkheim and Max Weber in the early part of this century? The main difference is that today people are not discharged from corporate religious-cosmological certainties into the world of industrial society, but are transplanted from the national industrial societies of the first modernity into the transnational turmoil of world-risk society (Beck, 1999b). People are expected to live their lives with the most diverse and contradictory transnational and personal identities and risks. Individualisation in this sense means detraditionalisation, but also the opposite: a life lived in conflict between different cultures, the invention of hybrid traditions. It is hardly surprising that various idylls – grandma's apple cake, forget-me-nots and communitarianism – are experiencing a boom. Even traditional (for example, religious) systems of interpretation cannot shut themselves off from what is happening; they collide with one another and end up in public competition and conflict, at both a global and a local level. Fundamentalism too, in its European and non-European variants, is in this sense a reaction to both individualisation and globalisation. The crucial point here is that the public realm no longer has anything to do with collective decisions. It is a question not of solidarity or obligation but of conflictual coexistence.

Nine: if globalisation, detraditionalisation and individualisation are analysed together, it becomes clear that your own life is an experimental life. Inherited recipes for living and role stereotypes fail to function. There are no historical models for the conduct of life. Individual and social life – in marriage and parenthood as well as in politics, public activity and paid work – have to be brought back into harmony with each other. The restlessness of the age, of the *Zeitgeist*, is also due to the fact that no one knows how or whether this can be achieved.

Ten: your own life is a reflexive life. Social reflexion – the processing of contradictory information, dialogue, negotiation, compromise – is almost synonymous with living your own life. Active management (and that does seem the right word) is necessary for the conduct of life in a context of conflicting demands and a space of global uncertainty. Self-realisation and self-determination are by no means merely individual goals; they are often also public stop-gaps, the reverse side of the problems that all partial systems unload onto citizens by suddenly deeming them 'mature and responsible'. This compulsion to self-realisation, this departure for the foreign continent of your own life, goes hand in hand with integration into world-wide contexts. Something like individual distinctiveness really appears for the first time through the combination of social crises in which individuals are forced to think, act and live. It becomes normal to test out a number of different mixes; several overlapping identities are discovered and a life is constructed out of their combination. The social structure of your own global life thus appears together with continual differentiation and individualisation – or, to be more precise, with the individualisation of classes, ethnic groups, nuclear families and normal female biographies. In this way, the nationally fixed social categories of industrial society are culturally dissolved or transformed. They become 'zombie categories', which have died yet live on. Even traditional conditions of life become dependent upon decisions; they have to be chosen, defended and justified against other options and lived out as a personal risk. Not only genetically modified food but also love and marriage, including the traditional housewife marriage, become a risk.

Eleven: living your own life is, in this sense, a late-modern form which enjoys high esteem. This has not always been so. In traditional, nationally closed societies, the individual remains a species concept: the smallest unit of an imagined whole. Only detraditionalisation, global opening and a new multiplicity of functional logics give social space and meaning to the emphasis on the individual. The positive evaluation of the individual is thus a truly modern phenomenon, which at the same time continues to be vigorously combated even today (as talk of the 'me-first' or 'push-and-shove' society shows). All through history, individualist behaviour has been equated with conduct that is deviant or even idiotic. When individuality features in the consciousness of a world picture, it is tainted with a flaw or defect. This was true in ancient Greece, or during the early Middle Ages in Europe, when individuality was mainly interpreted as deviant or sinful behaviour to be avoided. This deprecatory sense of individuality persisted in the sciences and 'the bourgeois world, up to the epigraph of Sartre's *La Nausée*: "Ce type n'a aucune valeur pour la société, il n'est qu'un individu." A mere individual – that is the most concise formula expressing the opposition to the early Romantic rehabilitation (and redefinition) of the essence of individuality.' (Frank, 1988: p. 611). Interestingly enough, this revaluation of individuality succeeded precisely because that which had for centuries been the reason for its low value now became the reason for its high value: namely, that the individual cannot be derived from the general. The point now was that the general could only be surmised, and thus paled beside the verifiability and indeed immemoriality of the individual. The 'essence of individuality' may therefore be understood as 'radical non-identity'.

Twelve: your own life, seen in this way, is a radically non-identical life. While culture was previously defined by traditions, today it must be defined as an area of freedom which protects each group of individuals and has the capacity to produce and defend its own individualisation. To be more specific, culture is the field in which we assert that we can live together, equal yet different.

Thirteen: living your own life therefore can mean living under the conditions for radicalised democracy, for which many of the concepts and formulas of the first modernity have become inadequate. No one knows how the conflicting transnational identities can be politically integrated. No one knows how the ever-growing demands for family intimacy can be linked to the new demands for the freedom and self-realisation of men, women and children. No one knows how the need of mass organisations (political parties, trade unions) to obligate individuals can be made compatible with claims for participation and self-organisation. People are better adapted to the future than are social institutions and their representatives.

Fourteen: the decline of values which cultural pessimists are so fond of decrying is in fact opening up the possibility of escape from the creed of 'bigger, more, better', in a period that is living beyond its means ecologically and economically. Whereas, in the old value system, the self always had to be subordinated to patterns of collectivity, these new 'we' orientations are creating something like a co-operative or altruistic individualism. Thinking of oneself and living for others, once considered a contradiction in terms, is revealed as an internal connection. In fact, living alone means living socially. The politics based on the defence of life as a personal project is the rejection of its adversaries: a powerful market system on the one hand, and a communalism that imposes purity and homogeneity on the other.

Fifteen: the dominance of living your own life thus leads to an opening and a sub-politicisation of society, but also to a depoliticisation of national politics. Two of the basic conditions for national representative democracy are being especially called into question. The first of these conditions is the general trust that enables parties (and other collective actors) to mobilise citizens and party members, to some extent blindly and independently of their personal preferences, around certain issues of the day. The second is the limited number of collective actors and their internal homogeneity. Both these premises are becoming questionable as a result of individualisation processes. It cannot be assumed either that citizens are party members and party members are party troops, or that parties and trade unions are intrinsically capable of achieving consensus – because large organisations are also pluralised in respect of their content. In the wake of the processes of individualisation and globalisation, collective actors are themselves being hollowed out and summoned to programmatic revolutions behind an unchanging façade (New Labour, for example). Unpredictable dilemmas arise, however, for the organisation of politics at the level of the national state. Here we see the impetuous development of what Kant already noted in his critique of representative democracy: namely, the contradiction that democracy appeals to the individual as the subject of law-making, yet filters out, glides over and holds down the expression of individual will in the forms of representativity. On the one hand, the 'living your own life' society validates at the heart of national politics the basic proposition that the individual – and only the individual – counts as the source of democratic legitimacy. On the other hand, the corporate and representative organisation of the mediation of interests rests precisely upon the fact that it is not individuals but collective actors, constructed in accordance with the constitution, which take political decisions of major importance and scope. Conversely it is not possible to admit more and more actors into the game of political power, because that would multiply the arenas of conflict without increasing the potential for consensus. The number of negotiating systems cannot grow indefinitely, and it is by no means the case that many individual negotiations add up to a single all-integrating power of decision. It thus becomes apparent that the politicisation of society in the wake of cultural democratisation does not at all translate into an activation of politics. This takes the steam out of the frequent objection that the numerically larger involvement of modern individualists in a wide range of local initiatives or (to use the fashionable expression) networks – from sports clubs to campaigns against xenophobia – integrates or socialises modern society in a way that is functionally equivalent to that of the traditional political forms of large organisations or the national state. Even the widespread talk of a 'networking of networks' cannot obscure the fact that the increasingly fragmented political structure of society, which is expressed in the individualisation of political behaviour and the waning capacity of the old large organisations for integration and aggregation, weakens the potential of political societies for purposive mobilisation and direction. (Greven, 1997: pp. 246 ff.). The ideal of integration through conflict, which is the basis of national democracy, here breaks down. It becomes ever more difficult to guarantee the two sides of democracy: consensus among individuals and groups based upon free agreement, and representation of conflictual interests. But this is where a real political dilemma of the second modernity becomes palpable. On the one hand, political imagination and political action are confronted with challenges of a quite unprecedented scale. We need only think of the sweeping reforms needed to give the social state a new foundation with regard to insecure forms of employment and the working poor; or of what is required to reorganise the nationally calibrated key institutions of parliamentary democracy so that they are more open to transnational identities, life situations and economic link-ups; not to speak of the once totally neglected question of ecologically reforming the autonomous and ever faster world industrial dynamic. On the other hand, processes of individualisation are eroding the social-structural conditions for political consensus, which until now have made possible collective political action. The paradox is that this happens because political involvement is increasing at the microcosmic level and subpolitical society is governed from below in more and more issues and fields of action. The closed space of national politics no longer exists. Society and the public realm are constituted out of conflictual spaces that are at once individualised, transnationally open and defined in opposition to one another. It is in these spaces that each cultural group tests and lives out its hybrid.

Bibliography

Beck, U. (1999a) *What Is Globalisation?* Cambridge: Polity Press.
—— (1999b) *World Risk Society*, Cambridge: Polity Press.
Beck, U., and Beck-Gernsheim, E. (2000) *Individualisation*, London: Sage.
Frank, M. (1988) 'Einleitung in Fragmente einer Schlussdiskussion', in M.

RICHARD SENNETT

Street and Office: Two Sources of Identity

Identities and Narratives

'My what, young man?' an elderly Boston matron replied when I asked her to describe her identity, point-blank over tea in the Somerset Club. I was still of so inexperienced an age, as a man and as a researcher, that I believed frontal ambush was the best way to elicit information from others. It was 1966, and the sociologist David Riesman had just sent me on my first research job, interviewing members of Boston's upper class about their identities in the city.

My informant had a clear image of herself and other Boston Brahmins, and equally clear images of people lower down the social ladder. These would be called in Latin *personae*: that is, images of self and other, which are instant markers; her own persona was a mask she donned without hesitation. An identity involves a life-narrative rather than a fixed image of self, I kindly explained to her, citing Erikson and Freud – and a recognition that others' lives intrude into one's sense of self. Equally kindly, she wasn't having any of it: 'We go our separate ways, dear.' Nor did I do much better with a senior banker at the Harvard Society of Fellows, who declared, 'I know just what you mean by "narrative".' He patiently took me through his family's genealogy – implying, as we neared the present, that references to various living kin were to persons I had inevitably met. In fact, I had grown up on a public housing estate in Chicago, but he had taken a liking to me.

Modern culture is flooded with identity-talk, particularly about marginal, subaltern, transgressive, or oppressed identities, but this chatter tends to be about *personae*, those images and masks – or of crude stories about 'how I discovered the person I really am'. Such identity-talk isn't much use for making sense of personal life today in the global economy, because an ever-shifting, external market reality disturbs fixed pictures of self. The new capitalism has radically changed, for instance, people's experience of work. Corporations are shifting from being dense, often rigid, pyramidal bureaucracies to be more flexible networks in a constant state of inner revision. In flexible capitalism people labour at short-term tasks, and change employers frequently; lifetime employment in one firm is a thing of the past. As a result, people can't identify themselves with a particular labour or with a single employer. They are frustrated, as I have found, in scripting a sustained life-narrative from their labours.

The new capitalism has also disturbed identities based on place – that sense of 'home', of belonging somewhere particular in the world. The disturbance occurs particularly in the places where the new sort of work gets done, cities which are increasingly homes to the global elite as well as lower-level migrants. An investment banker in New York will identify far more with peers in London and Frankfurt than with other New Yorkers; the janitor cleaning his office is likely to have a mother in Panama and a brother in Buenos Aires. Where do such people belong, where is home? Like Odysseus, they need some orientation for their life-journey. As traumas go, globalisation does not rank with war; so far no one seems willing to die for it. Yet any great change is disturbing. Some analysts believe people will seek to defend themselves by asserting seemingly stable cultural values against the chameleon indifference of the economy: the conflict will be between an idealised home and the realities of labour, place versus work. Here's how the sociologist Manuel Castells evokes that conflict: 'This is a defensive identity, an identity of retrenchment of the known against the unpredictability of the unknown and uncontrollable.' Suddenly defenceless against a global whirlwind, people stick to themselves: whatever they had, and whatever they were, becomes their identity. The janitor dreams of his abandoned farm in Panama, the banker perhaps of Yorkshire, where people seemed more rooted. I think people's actual experience is likely to be just the reverse. The complexities of globalisation will prove easier to digest in the city than on the job. While modern cities are becoming more cosmopolitan, people are still looking for some version of 'home' at work.

The Importance of Edges

Since we so commonly think in pictures, it would be foolish simply to rule out self-images in understanding identity. As an unfolding story, an identity originates precisely in the conflict between how others see you and how you see yourself. The two seldom fit, and people are seldom indifferent to that lack of fit, so comfortable in themselves like the old Boston Brahmins. Instead, people tend to focus on what could be called the edges of an identity, how those two images might fit together like pieces of a puzzle.

Imagine, for instance, a poor woman in Boston declaring, 'I am a black lesbian mother.' Here, 'lesbian mother' might be a more active element in her identity than 'black mother'; she would concentrate more on the two aspects of experience which, conventionally, did not fit neatly together. She would attempt to explain herself. Self-explanation is one thing people seek to accomplish through constructing life-narratives.

In real life people lack the control over events and other characters that a novelist possesses. A person's life-narrative therefore has to be continually recast in the course of experience; you need continually to make a fresh explanation of yourself. Far from plunging into a subjective abyss, the capacity to recast your life-story is a sign of strength in attending to the world outside.

Correspondingly, a weak identity means clinging to a rigid image of self, a lack of capacity to revise when circumstances require it. Despite themselves, even my Boston Brahmins were so obliged: upwardly mobile Jews and Irish immigrants in the city were joining their clubs, marrying their children and taking their jobs; the WASPs in fact continually recast the meaning of these disturbances to themselves; they had to fit these pieces of the puzzle together. How to narrate what happens at the edge, when you try to fit unlike pieces together? That's the challenge for modern fiction writers from Joyce to Salman Rushdie, who have pieced together stories out of events which have no forward thrust and characters who have no logical relation to each other. I was surprised to find something akin to this among manual workers as well as among younger members of the elite whom I began interviewing in Boston forty years ago. They evinced what might be called a capacity for 'cross-referencing' disparate experiences.

One budding lawyer, for instance, recounted the leading characters in his white-shoe, old-school Boston firm; he displayed pride in the family pedigrees of his elders, but retailed in equal measure their professional incompetence. I found members of the Boston working class shoving up similar incongruities in their own families, boasting about the achievements of the sons for whom they sacrificed their small savings to put them through university, even while complaining that these jumped-up youngsters often became ashamed of their family origins; sacrifice and betrayal were inseparable in their life-narratives. Such cross-referencing is like scanning the index of a book and finding under the entry 'memory' the direction 'see incompetence', or under 'sacrifice' the pointer 'see eclipse'. By making cross-references of this sort, people set about welding dissonant experiences together.

From the psychological point of view an important, if unexpected, thing about cross-referencing is how it can strengthen a person's sense of self. Interview sessions in which cross-referencing becomes important usually begin, during their early hours, with the subject keeping unlike people or events categorically apart; as the interviews proceed, and the subject becomes engaged, people and events are shoved ever closer together. The act of compression creates the 'edge', in the sense I'm using that word, and imparts weight and density to the life-story. A janitor who feels both pride and class anger at his son has a density of self; so does a young lawyer who feels affection and solidarity for elders he does not professionally respect. Such transactions have a simple but important consequence. Over the past fifty years, psychological studies of the phenomenon of 'cognitive dissonance' have documented ways in which higher mammals become attached to precisely those challenging experiences which lack symmetry and fitness. People, like chickens or hamsters, return again and again to scenes or problems which are puzzling: ambiguity and difficulty breed involvement.

The 'edge' is a zone of engagement – but by no means inevitably. In the psychologist's laboratory, how the experimenter rigs conditions in the environment determines whether mammals will engage or withdraw. The human question is: what are the conditions of social life which might similarly make the edge a zone of engagement? It would seem that the mobility and uncertainty of the current political economy ought to provide just such a human laboratory, spurring people to constantly revise their life-stories, to refresh their self-explanations. Indeed, global capitalism ought to be a compelling breeding ground for cognitive dissonance; you withdraw from attention and engagement in this dynamic milieu at your peril.

Yet the modern world doesn't work this way. 'Attachment' is not a operative category in the labour market; employees feel little loyalty to chameleon corporations, and little collective involvement with each other; more largely, the workers I've interviewed in flexible, leading-edge companies have a great deal of trouble creating viable work-narratives, or recasting these stories as their circumstances change. Here precisely a divide has opened up between work and place. The act of forging a fluid narrative of place is often much stronger, particularly among urbanites caught up in the global jet stream, interpretative acts focusing on the 'edges' of experience in the city, involving a great deal of cross-referencing among puzzling phenomena. Such narratives breed strong attachments to the city itself.

The Theatre of Struggle

To understand why this should be so requires us to look askance at another cliché, rootedness. The image of putting down roots in a place is a common way of measuring communal identity, but it is inherently misleading; plants do not walk, and people do. The cliché confuses immobility with the sense of belonging somewhere particular in the world. Instead of coming to rest, people orient themselves in both space and time by thinking of cities as necessary stages on which to do combat with both the opportunities and the difficulties of the new economic order.

I can best explain this by a prosaic example. For several years I've been going to a laundry in New York run by a Korean family. From washing shirts and socks, they in time expanded to dry-cleaning, then to the addition of a resident tailor – surprisingly, a well-turned-out young man dressed as though for the office; now the laundry has begun selling cuff-links, bow-ties, and women's scarves. It would seem the Koreans have come to rest in New York; however, they don't think so. The patron confided to me: 'We are not immigrants.' Why not? The middle-aged couple who started the laundry were once middle-class; they came to New York as political exiles from Korea in its bad old days. As Koreans, they have suffered in New York. The city's black and Asian communities famously do not get along; the Korean family could at first find a place to live only in a black slum where they did daily battle with their neighbours.

Their white, middle-class customers disturb them for other, less violent reasons. Added to the usual complaints about American individualism and lack of family coherence, there is a surfeit of material goods in the city and a negligence of possessions that disturb them – men careless of their cuff-links, women who buy scarves only for a season, these appear signs of a people spoiled by abundance, to these once impoverished foreigners, for whom possessions remain scarce objects carefully to be conserved. If ethnically their experience has

179

rough edges, the narrative of their own struggles also doesn't seamlessly cohere.

For instance, the wealth they've accumulated has been dedicated to putting their children through university; the well-turned-out tailor turns out to be a son studying electrical engineering at night. He intended to go back to Korea as soon as he finished school; now he has graduated but remains in New York. Similarly, his parents frequently tell me they intend to close the business and return home to retire, but they've just bought two other stores and are working harder than ever. Their very struggles are, I think, partly the reason why they have stayed. They've done combat against an alien culture and, as combatants, in time have become deeply engaged in it.

For the same reason, the father refuses the identity of 'immigrant' because that label suggests a trajectory of absorption, it denies the battle that they've waged while maintaining their separateness. New York is the stage on which the great drama of their lives – exile, poverty and renewal – has been played out. If they left, their life-narrative would cease; they are 'rooted', if we must use that word, in their struggle.

When the globalisation of the political economy began, it was often said that place would lose its importance. Yet despite modern information technologies, leading-edge firms are crowding into cities like London and New York. There are some simple reasons why. Density and compression on the ground sharpen both comparison and competition. Chance social encounters in bars or at parties probably generate more opportunities than do formal business plans disseminated over the office intranet. But global cities are not just about high-flown global business. They are places open to poor economic migrants, people who, as Saskia Sassan has shown, were usually entrepreneurially minded, and so restless in their countries of origin. Even the Koreans who were political exiles showed themselves so minded, by taking advantage of a crack in New York's service economy. In a way, the very term 'globalisation' keeps us from connecting the tide of economic migrants to the massive expansion of the service economy at all levels which has taken place in cities like London, Berlin, New York, São Paulo, or Tel Aviv – in such mundane activities as plumbing and electrical work in construction, or in the supply of goods and services to the tourist industry, which in both London and New York is the single largest category of urban labour. The urban service sector is anarchic, plunged into constant turf battles, niches and the search for new markets; these competitive dramas, Jane Jacobs has argued, are the life-blood of cities, and the service-based city open to migration has indeed sprung back to life. Moreover, the competition which open cities foster is not just economic. People contest with each other for places in schools, use of street space, the imprint on leisure spaces like parks and pubs. These are the city's raw social edges, but they have a defined class character. The realm of the city where such dissonances and conflicts are played out among strangers has been 'abandoned' to the middle and lower classes.

I use the word 'abandoned' because the signal feature of the new elite in these cities is that it has withdrawn from the public realm. This abandonment is most evident in the transformation of the urban centre, the geographic place in the city bearing the brunt of the new economy. Massive income gains for people at the top have pushed the middle and lower classes out of the centre of cities like London and New York; neighbourhoods, no matter how decayed, can be quickly evacuated and refilled thanks to the piston of gentrification.

That change is daily evident to me in London's Clerkenwell, where I now live. Once home to printers and small manufacturers, Clerkenwell is now becoming a neighbourhood of lofts, sold to young financiers working nearby in the City, or to the officer class in the army of graphic design, fashion, and advertising which has occupied London. What's happened to Clerkenwell is not quite the repeat of the gentrification which occurred in New York's Soho, another former manufacturing district where I used to live, close to the Wall Street colossus: Clerkenwell passed from desolation to chic without an intervening era of poor-artist habitation as occurred in Soho.

Still, both places bear the impress of a new global elite living in the city but withdrawn from the public realm. New money uses the city but makes little effort to run it. This elite therefore looks nothing like the new men of Balzac's Paris. In the *Comédie Humaine* we are shown driven new men (and women) who want to wrest power over the city from the entrenched ruling class. They want to rule the place in which they live. Though Rastignac or Vautrin imagine themselves free of the past, in fact theirs is an old story: fealty, submission, obedience. This was the story of power and the public realm in the Italian medieval communes; it was the essence of *Burgherlich Gesellschaft* in the Hanseatic towns of the north. And in America, it was the story of the Boston Brahmins, who sought to leave their imprint on the city's schools, libraries, hospitals and parks, as well as on its businesses.

If the new elite of London or New York reigns over restaurants and flats, it has shown little desire to govern those hospitals, schools, libraries, or other public aspects of the city. Indeed, one of the great dramas currently unfolding in New York is the financial crisis which has resulted from the new elite's withdrawal from the public realm; the new monied classes, particularly in the information and high-tech sector, have failed to continue just that kind of civic domination, one that stretched out in New York's history from the time of the Dutch in the early seventeenth century up to the arrival of Italians, Irish and Jews into the city's elite 250 years later.

And this, I fear, will also be London's fate as a global city. Money from the global cornucopia will not diffuse if the captains of that money do not feel connected to the whole city. The contrast between a privatised elite and a mass of citizens below, struggling for both economic and social goods in the public realm, also establishes the class character of the kind of urban identity I wish to describe.

It is indeed working-class or at best petty bourgeois, immigrant-based. It has coped well with drastic change in life-circumstances, often with little government support or charity from above. Neo-liberal ideology has found a certain, perverse virtue in that lack of assistance; individuals and social groups have been forced to confront one another in public, rather than become supplicants like the clients of ancient Rome who fed parasitically on their masters – though competition does nothing to remedy the scarcity of social services or public goods. Whether for good or ill, the rough edges of social life in the public realm mean that differences have had to be negotiated every day.

Identities in the city form not in a grand scheme but in seemingly microscopic social exchanges, negotiations that divide between how others see one and how one sees oneself. Last year, for instance, I informed the Korean cleaners that my son had married; the next time I went in – to replace yet another set of lost cuff-links – the mother gave me a little package of sweets she had made. In the holiday season, however, when I brought her a jar of caviar in return, she accepted the jar across the counter but looked at me with what I can only describe as fear – as though my reciprocal gift made a demand she might not be able to handle. It is the principle of the potlatch; he who makes the gift remains in control. But now it was applied to a situation in which the boundary between customer and friend had become blurred, and that by her own initial, generous impulse. This little incident underscores how unrealistic are images of urban community based on reciprocity and mutuality, a legacy of nineteenth-century thinking about *Gemeinschaft*. Like rootedness, *Gemeinschaft* is a cliché that gets in the way of understanding the unbalanced relations between self and other in places like New York, with its extreme mixtures of class, ethnicity, and race.

People may draw towards one another, but not in order to consummate the union by erasing boundaries. If it is true that globalisation is creating cities with an ever greater mix of peoples, still the definitions of identity lie in the negotiation of those borders, particularly in determining those lines that cannot be crossed, evinced even in so trivial a detail as the unequal exchange of gifts. This detail helped to maintain an important sense of self-control and refusal to 'melt' in a city long considered the world's melting-pot. Negotiation of dissonance is the plot of identity, the city its necessary stage.

The Narrator at Work

Early writers on capitalist labour, such as Adam Smith, believed work-narratives would disappear in the industrialised world, since unchanging routine would ever more dominate the labours of men. This has proved not so. Just as we learn skills through repetition and routine, so in the work-world even the most numbing routine can be used to construct a cumulative life-history. I've interviewed a janitor who composed a dramatic work-story from slow and steady wage gains earned through routine work; now as an unemployed street-sweeper he felt deprived of anything significant or honourable to be recounted about his life, since he had lost what more favoured people might consider deadly dull work.

The labours of the modern, flexible workplace pose quite a different challenge to the task of narrating one's work: how can one create a sense of personal continuity in a labour market in which work-histories are erratic and discontinuous rather than routine and determinate? In one way, what has recently happened to global capitalism is quite straightforward. After the Second World War, the capitalist system solidified into large, pyramid-shaped bureaucracies tied to the fortunes of nation-states. These pyramids began disintegrating in the late 1970s. Today the cord between nation and economy has been cut, and businesses have replaced their bureaucratic solidity with more fluid and flexible networks connected around the world. These historical changes in bureaucratic form have altered the way people experience the passage of time inside institutions. In old English, a 'career' was a straight and well-marked roadbed, while a 'job' was a load of coal or wood that could be moved about indiscriminately. In that sense jobs are replacing careers in the modern work-world. Few people now labour for life for one employer; a young person in Britain or America with a few years of university can expect to work for at least twelve employers in the course of a lifetime; his or her 'skills base' will change three or more times so that, for instance, the computing skills learnt in school will be out of date by the age of thirty-five.

The shortening time-frame of employment coincides with the shortened institutional life of employers, companies merging and restructuring themselves at a rate unthinkable a generation ago. Though the publicity for these institutional changes invokes an aura of precision as 're-engineering', the majority of company make-overs are chaotic: business plans appear and collapse, employees are fired only to be rehired, productivity falls as the company loses sustained focus. Workers can hardly be expected to make more personal sense of this chaos than their bosses. Even in well-disciplined firms, work itself is shifting from the steady-state repetition of tasks envisaged by Adam Smith to short-term tasks performed by teams, the content of the task-labour changing in flexible corporations in quick response to changes in global demand. The shifts in task-labour are, again, beyond the individual's or the team's control. All these material changes challenge the effort to forge a sustained work-narrative. Indeed, I've found that the employees of leading-edge, flexible businesses have a great deal of difficulty in doing so, or in deriving a sense of personal identity from work. This blanket assertion needs one immediate qualification: the lack of a sustained work-narrative doesn't bother many younger employees. Once, however, a man or woman marries, begins to have children, takes on the burden of a mortgage and the other accoutrements of middle age, the aimlessness of labour begins to tell; with advancing age, people need to make more sense of their lives than seeing them simply as a random series of events. This is a practical need, because a work-narrative is more than a mere report of events occurring on the job; it serves a critical and evaluative function.

The judgement of work usually falls in three parts: the narrative defines long-term purposes, it prospectively measures the consequences of risk, and it orchestrates the pace and extent of family consumption. 'My job history', a computer technician said, 'is moving from one thing to the next, paying attention to today.' This seemingly innocuous remark proved, in the course of interviews, to be the source of real unease.

'I lost my own professional goals,' he later said, under the pressure of responding to the demands of four different employers; his job continually on the line, he had trouble evaluating whether he ought to leave before he was fired; as to pacing his consumption, which in his case means shouldering a larger house mortgage for a growing family,

'I'm afraid of being trapped by responsibilities I can't manage.' The work-world seems illegible to him – and it is in fact illegible. But simply leaving the matter there would 'make me feel stupid, and I'm not'. Interpretative acts do not, of course, master social realities. But interpretations do provide people with a sense of personal 'agency' – a cliché, though admittingly only to sociologists, which needs to be made concrete. The phenomenon of agency in a real-life narrative resembles what novelists call 'voice'.

Flaubert once succinctly defined voice by declaring: 'The author should be everywhere present in his story and nowhere identified.' In literature, the phenomenon of voice makes us aware of someone telling us about people or things, clipping and editing and organising what is told. We feel that presence even in accounts like Primo Levi's *The Periodic Table*, a story of the Nazi concentration camps in which the author is totally subservient to his guards. 'Agency' works the same way in ordinary life. Take what happens when people must confront traumas at work such as redundancy, a frequent event for middle-aged employees in the new work order. Here agency consists in stepping back, in creating some space between oneself and the event. Even the trivial act of telling can help people step back: for instance, a secretary recounted to me, 'As X was explaining why they had to let me go, I noticed the wart on his nose seemed darker.' In evoking the wart, she signalled she wasn't overwhelmed by the rejection.

This is narrative agency. Agency must follow Flaubert's command rather strictly. That is, the ordinary story-teller weakens himself or herself, becoming vulnerable to events, by intruding his or her 'I' as a protagonist. A file-clerk made redundant, for instance, said to me: 'Suddenly a machine did my job better and they let me go, and the first thing I thought was, "What a fool I was those days I stayed at the office extra time just to get the job done." ' The loss of work constitutes a moment of betrayal; her long hours, her self-discipline meaning little in constituting her work-history. Moreover, she tells about the event in a way which accentuates her vulnerability – while her 'I' is nakedly exposed, her sense of agency is weak.

Some analysts, like the Harvard Business School guru John Kotter, believe such experiences of betrayal signal the failure of workers to adapt to a work-world which admits of no narrative, at least of the long, three-decker Victorian-novel sort. His view implies that the file-clerk erred in imagining her work identity as a sustained story with a denouement – she invests time and effort, she receives at least the minimal reward of keeping her job. This, Kotter argues, is an outdated story; she should have harboured no such expectations. But very few people can put in the hours and cope with the stress of the modern economy by simply believing themselves chameleons, their work promising no more than a disconnected series of jobs. The operations of personal agency, clipping and shaping experience, standing back and resisting, judging practically, are missing in many modern work-narratives. The reason has to do with the work itself, rather than emotional or cognitive failure on the part of employees.

An identity, as we have seen, takes form through the social interaction of people at the edges of their personae, those boundary negotiations between self and other. But in the modern workplace, the other – embodied in the person of an authority figure – tends to be absent. As in the city, the people at the top of the corporation seek to absent themselves from daily interaction with the mass of their employees; in the office, this flight from engagement leaves employees without a necessary antagonist.

Working without Recognition

An absence of authority in the office is one consequence of changes in the bureaucratic form of the new capitalism. The modern corporation has sought to eliminate layers of bureaucracy, to operate via work-teams and work-cells, but very few such reformed businesses become flat playing fields. If anything, the effort to create a more flexible organisation centralises power at the top. Thanks to the way information technologies are currently deployed, it is possible to transmit orders from this inner elite core quickly and comprehensively, with less mediation and interpretation down the chain of command than occurred in old-style pyramidal bureaucracies. The top can also reckon results instantly and for itself, thanks to the computerisation of corporate information.

In such flexible corporations, a split opens up between the command function and the response function. That means an inner core will set production or profit targets, give orders for reorganisation of particular activities, then leave the isolated cells or teams in the network to meet these directives as best each group can. Those outside the elite corps are told what to achieve, but not how to achieve it. The split between command and response often appears at the moments when an enterprise is trying to remake itself, feeling its way towards another structure.

At Microsoft mid-level programmers were suddenly told in 1995, 'Think Internet,' without much indication of what 'thinking Internet' might practically entail. This command expresses an intention rather than an action; at Microsoft, the burden of responsibility was thus shifted downwards, the middle ranks trying to figure out what exactly to do about their bosses' intentions.

Today, corporations like IBM practise this division between command and response, shifting responsibility downwards, as a permanent fact of institutional life; the practice marks a stark contrast to the paternalistic, tightly organised chain of command which orchestrated the corporation for most of its history. The economist Bennett Harrison characterises the split as a concentration of command without centralisation of execution. The polite phrase for this in New-Labour-speak is 'deregulation of the workplace'. In reality, it amounts to a regime of indifference. Commands have not disappeared, nor has the stringent assessment of results. Engagement in the actual work process has diminished, as has that cornerstone of authority, the willingness to be held accountable for one's orders. The necessities of the flexible economy, it should be said, often force the boss to act as a *deus absconditus*. 'We are all victims of time and place,' a consultant said, observing the chaos of a business in the throes of reorganisation.

Of course, as one of the architects of change, in so saying he ducked being held personally accountable. But deregulation is a more apposite term than many of its apostles realise; the consultant understood that most flexible enterprises teeter on the brink of disorganisation, barely stable – and so he protected himself by disappearing down the Nietzschean rabbit-hole in which the ruler does not pretend to be the master of Fate.

The same disappearance occurs in flexible management's favourite image of collective effort, the team. Teamwork engaged in flexible labour is the creation of Japanese auto and electronics manufacturers; in its exported form, particularly into Britain and the United States, it often changes complexion. Whereas Japanese managers are usually on the shopfloor, arguing with (or, to Western ears, shouting at) the workers in various teams, in export form the team experiences much less interaction with the manager. He is a 'coach', as in sports, urging the worker-players on but not playing himself. In Anglo-American forms of teamwork, each group holds each individual responsible for collective results, usually with one exception: the manager-coach. Nor are these teams really self-determining: the group puzzles out how to meet production or output demands often set purposely too high by management; their immediate coach does not translate these into action – and seldom, in my experience, risks defending orders from on high as legitimate – but rather 'facilitates' discussion about how the workers themselves will obey. As a result fraternal recrimination marks Western-style teamwork much more than it does Japanese team-labour.

For workers on the receiving end of the split between command and execution, what most disturbs them, I have found, is that they lose what could be called a work-witness. The employee labours in a vacuum, even in Western-style teams, and the burden of making sense of his or her work becomes internalised. It might seem, logically, that this would free up the individual to contrive whatever meaning for work he or she wills. But in fact, without a witness who responds, who challenges, who defends and is willing to take responsibility for the power he or she represents, the interpretative capacity of workers becomes paralysed.

An essential quality of productive cognitive dissonance has gone missing: interaction with others in the environment, so that difficulties, dissonances and differences can be renegotiated. As a result, employees often contrive an idealised version of 'home' in their heads: what they would do, if they were really free; the perfect job, which would make use of their abilities. A split in time-consciousness occurs so that on the one hand there is a sheer chronicle of events and, on the other, an image of what ought to be.

This idealised ought-to-be image of work does not interact with the chronicle. It retreats into the realm of 'if only'. The computer technician told me, 'If I could just get a hold of some start-up money, only a few million, I could start a great company.' But he knows the chances are slim.

In point of fact, only 4 per cent of start-up firms in the USA find outside investment capital, and of these firms, over 90 per cent fail within three years. So the dream of a work identity in which the individual comes into his or her own becomes the employee's secret.

Put in sociologese, the lack of a witness diminishes the power of agency. I revert to this bastard diction in order to emphasise that it is a social breakdown that causes the weakening of agency, not psychological weakness. Recognition, we might think, is a matter of acknowledging results: the promotion, the raise in wages.

But the actual work process – the time spent working – has quite another logic of recognition: the employee needs to be in contact with someone who embodies institutional power and is willing to speak in its name, particularly when things go wrong or the demands are impossible. Yet the split between command and execution means that power is retained while authority is surrendered.

Conclusion

My argument therefore comes down to this: you can do without authority in your sense of place, you cannot do without it in your sense of work. The eagle-eyed reader will no doubt object, but this abstraction mixes up two different kinds of people.

The Korean immigrants owned a very traditional kind of small business; the computer technician lives in a suburb. But this objection only sharpens the issue I wish to raise: what is personally at stake in global, flexible capitalism? It seems a truism that all people have compound identities – that is, different kinds of stories they tell to explain themselves, depending on what they want to explain.

My elderly banker, who happened to be gay, forged a very different narrative of exclusion and inclusion in Boston society once our discussion turned to sex; the Koreans told another story of personal conflict when we talked international politics, one in which New York life was a side-bar. The truism of compound identity becomes weightier when identity is distinguished from self-image *per se*; identity is the process of negotiating in the world one's self-image, however internally fixed, and diplomatic activity of this sort usually occurs simultaneously on many fronts.

In modern capitalism these negotiations have broken down on the labour front. The regime of power and time in the modern corporation puts serious obstacles in the way of deriving an identity from work. When employees succumb to this regime, they find it hard to integrate work experience in the compound of identity.

In a way, distinguishing place and work might serve the defenders of globalisation, at least partly. The promise of globalisation is a deregulated, mobile, ever renegotiated life-course. This evokes an indubitable contemporary reality with genuine personal value – but not in the social sphere where it is supposed to occur.

What neo-liberalism wants to achieve in the realm of work is more possible in the places, particularly the cities, in which globalised people live. To me, however, making this contrast helps sharpen the critique of globalisation. The struggles of globalised people to make a place for themselves in work point out what is missing at the economic heart of the global system.

There is a regime of power operating on the principle of indifference to those in its grip, a regime seeking to evade, in the workplace, being held accountable for its acts. The essence of the politics of globalisation is finding ways to hold this regime of indifference to account. If we fail in this political effort, we will suffer a profound personal wound.

Global culture and its detritus wash up everywhere, nothing sacred, nothing wild, nothing authentic, original, or primitive any more. These modern travellers' tales tell of cultural vandalism, Western Goths contaminating ancient civilisations and traditions untouched for centuries. If the West were to set out on a mission of global imperialism deliberately planned we would surely choose better cultural ambassadors. It is not pages from Shakespeare or scores of Mozart that litter steppe and savannah but some marketing man's logo from last year's useless, meretricious product, or a snatch of that maddening theme tune from *Titanic*.

Glum thoughts and morbid fears such as these I call 'culture panic'. We are all seized by it from time to time for it's easily sparked by tripping over some new abominable vulgarisation or Americanism. 'Culture panic' is a close cousin of 'moral panic' (moral decline), 'intellectual panic' (dumbing down) and 'patriotic panic' (loss of national identity). These panics spring from a rich vein in the human psyche dating back to our expulsion from Eden: the world is getting worse. We are all slip-sliding down the primrose path to perdition and nothing is ever as good as it was. Our parents' generation was better than our own, our grandparents' better still. Whatever improvements there may be in our physical and material circumstances, that doesn't compensate for the ways we are morally, spiritually and culturally impoverished compared with our great forebears. They learned Greek, our kids watch *South Park*. They created their own entertainment around the family piano of an evening, we watch *ER* and *Friends*. They had tradition, we want what's new. They were serious, we just want to have fun. We lack the self-discipline to try anything difficult, that's why we are dumber, intellectually self-indulgent and idle. Who made us lazy? Those who seduced us away from serious pursuits by offering us easy pink stuff – the Americans of course. They are to blame and they are spreading their short attention-span around the globe.

Every generation has always been shocked by its youth. In *Hooligan*, the sociologist Geoffrey Parkinson looks back over many generations and notes that in all contemporary writings youth fashion and youth culture was always demonised as a sure sign that the future of civilisation was doomed in the hands of these decadent offspring. From apprentice boys to teddy boys, mods and punks to goths and ravers, the next generation always looks like degeneration: 'generation panic' if you like. But it must be an illusion. It simply cannot be true. For no one can quite pinpoint the perfect age of grace, that golden time we should be striving to recapture. Some things may get worse, but others get better and in reality few would choose to go backwards.

The panic perspective believes that cultural, intellectual and moral decline have largely wafted like a plague across the Atlantic from the Americans, who lack intellectual rigour and moral fibre. Sex was invented in the States, first imported by over-sexed and over-here GIs in the war. It is they who keep knocking over our boundaries of decency, their movies, their popular music, their gyrating pelvises that have sexualised us as never before, so that now nothing moves or breathes without sex and innuendo. Moral panickers usually find the root cause of what they melodramatically call 'the collapse of the family' in the USA, where divorce 'began'. See how it has undermined that 'fundamental building block of society'. See too how it is spreading across the globe, destabilising other cultures just as it transformed ours out of recognition. Hollywood sells sex packaged as romantic love with happy endings: in traditional societies that translates simply into sexual licence and destruction of the family. Self-fulfilment spells the end of family duty. Where American morals invade, religion and tradition recede. Even American religion is prettified pap. The fine old rigours of Christianity are repackaged and marketed with a kindly Father Christmas of a God, a free guardian angel with every prayer book and a guaranteed easy ticket to an American heaven – no hell, or your money back. So goes the rubric of global moral panic.

Was ever an empire so monstrously self-assured and ambitious? Western cultural imperialism reaches right into the hearts and souls, the sexual behaviour, the spirit, religion, politics and the nationhood of the entire world. It happens haphazardly with no master-plan or empire-building blueprint, but with a vague and casual insouciance that drives its detractors to despair.

So when we consider the globalisation of culture most of us bring to the subject a jumble of deep-seated alarms – moral, intellectual, political, spiritual, artistic and nationalistic, melting into a great pot of 'globalisation panic'. It causes deep pessimism about the cultural future of a world turning homogeneously horrible. It makes America hated, for try as you might to describe it any other way, globalisation is by and large the spread of American culture, ideas, products, entertainments and politics. If you view America primarily as a place of vulgarity and avarice, coarsened sensibility and rampant global ambition, you will shudder for the fate of the world. Much of the debate about cultural globalisation is a surrogate debate about America and the value or damage done by its growing influence.

In this chapter I shall try to swim through this sea of emotions and sort out what seems to me to be good about cultural globalisation, what is dangerous, what is inevitable and what might be tamed and regulated to our advantage. Confronted with frightening things I shall try to set aside panic, though like anyone else I feel it clutch at me from time to time. I shall try to distinguish between that primal fear of perpetual pejoration and those things that are genuinely getting measurably worse. I shall also inject some thoughts about the trade-offs in cultural globalisation between elites and peoples, for sometimes spreading more culture about may mean spreading it thinner, making the elites distraught but improving the lot of the rest. In the end each of us calculates our own balance of better and worse, probably depending more on our individual character (optimist or pessimist) and on our political perspective (conservative or liberal), than on 'the objective facts' which frankly are few and far between: culture is mercurial.

To start with, let's go back to Tony Giddens's Cambodian village and the disappointed anthropologist who found *Basic Instinct* had got there before her. That story is a very good example of our ethnocentric view of globalisation. What did she hope to find? Some ancient traditional entertainment, lays of old Cambodia as recounted down the centuries from the voices of the village elders, living oral myth and history in poem and song, perhaps. What a wonderful, rare, authentic experience that would have been for her! How her tape recorder would have whirred, with her pen flashing through voluminous notebooks. All of this she would have taken back to us in the West, tales of unspoiled Cambodian life, a reflection of our natural selves before our descent into so-called civilisation. She wouldn't, of course, have been planning to stay there for ever, just to visit and bring home her academic booty. For her an evening watching *Basic Instinct* was a bitter disappointment. But what of the villagers? Would they prefer to hear grandma's song yet again or would they rather watch Hollywood's latest?

Probably not a hard choice. What's more, if our anthropologist were to stay there for ever, she too might quite soon come to look forward to the next video arrival, rather than another evening of Cambodian bell-ringing. Read the acid lines of Jane Austen on the less-than-joys of the home-made musical evenings of her day and be thankful for the CD player.

There is some ethnocentric disingenuousness about our concern for the preservation of traditional cultures and our disgust at the way Western culture invades the arts of other peoples. Western explorers and tourists to remote places are just visiting for a quick look before beating a retreat to London, Paris, or New York, so we want other people to stay just as they are, while having the newest things for ourselves.

We worry that, by the very act of visiting it, we will spoil the thing we love. For our own belief in our elemental selves we need there to be an idea of Eskimos and nomads, Red Indians and Yanomami, living as close to their ancient, natural ways as possible. It reassures us that there is a 'natural' state of mankind in the wild for us to reconnect with when we feel lost. We steal from them all kinds of cultural icons and ideas – Eastern mysticism, Bangra music, world music, Japanese tea ceremonies, Sufi dancing, Thai batik, Tai Chi – tasting an exotic *mélange* of other traditions, adapted and Westernised, often reinvented altogether to suit our own cultural needs. Those who fear globalisation seem to want those traditional cultures to stay as they are for ever, a permanent primitive resource for us, though they, the 'natural' people, may or may not choose to live as they do, depending on their circumstances and what other realistic choices they have. As for the dangers of contamination, cultural cross-fertilisation is the essence of art: static art is dead art. Remember the decree in Tsarist Russia designed to keep out foreign influence which banned all kinds of painting except traditional flat icons for centuries – and so Russian painting ossified and died.

Boredom is the greatest driver of human endeavour. It is what separates us from animals who are happy enough to go on in the same old way for eternity without bothering about progress, innovation, change, fashion, or adventure. That human thirst for the new is very easily awakened in people everywhere once they come in touch with worlds beyond their own narrow horizons. Give them a taste of a life beyond their own and they are drawn towards it. All over the world people try to leave claustrophobic subsistence farming communities for the bright lights of something more.

There may be a great global conspiracy to Americanise the planet, a Coca-Cola push into remotest corners, but there's no doubt it is often greeted with a warm welcome, creating just as strong a pull to suck more of it in. (Remember trips behind the old Iron Curtain and how everyone begged for jeans or any artefact that symbolised the West.) For them the clash of cultures is a draw, but for Westerners it can make us ashamed. Visit a popular holiday resort in the Gambia or in Kenya and you find yourself staying in enclaves that are perfect little replicas of life in Florida plonked down in the midst of such poverty that the schoolchildren, carrying water home for miles, stop to beg for old biros outside the heavily guarded hotel compound gates. The hotel probably uses more electricity than the whole surrounding district. No holiday is better designed to make Westerners feel their own lives to be greedy, idle, rich and wasteful in comparison, though infinitely desirable to those denied it.

Naturally they want more of what we have got. Cultural globalisation for them means seizing the opportunity to have our wealthy life-style, even if, sadly, a baseball cap is as much as they can get their hands on. It may be relatively easy for the Taliban and the Iranians at their strictest to stop this Western filth crossing their borders, to ban television and every outward sign of decadence. But they know the real battle is in the hearts and minds of their own people: unless ruthlessly suppressed by culture police, people can't be trusted not to watch Western television.

Why? Is it just the cry of poverty for more wealth? Often no doubt it is, though something more important may lie beneath. In the artefacts of the West they glimpse not just a world of plenty, but of freedom and opportunity – the American dream symbolised in that baseball cap. It may be dangerous folly for we know how savage Western society is and what the West has done to exploit and destroy native and alien cultures everywhere. Western 'freedom' traditionally tends to arrive as it does to the Yanomami in the rain forest – in the form of hired killers and bulldozers. Some dream.

But for many others the dream is real enough: opportunity lies in the West even if you have to swim there. Those harmonious village communities can be stifling with their rigid hierarchies and an immutable social predestination for every baby born. Getting away may be dangerous and lead to much worse, but the wide world still beckons seductively, every ancient fairy story starting with boys setting out to seek their fortune.

We are selective in our feelings about global culture. We may regret the Coca-Cola bottles but we will strive with missionary fervour to spread our most important values. In our political and social culture we have a democratic way of life which we know, without any doubt at all, is far better than any other in the history of humanity.

Deeply flawed maybe, but the best so far. Western liberal democracy is the only system yet devised that maximises freedom for the many. We preach and struggle to practise a doctrine of freedom for women and multicultural optimism – by no means perfected, but probably the best there is. Modern urban society may sometimes be frighteningly free, alienating and lonely, but (for those above abject poverty) it offers a welcome escape from social pressure, superstition, patriarchy and hierarchy.

Is it possible to proselytise these new freedoms while preserving what is best in alien cultures? Probably not. Some of the outward charm of old ways may survive an entirely new intellectual culture but those old traditions will quickly become an ersatz heritage industry as Western ideas take hold. There is a trade-off between the charm of ancient monarchies, tyrannies, or theocracies, and the spreading of democratic freedom.

Is there really a choice? Decorative autocrats make good postcards, not good lives. So convinced are we of the rightness of democracy that most Westerners believe it is only a matter of time before the world eventually succumbs to its obvious merit. Theocratic imams, military dictators, ethnic-cleansing demagogues and the few remaining communists will all fall in time. Historical inevitability is with us and the onward march of the human rights culture. But that also means a far greater degree of globalised culture – a price well worth paying.

As democracy flows across borders over the years it starts to erode the borders themselves, inducing 'patriotic panic' in many. What hope for the culture of the nation-state when we all share so much culture in common? Just so. Slowly, inch by inch, Europe is starting to build itself a democratic identity that, if it succeeds, will in many spheres supersede the boundaries of its nation-states. National identities may fade, but that doesn't mean a spread of bland homogenisation – quite the reverse. Frontiers blur because of a sharpening of stronger identifications elsewhere that bind particular groups far closer together across national borders.

A British social democrat has far more in common with a German social democrat than with some Thatcherite who happens to live next door. Admirers of Monet or Madonna have more in common with each other than with those some accident of geography has made their neighbour. Community of interest, passion and belief will come to matter at least as much as mere topography now that we can go anywhere fast and communicate at the speed of light.

The ideas of the Enlightenment proclaim that essential elements of culture are universal. Universal human rights know no national frontiers. That, of course, is anathema to those who already regard the European Union as a monstrous encroachment on national sovereignty. But we are entering a new era where the nation-state will become decreasingly important. In any case, nations frequently created artificial cultural identities for themselves within their arbitrary physical borders. Nationality was often brutally imposed by the suppression of competing minority languages by the sword. Ethnic cleansing was in at

197

the birth of many nations: ask the Irish, Scots, Cornish, or Welsh. A nation-state invents for itself a semi-fabricated history and an artificial collective identity that may mirror the actual ancestry of relatively few of its citizens. The cry of nationalism seeks to hide and suffocate profoundly different interests across class, gender, race, religion and ideology. The 'kultur' of the Third Reich or Greater Serbia lurks only just beneath the surface of most nationalist emotions. What binds a nation together is external threat. Now that the threat is past for Western democracies, the bond of nation-states begins to weaken. The last few centuries created the warlike nation-state: the next century may improve on that by creating an ever-growing global alliance of democracies spreading out across the world.

European nations who used never to suffer from self-doubt find themselves now debating who they are. Tony Blair made an embarrassing attempt at it with his multi-cultural, young country, all hot design and new music: Cool Britannia. At least it was marginally better if no more accurate than John Major's vision of spinsters on bicycles peddling to church, warm beer and cricket bats. What are we? Europeans now are too self-aware, too diverse and pluralistic to want to accept any single vision of themselves. Scientists, artists, musicians, computer programmers and all other specialists are primarily interested in connecting with the best wherever it is in the world, never mind the frontier posts. Likewise their consumers and customers happily cross any borders to buy the best. Campaigners for the environment, peace, religions or women's movements draw strength from globalising their organisations, linking across countries.

For some things people may want cultural devolution to the most local cultural level, but they pick and choose parts of their identity from different concentric circles of power, demanding the best from whatever level of power can best deliver it – the UN or Europe for campaigning against environmental vandalism, the world for state-of-the-art technology, the region for the best medical specialist, the parish hall for the smallest planning decisions.

As for those in a moral panic about the way Western sexuality is corrupting the world's more dignified cultures, they look only at the worst and not at the best outcomes. They see only how family life has broken down in the West, divorce spreading like a plague with lewd, tawdry images breeding disrespect for women and old sexual customs.

To moral panickers, globalised culture means globalised no-knicker shots of Sharon Stone in Cambodian villages. Sexual liberation in the

West is seen only for its tacky side, never for what it really is – harbinger of most fundamental freedoms. We worry so obsessively about how to contain its less desirable side-effects that we too easily forget the freedom it also represents. Worlds of misery and repression are swept away once people seize the freedom to choose whom they love, live with and marry.

Divorce frees people from disastrous mistakes made early in life, releasing them from relationships made in hell. For many people freedom from violent or deeply unhappy marriages has meant far more than political freedom. Who wouldn't rather be with the partner they love under communism, than be chained by social pressure to some monster under the democracy of the 1950s? Personal freedom can be even more important than political freedom.

The tidal wave of divorce that follows Western cultural influence isn't an unfortunate disease but an integral part of the spread of human rights because everywhere it is the result of the emancipation of women. That's how it began in the West, women free to walk away from violent, abusive, unequal and unhappy marriages. Once they have the power to do that women are liberated to find the power and the voice to be more than chattels for the first time in history, which also frees men from the obligation to care for them for life as they did.

Breaking down the laws and customs that make a woman the virginal possession of a husband is the first great step in women's rights. It changes the family bond and traditional family power structures for ever. Those who consider Westernisation an invasion of ancient traditions are usually looking at the world through male spectacles. The emancipation of women is the most radical cultural revolution the world has ever known, reaching right into the most elemental aspects of humanity.

It is a revolution still only half-made in the West, with socially disruptive consequences and uncertainty as to how it will quite end up or what will happen to families in the next century. This revolution was unplanned: women just voted with their feet once they had the economic and social freedom to do it. Our economies have yet to adapt to ensure women have the same ability as men to be breadwinners for their children.

This disjunction has left Western governments with a huge problem, not least a vast social security bill paying for the children whom mothers cannot support alone. But there's no going back and the world's women are all being swept up in its path. Cultural globalisation means global feminism, freeing women everywhere. What has been a great unequi-vocal good for women of the West can't be denied indefinitely to others in the name of preserving indigenous (male) cultural tradition.

All these are reasons to consider that much cultural globalisation is essentially a force for good, something worth promoting. We may be coy and self-deceiving about it, but in fact the West is quite rightly intent on spreading its culture across the world. Even if we don't like to admit it, we are all missionaries and believers that our own way is the best when it comes to the things that really matter – freedom, democracy, liberation, tolerance, justice and pluralism. Our culture is the culture of universal human rights and there is no compromise possible.

These principles are the only hope of long-term peace in war-torn places. We may be easily dismayed by our less attractive exports reaching far-flung corners before the things we really mean to impart – the used plastic bottle or the rapacious greed of uncontrolled capitalism often arriving long before the freedom message. But squeamishness about globalising Western ideas is often frivolous and, paradoxically, profoundly ethnocentric, regarding other people's freedoms as optional when our own are not.

The question remains as to whether we believe strongly enough in human rights to keep pressing for the spread of that culture of freedom and at what cost to ourselves. The liberal idea, conceived in the age of Enlightenment, born in the revolutions of 1848, has not looked in the past 150 years like a certain and inevitable winner. From 1917 to 1989 it has been in mortal global combat with communism, with fascism attacking on the other flank, though it has emerged the undoubted winner.

Still, however, great swathes of the world are only brushed by its mantle. Does the West have sufficient will and confidence in the liberal idea to carry that crusade to the ends of the earth? It should. If globalisation means no more than letting our industries conquer other people's in a form of world domination, and in the process chipping away at our own democratic power to control our lives, that's not enough. Globalisation has to progress with a mission to spread Western political culture and ideas too.

Possibly the war in Kosovo was the beginning of the realisation that Western societies have a moral duty to ensure that the political culture of human rights reaches right inside foreign borders where dictators and ethnic cleansers think they are safe. The weakness and ambivalence with which the war was fought by most of the Western democracies, dithering about ground troops, some trying to pull out halfway through, might have been the birth pangs of a new world order where it will be accepted that the rich world does have a moral duty to spread human rights everywhere.

Or it might be the one and only time it is ever tried before the rich West retreats into selfish don't-care isolationism, losing all sense of global responsibility. I remain optimistic, believing that liberalism is a naturally missionary culture and inevitably seeks to spread itself across the world. Only the Cold War and the threat of annihilating the globe in the process have prevented the liberal world from seriously pursuing universal human rights until now.

However, there are aspects of cultural globalisation that we should and can resist. Proud though we may be of freedom and democracy, too often it comes linked to a culture of the rampant free market and economic theories entirely predicated on insatiable greed. We deliberately encourage the greed ethos everywhere in order to create new markets, only lending money to those who profess to share our belief in it. Western economies only know how to grow or die, over-producing and over-consuming without any concept of satiety.

With shameless triumphalism at the end of the Cold War the West sent in nothing but the hard culture of Thatcherism which has brought the former USSR to its knees, allowing privateering banditry to run riot. Worse still, it has risked the reputation of liberal capitalism and democracy with a disillusioned people. The unfettered market is not the best ambassador of freedom, unmitigated by real human rights ideals nor softened by the policies with which we ourselves regulate and tame it at home. The communist world discovered you can't have a thriving competitive economy without political freedom – but the West knows it is also difficult to control the worst savagery of the free market within a politically free system.

However, it can be held in check and nowhere is that more needed than in the cultural sphere. Guarding those elements of our cultural life we prize beyond greed now usually requires global or at least multinational action. Global cultural industries require global regulation. One of the most important functions of the European Union will be to prevent the international monopoly of the chief sources of all our culture in future – information, communication, education and entertainment. I shall here examine the ways in which our most precious cultural assets can be protected from the less desirable aspects of globalisation, those ambassadors of universal freedoms we wish to promote which are themselves in most danger if left to an unregulated free market. Here I pick out the dangers for the press, broadcasting, television and films, the internet, music and tourism.

Start with the media. The multinational power of the EU has the potential to impose far better media ownership rules. By banding together, its members can take braver political action collectively and establish more effective regulation of their airwaves than each could hope to do alone in dealing with global broadcasting.

Already a few global players control the main international sources of information and its dissemination, a potential danger to democracy. On the one hand the new technology of electronic media makes it possible for people everywhere to reach each other and the rest of the world on the net at a click of a button. At the same time media moguls are threatening to kill off the diversity which the new technology promises.

The danger is that only one world-view will pump out of every television and PC across the planet: one view of who is right and wrong in any dispute, one management style, one business format, one economic theory. That one view will probably be designed by the successful for the successful, the devil taking the hindmost. Spreading the ideas of universal human rights and freedom of speech across the world must not mean any less a diversity of views than comfortably exists in Western cultures with a broad democratic spectrum from far left to far right.

In Britain we can see a threat to cultural diversity from global players with political agendas of their own. Rupert Murdoch is as good a case study as you could find of a phenomenon the world will see more of in the media business. He is a mogul who uses his newspapers to intimidate politicians and promote his political ideas, not for some personal ideology but to push policies designed to maximise the global profits of his business. His rabid anti-European Union ideas come from his fear that the EU is a powerful forum which could control his operations more effectively than any British government alone would do.

Back in the 1980s when Rupert Murdoch first set out to break the stranglehold of the old print unions, he promised to be a liberator by bringing in new technology that might in theory allow anyone to produce their own newspapers through desk-top publishing at very low cost. New technology was going to liberate print not just from union power, but from the stranglehold of the usual maverick bunch of press barons all across the globe. Technology did all it said it would, but the social consequences predicted have been entirely wrong. It liberated no one except the proprietors.

Readers in Britain haven't gained as there is no greater diversity of newspapers: one has closed, two are in dizzying descent and two are in mortal danger. The quality of newspapers has not improved – bigger but not better. Technology means all the journalists can now turn out many more stories just sitting at their desks: real reporting is in retreat, with less time to explore speculative or investigative stories.

Journalists are often little more than reprocessors of information taken from government and other press releases. These are digested and spun according to the taste of their proprietor. It's an irony that at a time of globalisation and greater world interdependency, most newspapers have slashed their foreign bureaux to around a quarter of the number twenty years ago and have cut back on specialist correspondents.

Nor has it done anything for diversity of ownership, which has always been heavily Conservative, media magnates being rarely left-inclined. Despite Labour being likely to stay in power for at least another decade, the press is overwhelmingly Tory. Only a few relatively weak papers stand against the massed ranks of Rupert Murdoch, Conrad Black and Lord Rothermere. Murdoch alone commands 41 per cent of the total newspaper readership.

There used to be tough rules about media ownership preventing any one player from owning too much or from owning both television and newspapers. All these regulations were set aside in the 1980s by Margaret Thatcher to allow Murdoch to acquire five dominant titles. She also ensured favourable regulation to help him set up Sky TV, in exchange for his unstinting support. As he acquired this major control of the media so he gained political power over her and all future prime ministers. There is no reason why Parliament should not pass new legislation now to reimpose a restriction on the percentage of the media one owner can control. Will this government do it? Unlikely, though not impossible.

Why is Murdoch using his newspapers to campaign against all things European? Because it would be easier to regulate media ownership through the EU, with rules right across Europe. The EU could decide to ban any ownership by non-Europeans, which would knock Murdoch out altogether. The only reason he took US citizenship when he acquired heavy television as well as newspaper interests there was because America does have these wisely self-protective rules about foreign ownership of its media.

Consider how in Britain Murdoch has used his newspapers to bully successive governments into getting his way over regulation and commercial deals, consider how he has escaped virtually all taxation for his enterprises, and there is the important reason why no media owner should be allowed to become over-mighty. There too is the reason why a pressing need exists for more multi-national co-operation along European lines – it is the only way of regulating these giant global press barons.

New technology has had much the same effect on the newspaper industry all over the West, shrinking diversity instead of growing it. In the USA not long ago there were 1,500 independent newspapers owned by long-term proprietors – now there are only 300. Most have been bought by large chains who seek only to make money out of them, like any other commodity, and they are constantly changing hands. With new technology and a local monopoly status they have become vastly profitable, regularly earning 20 per cent dividends for their new owners.

How have they achieved these phenomenal profits? Largely by cutting staff, including flotillas of journalists. Bean-counting managers from non-journalistic backgrounds have been brought in to impose productivity quotas on reporters. A standard calculation among these new corporate proprietors is that a reporter should be able to produce an A1 category story in 0.9 hours and thereby turn out 40 stories a week. This is the kind of madness you get if you allow the free market unfettered control over cultural industries.

The European Union could and should set about protecting its media by:

- creating an EU-wide limit to ownership by any one company or individual within one country and across the EU
- banning the ownership of any television or newspaper by non-EU nationals or companies
- establishing an EU code of conduct for proprietors, to run alongside an EU-wide general press code of conduct for journalists
- establishing agreed rules regarding the freedom of information for all countries, to run alongside privacy rules, since neither information nor privacy can be guaranteed within the frontiers of one country

Acting collectively, there is a chance – only a chance – that the EU could secure minimum standards for the news media and a measure of protection against global predators. It is not a matter of governments telling the media what to say, but of trying to ensure a diversity of voices in their ownership. De Tocqueville said rather sententiously in 1830: 'It would diminish the importance of newspapers to believe they only serve to guarantee freedom; they maintain civilisation.' De Tocqueville, of course, hadn't read the *Sun* and few would be entirely certain that even the best of the broadsheets are necessarily devoted to the cause of civilisation. But he had a point. A nation's news media tell us a lot about the nature of that society.

Although we can't satisfactorily quantify the cultural importance of newspapers, most would acknowledge that they still retain extraordinary power in our democracies. Even with shrinking readerships they punch politically far above their weight. Newspaper reading time is going down around the world, with AOL claiming more young people now read their news on the internet than read newspapers or watch TV news.

However, all my professional life, I have been assured that newspapers are dying if not dead and are definitely the medium of the past – and yet I see no sign in Britain or around the world of any lessening of the power of their voice in politics. There is also a symbiotic relationship between press and television that means newspaper reporting and comment still tend to set the tone for debate and reporting in broadcasting. Keeping both free of state interference and free of unfettered market forces is equally important.

The French have a strong tradition of attempting to protect their language, their culture and their cultural industries from the global steam-roller. It is they who seek to persuade the EU to protect our film and television industries. But it was the British under Mrs Thatcher who did their best to prevent and undermine this useful initiative in a short-sighted act of folly, for as Europe's largest television exporter Britain has most to gain from self-protection.

The EU tried to pass a directive insisting on a minimum quota of 51 per cent European-originated programming on every TV channel. This was being debated at the time when Murdoch was about to launch his Sky satellite enterprise. Sky was a financially risky business which brought his whole empire within days of bankruptcy. It was launched with almost entirely wall-to-wall cheap American TV programmes: apart from news and sport, his channels still produce virtually no home-grown programming. To ensure that he could launch Sky without having to make expensive programmes of his own, Murdoch persuaded Mrs Thatcher to use the British veto to insert a loophole in the EU directive through which Sky could escape. So the British government added a key clause: quotas would only have to apply 'wherever practicable'. Sky, of course, found it wasn't practicable for them.

Since then new satellite and cable channels all over Europe have started up making use of the same Murdoch let-out clause. Europe's airwaves are flooded with cheap American programmes which Hollywood sells in large bundles, forcing networks to take the bad alongside the good. All costs have already been recouped within the huge US market so US producers can sell American programmes abroad at such low rates that indigenous programme-makers can never compete, especially in countries with small populations and exclusive languages like Swedish or Dutch (though the Portuguese have some outlets in Brazil).

This has had a disastrous effect on the European balance of payments in the burgeoning entertainment sector. Before cable and satellite, Britain was a net exporter of programmes. By 1997 it had a deficit of £272 million. This is partly because of importing more US shows but also because competition from Sky and others has pushed up the cost of the most popular American films and programmes such as *Friends*, *ER* and *The Simpsons*. Britain is the second biggest exporter of programmes after America but still has only 9 per cent of the global programme market, compared with America's 72 per cent. The USA is the single biggest exporter to every country in the world but it's a one-way traffic: it buys only 2 per cent of programmes from abroad. Extra digital channels are never matched by equal indigenous programme-making capacity, so the trade deficit with the USA is increasing right across the globe.

A recent report commissioned by the Department of Culture, Media and Sport investigating reasons why Britain doesn't export more programmes concluded that we needed more co-production with foreign companies to raise sufficient capital to make series and dramas with the same high production values as Hollywood blockbusters. This brought a groan of distress from many British producers who have suffered the creative limitations of co-production. All the same, the economic imperative for Europe is clear and the EU should set up an effective co-production network able to compete. Globalisation can be mitigated by those willing to take action.

Most worrying is the rapid growth of multinational corporations eating up television stations across the world in mergers that will soon threaten diversity. As television increasingly becomes an adjunct of the whole colossal telecommunications industry, combines could soon grow powerful enough to control the global media. Government regulation used to be tighter over broadcasting than any other media but with global satellite and cable networks, everywhere this has been weakened. As with the example of Murdoch in Britain, the power of dominant broadcasters to intimidate politicians in their own country has often caused the relaxation of regulations, especially those concerning cross-ownership of media.

Many EU politicians are intimidated by their most powerful media magnates, which makes acting together under EU regulation the best way to protect independent news sources. Italy provides an excellent warning. A few years ago Italian politicians tried to diminish the overbearing media power of Silvio Berlusconi. Instead of daring to confront him directly, they called a referendum to let the people decide whether there should be new media ownership rules preventing any one owner from becoming too powerful. The campaign was a fiasco as Berlusconi used all his TV channels to blast viewers with mendacious messages that implied their favourite shows would be stopped, the state would control everything and all television would be boring and political. Not only did he win the referendum but he went on to win an election and become prime minister largely by using the sheer brute strength of his media empire to get himself voted in. That should stand as a warning right across the EU.

Television news is dominated by a handful of providers who produce the news pictures for the world: these are channels from CNN, the BBC and Murdoch's News Corporation. Then there are the dominant news agencies WTN and Reuters. Their biggest buyer by far will always be the USA, something that is likely to slant their news priorities and ensure they will always reflect US interests. It is leading to greater homogenisation of news, so that even if there are many new TV news channels globally, they all still rely on the news agenda set by these few outlets, recycling the same old pictures and news priorities provided by them.

In view of this, Britain is extremely lucky to have the BBC and that the BBC is – just – a real player on the world stage for news. If for no other reason, the BBC's independence of any commercial interest will make it an ever more important media asset, not just for us but for countries and channels who want a view other than the American eye on the world. Great empires like Time Warner, News Corporation, Sony, Kirsch, Bertelsmann, Berlusconi and the rest will always be driven by commerce: remember how Murdoch threw the BBC off his Star satellite in China when BBC reporting angered the Chinese government, revealing how low the principles of honest reporting come in his commercial priorities. Because of the BBC the British probably have less to fear from globalisation than many other countries. Its competitive power is demonstrated by the vigour with which Murdoch tried to argue in the EU that the BBC should be forced to do nothing but education and minority programmes. As a state-subsidised broadcaster, he claimed, it was trading unfairly against commercial competitors in popular programmes. Special status for state broadcasting will be challenged again and will need defending: state broadcasting is just not the same as state coal-mines and culture needs special rules of its own. The BBC ought to act as a model for other democracies to imitate, to combat some of the dangers of globalisation.

So will American television inevitably rule the world? Not necessarily. The alarming balance of payments deficit in imported programmes from the USA is due to cheap, thinly watched US fillers shown around the clock, not mass peak-time viewing. It disguises the fact that the British, like every other country, still prefer to watch their own programmes. In India, Murdoch made the mistake of launching his Star TV with a diet of American programmes and it flopped. He had to replace US with Indian-produced films and shows instead. Digital is in its infancy still, but the signs are that these multiplying channels will get low audiences with small niche tastes, while mainstream national channels making their own programmes will win out against US repeats. Even top shows like *Friends* score only some 2 million viewers, which is small beer compared with prime-time UK programmes that expect 10 million. Encouragingly, US programmes are less popular than they were: in the 1970s prime time on the BBC was dominated by the likes of *Dallas*, *Dynasty* and *Kojak*, so here TV globalisation has actually rolled backwards.

It's also worth asking whether the global culture of the whole world watching *Friends* and sharing that experience together is automatically, *per se*, a bad thing, since it does create a globally shared experience. (And not such a bad one.) Indeed many commentators are starting to bemoan the loss of a sense of community when people won't any longer be watching the same things. In the multi-channel era strangers at a bus-stop will no longer discuss together the latest shared episode of *EastEnders*. And people don't necessarily see the same things in what they watch. Some years ago a global study of how one episode of *Dallas* was viewed in different cultures found people saw quite extraordinarily different things in it, defining the plot and which characters were good or bad as if they'd been watching something else. The eye of the beholder does also protect from too much cultural homogenisation.

Film remains the most commercially important driver of all entertainment, dominating television as well as cinema, providing the prime source of stars and media excitement. Spin-offs from movies continue to multiply, from magazines, albums, merchandising, from global McDonald's themed Happy Meals to the vast new video game industry. Hollywood drives far more than just movies. That is partly why there has been a long tradition of countries trying to buttress their own film industries against unfair competition from Hollywood, who have often controlled the main chains of cinemas for distribution. France has a strong system of quotas and protection for its own movie industry. The result is that the number of foreign releases actually fell during the 1980s in France to around 65 per cent. In Britain where protection for our industry was abandoned long ago, US films amount to 90 per cent of new releases. This is partly powered by Hollywood's ability to sell good and bad films together in bundles.

The British used to have a rule that American movies had to be balanced by distributors with British-made movies. It led to some absurdly bad, very cheap 'quota' movies being made just to obey the law. Certainly all quota systems create oddities. (France makes many subsidised movies that never get a single showing.) But the evidence is that they do help keep a thriving local movie industry alive. Again, it is something that could be done at EU level, especially in forcing a fairer film distribution system, keeping the door open for European movies. It is not a matter of denying the brilliance, imagination and sheer mega-production values of the US film industry. It's a matter of holding open a crack in the door to allow small indigenous industries to thrive alongside this leviathan.

The WorldWide Web has been a good force for global pluralism and even for global anarchy. So far its merit has been its uncontrollability. Unedited, speaking in many tongues, it is cultural freedom personified. But since few internet businesses are making any money out of it yet, it is still early days. At the moment it is still driven by impulses that have less to do with money than almost any aspect of modern life. We wait to see whether a few players will before long take control over this sprawling new universe. It is still unclear whether it will become the key means of communication globally or will remain a relatively sectional tool of the global elite. But every effort should be made to keep it as wide open as possible in the coming years. It offers some of the best elements of cultural globalisation as it links together niche interests and specialisms around the world as never before, allowing a more flourishing range than could ever thrive in one country alone.

Music permeates global consciousness faster than any other cultural medium. Tunes, styles, new sounds float across the world with no respect for boundaries, influencing all listeners whether they want it or not. Pop pours out of radios in every market square, the latest chart-topper assaults the eardrums on every global street corner, under any jacaranda or palm tree. Just six music companies now control virtually all world recorded music sales: Thorn-EMI, Polygram, Warner and Sony hold over 70 per cent between them. The trickle of influence that flows back via world music and other sounds is infinitesimal in comparison with the blast of sound pouring out of the West into other global ears.

Is that all bad? There's no doubt the huge range of choice and the affordability of recorded music have grown vastly, even though the number of providers has shrunk. In the last ten years 10,000 albums have been produced in Britain alone. In music it is not immediately apparent that control of recorded music by a few companies is anything like as potentially damaging and dangerous as monopoly control of news media could become.

Tourism is the globalisation most of us in the West understand best. The world has turned into our oyster, nowhere too expensive or too inaccessible for most people determined enough to travel. We can see and devour foreign cultures for ourselves, no longer a luxury for the few, but a mind-expander for the many. By 1995 half a billion people a year travelled abroad. They spent $380 billion, travelling mostly between and within Western Europe and North America. The growth rate is astounding with a doubling in numbers expected by 2010 according to the World Tourist Organisation. That will mean an extraordinary one billion people on the move every year.

Travel will continue to make the world feel a smaller place, culturally closer together. The pessimistic will point to the despoliation of everything everywhere with the tacky and insensitive demands of Western tourism. The optimistic might hope that the plight of the Third World will become more real and of greater political concern to the First World as more voters visit and empathise with far-away countries.

Global intermingling has brought great cultural riches to the West. Throughout history discovery of foreign lands, arts, architecture, knowledge, science, horticulture, medicine, language and religions has brought waves of new inspiration, alongside the arrival and absorption of new citizens bringing with them new cultures. Food stands as a symbol for much that is best and worst about globalisation. The entirely beneficial foreign influence on British cuisine is a positive example of globalisation. It has turned London into a most unlikely culinary centre, a melting pot of global food successfully exterminating the revolting remnants of our own long-dead native cuisine. How easily and happily the West plunders every other culture under the sun, adapting it to our own palates. True, sending McDonald's to Rome or Beijing was hardly a fair cultural swap – back to that original global strawberry milkshake. But with the milkshake, they get other Western things they desperately desire.

So there is the balance sheet. Those who fear cultural homogenisation shudder at the sight of the mug imprinted with Monet water lilies on sale in street markets or the Mona Lisa emblazoned on global T-shirts. But to spread culture widely, even in ways not always to the taste of connoisseurs, is always a good thing, even if it gets spread thinly. In the end there is more to be gained than lost in this great global exchange. We think so because in our hearts we believe Western political and ideological culture will, or at least should, finally permeate the world to the advantage of all.

But each country can protect those elements of its culture it most prizes: local regulation can be made to hold back the pink tide when it endangers vital principles. Britain has provided some successful models of cultural protection in the BBC and Channel Four – both now national treasures others might emulate. If only the people can generate enough local concern and political will, free societies can always devise ways to guarantee cultural plurality and deny hegemony to any single over-mighty cultural threat.

These concerns, though, are still relatively trivial compared with the most fundamental cultural values the West seeks to spread around the world. Our culture rests on human rights and from that principle all the rest flows. Once all individuals have the right to live as they choose, free from political, religious, patriarchal, or social tyrannies, their cultures will inevitably change – and for the better. There will be some cultural losses and regrets, but the gains will always outweigh them. The West in its many cultural manifestations is a human rights crusader, though often reluctant to realise it or, until now, to play the part with sufficient honour. Those of us who take human rights as the essential first principle of all decent society should be wary of those who think globalising those values is cultural imperialism. Genuinely embracing the idea of human equality demands we take universal individual rights more seriously than anything else.

211

Acknowledgements

Many recent facts are from the excellent encyclopaedia of global information by David Held, Anthony McGrew, David Goldblatt and Jonathan Perraton, *Global Transformations* (London: Polity, 1999).

See also *Building a Global Audience – British Television in Overseas Markets*, David Graham and Associates, Department for Culture, Media and Sport, 1999.

Many thanks for information and advice from Mathew Horsman, Media Analyst, Henderson Crosthwaite; and also to Chad Wollen, co-author of the Henley Centre for Forecasting's Media Futures.

ANTHONY GIDDENS and WILL HUTTON

Fighting Back

We live in a period of multiple revolutions. We witness extraordinary technological change centred on digitalisation, information technology and extending into biotechnology. New global capital markets have a reach, liquidity and speculative capacity that is unparalleled. The changing role of women, no longer confined to old sterotypes, is the source of tension and opportunity in the developed and less developed world alike.

The risks confronting the global environment are on a scale and have a degree of uncertainty that is again unprecedented. Inequality of income and wealth, both within countries and between the developed and less developed world, has increased. And uniting all these trends is the vigour of the global market economy seeking more ruthlessly to increase the returns to shareholders. This in turn has generated another revolution: the emergence of glut and low inflation. Productive capacity and the size of the world labour market now far outstrip demand, sustained on a global basis very largely by American consumer spending. All these phenemenona co-exist and reinforce each other. Together they both drive and result from the processes we call globalisation.

It is both a glorious and a frightening time. This is neither a period of Empire building nor of the rise of great competing ideologies; communism and fascism alike have been tested, found wanting and failed. Our generation does not face the risk of global war in the service of flag, territory or ideology. Trade grows exponentially every year; living standards, pockmarked by horrendous poverty especially in the less developed countries, are nonetheless rising overall across the globe. Life expectancy is generally increasing globally; infant mortality decreasing. Women are being freed from the drudgery of domestic

213

labour in the home. The open global economy is a precious acquisition offering opportunity, creativity and wealth.

But it is a system, as the title of this book suggests, that is precarious and potentially dangerous – it is on the edge. The world's new financial markets have a propensity for enthusiasm and panic which because of their reach and power can be massively destabilising. At the time of writing there is growing concern that Wall Street has reached 'bubble' levels and could suffer a sharp setback or even crash, which would have depressionary ripple effects across the globe. The causes and consequences of the Asia crisis do not need rehearsing again, but they are part of the same story.

Nor is that all. As Manuel Castells explored in his essay, although productive capacity is galloping ahead it is not clear that demand will keep pace; inflation has all but disappeared and in continental Europe, Japan and even the USA prices of commodities and manufactured goods are falling – a potential harbinger of recessionary times. More importantly still, a growing number of people around the world reject what he calls the 'Automaton' whose logic either ignores or devalues their humanity. Whether as religious fundamentalists, fervent nationalists, or the rebels protesting at the WTO meetings in Seattle, there is a growing backlash against the anonymous forces of capitalism that are one element of globalisation.

It is a moment of great unpredictablity. Nobody fifteen years ago foresaw the collapse of the Soviet Union and the great boom in the USA in the 1990s; the conventional wisdom in 1985 was summed up by Paul Kennedy's book, *The Rise and Fall of Great Powers*, in which the USA's gathering decline seemed unstoppable. Today American technological, financial, military and corporate power is unrivalled, while Japan has been mired in a decade of stagnation. Equally few anticipated the technological revolution or the collapse of inflation. Events ten years ahead are harder than ever to predict; there is almost certainly some change already under way whose future impact has yet to be identified.

Thus optimists and pessimists can write with equal fervour. The most sanguine view is that we don't have to worry. The international system's durability is guaranteed because there are no alternatives; in any case it is immensely resilient, with great powers of recuperation. The story of the Asia Crisis, for example, is not the crash of 1998 but the recovery of 1999. There may be fundamentalist forces, ranging from some fundamentalist Arabs to right-wing European nationalist parties, contesting globalisation, but the system is so powerful and the opportunities so great for those who play the game, that resistance will be episodic and weak.

And while there are always temptations for individual countries, and especially the United States, to put self-interest before the collective management of the system, the story of the 1990s is also one of more internationalism rather than less. This has been the decade of the Rio Earth Summit, of NATO intervention in Kosovo, of international peace-keeping operations such as that in East Timor, and of the detention of General Pinochet for possible trial. The spirit of the UN Declaration of Human Rights has more force rather than less, and multinational corporations find that the penalties for trading unethically or irresponsibly are growing, imposed by an increasingly well-organised and powerful international consumer movement. Globalisation is here to stay, and while there will be inevitable hiccups and setbacks, there is no going back for anyone. The next twenty years will be uneven but in essence the system will probably look the same then as now; and the world will be richer still.

But there is a pessimistic account of the future that is equally plausible. The decades ahead could be plagued by economic stagnation or recession in the aftermath of the 1990s boom, prompted by a Wall Street Crash which exposes the mismatch between global oversupply and lack of appropriate demand. The USA could turn away from world affairs, a trend already evident in its refusal to sign the Comprehensive Test Ban Treaty and reluctance to maintain its contributions to the United Nations, IMF and World Bank. It could become protectionist, undermining the multilateral free-trading system – a more real probability after the 1999 stalemate of the WTO talks in Seattle. These are circumstances in which the rise of the nationalist right in Europe and Asia, and the continuing strength of religious fundamentalists in the Muslim world, could become very dangerous. Globalisation and the current liberal world order would become seriously undermined.

After all the most analogous period of growth, technological change and global reach was that between 1880 and 1914 when urbanisation exploded, trade boomed and Europeans migrated in their millions to the New World. But it ended in war and recession; the dynamism of the underlying economy released ungovernable tensions over inequality and social injustice. Today could equally be the highwater mark of a second wave of globalisation for which the world has not yet acquired the political, cultural and social equipment to handle – and a relapse is possible.

But there is no alternative blueprint to hand. Global socialism is an exploded and defunct concept. Global autarky, in which economies turn their back on trade and seek to grow on a national or local basis, is equally unappealing; we know that protectionism produces lower growth and that the national rivalries unleashed can produce war. The last decade has seen too many local wars, from the Balkans to Africa, for there to be any confidence that in any other environment there would be less conflict – and with nuclear weaponry more widely available, the twenty-first-century wars will have deadly global consequences.

The task, surely, in the absence of alternatives, is to keep the current system going and improve it. It is all we have; it is both a source of creativity and global enrichment but equally it faces risks from all sides that need to be confronted and managed. Nation states face loss of power and autonomy: it is obvious that over the next century, if the system is to be successfully governed and regulated, sovereignty – and parallel systems of democracy and accountability – will have to pass to new forms of global agency. While we, the two editors, differ over the degree to which globalisation has been designed and managed to benefit the world's pre-eminent nation state, the USA, and the degree to which the USA will obstruct creative global initiatives in the name of unilateralism, both of us are clear that notwithstanding new global institutions need to be created if the system is to continue to prosper.

We see this as urgent. The paradox is that just as interdependence and prosperity are mounting, so the suspicion and resentment of 'foreigners' is growing – although who and what is 'foreign' in today's context is more problematic and ambiguous than ever. It is wrong to dismiss the new fundamentalists as likely to be at the margins of debate and influence. Globalisation gives modernity its tremendous sense of irreversibility in which, as Ulrich Beck argues persuasively in his essay, every individual is forced to make his or her own life; the traditional constraints upon individual activity have been largely dissolved. Women in particular have gained hugely from this process.

Intriguingly resistance to the growth in equality of women and men is one of the driving motives of fundamentalist doctrines. The emancipation of women is itself a main feature of the processes of globalisation. There are very few countries where the future of the family isn't intensely debated; where there is no debate it is actively suppressed. The traditional family everywhere was based upon the legal and cultural dominance of men; new family forms are now emerging in all industrial countries.

As Arlie Hochschild shows, the consequences for women on a global level are mixed. Middle-class women in the affluent countries are freed to enter the labour market by employing women from Third World countries as child-minders. Both sets of women are faced with difficult choices, although those of the Third World women are much harsher. While affluent women are trying to balance work and home, the poorer women who work for them often leave their own children thousands of miles away in order to earn money and send back support.

Ulrich Beck and Richard Sennett both show that the rise of individualism is a mixed blessing. Individual choice alone – the key element of neo-liberal philosophy – cannot supply the social bonds necessary to sustain a stable and meaningful life. If individual freedom is to be extended then it must be accompanied by the construction of new cosmopolitan communities – otherwise the result is a generalised personal insecurity.

Individuals are beset by new forms of anxiety and rootlessness. On top the wider system is palpably not self-regulating. Neo-liberalism thus fails at two levels: at the level of individual conviction and as a compass to inform the intellectual discussion over the economic and political framework in which globalisation can take place. The new far right has its origins in this situation. Western conservatism is developing a nationalist and sometimes, as in Austria and Switzerland, an overtly racist tone. Support for internationalism, whether of the European Union or the United Nations, is uncertain and hesitant.

A start has to be made in fashioning a philosophy that can underpin globalisation which is not neo-liberal but no less importantly represents a clear rupture with the old framework of nation-states or of a utopian internationalism that rested on extending socialism on the globe. The philosophy to hand, in our view, is an internationalist third way, blending more effective economic and social governance around social-democratic values, passionate belief in democracy and an intense concern with human rights. We need to equip the emerging global civil society with the institutions and intellectual framework in which liberalism, in its best sense, is no longer associated with fatalism about being unable to govern the global market economy. It is a philosophy that could underpin the creation of global institutions that will help promote global security, policing and international criminal justice; create the conditions for the alleviation of poverty in the Third World and inequality in the First World; and propel the renovation and reconstruction of a system of world economic and environmental governance, notably the regulation of the financial markets.

These initiatives require in turn new systems of international democracy and accountability. We need to lay the groundwork so that eventually an elected second chamber for a revitalised United Nations is no longer seen as far-fetched; for this it is vital that the European Union succeed in pioneering the world's first system of international democracy in the European Parliament. And as we build global democratic institutions so we believe that the nascent 'bottom-up' transnational political organisations – the more than 10,000 non-governmental organisations – will start to have more political leverage and thus attract members and more energy. We have already noted how they, and international trade unions, have begun to develop in response to global companies – and have already achieved a striking record of success. As their political purchase grows, so they will be one of building blocks in the creation of a new global civil society that is no longer the dream of idealists.

The most pressing area of action, which has preoccupied all our contributors, is to alleviate the dangers presented by the operation of the current international financial system. We cannot share the view that any intervention to regulate, govern and even tax the financial system is likely to offer intellectual and political justification to those arguing for protecionist measures to control trade, and thus must be resisted. In this view free finance and free trade are indivisible; we have to live with the global financial market as it is, warts and all, because it is indisolubly linked to free trade.

But as Robert Kuttner argues, there is an important intellectual distinction to be made between the dynamics of how financial markets work and the dynamics that govern trade in goods and services; it is the heart of a Keynesian outlook that even notable defenders of free trade, like Jagdish Bhagwati, have come to accept. The reason is simple. While there may be some self-regulating tendencies in the markets for goods and services, these tendencies, already weak in domestic financial markets, are even more limited in global financial markets. Finance has to be regulated, paradoxically, in order to protect free trade. Capital controls are essential in order to keep the markets for goods and services open.

The Keynesian argument has always centred around the proposition that different markets in a capitalist economy adjust with varying speed and efficiency, thus affecting the performance of the whole. In particular the financial markets necessarily move prices of financial assets much more quickly up and down than the labour markets can ever do with wages – and it is this conundrum that is at the heart of the difficulties that capitalist economies have in maintaining an even pace of economic growth. However, in the neo-liberal rush to bury Keynes and his work, this insight has been lost. The principle has been – which as

Paul Volcker argues is now no more than ideology – that the best way for every market in the national and international economy to be organised is as a spot market: currencies, labour, products, capital – all should be freely bought and sold at will. If there are problems of adjustment then the solution is to intensify the market process rather than resort to regulation and government intervention to solve economic underperformance.

But the difficulty in the global capital market is not just the different speed at which financial asset prices move compared to prices in the real economy, it is that the prices massively overshoot. Volcker points to the extraordinary variation in the dollar–yen rate – with the yen devaluing 50 per cent in a couple of years and then appreciating as quickly – as witness to the virus at the heart of the international financial order. This confronts smaller countries with an impossible dilemma. If they float their currencies, then they will face the same extraordinary and destabilising sudden capital inflows and outflows; but pegging their currency to a larger one is no answer either because they swing in value too. Volcker, while careful to say that the Asian economies need more transparency and better banking systems, places the cause of the Asian financial crisis not in these shortcomings but firmly with the systemic faults of the international financial system.

The countries at the periphery of the global economy are thus continually vulnerable and exposed to economic instability, as George Soros emphasises. Both Soros and Volcker indict the conventional approach of the IMF, which has interpreted each national economic crisis individually in terms of domestic imbalances and policy mistakes rather than as the fault of the international system. There is a consensus between them, Robert Kuttner and Manuel Castells that it is simply inappropriate for capital to move into less developed countries with the free right to exit so easily; and the same applies to the massive swings in currency rates now experienced by the big three, Europe, Japan and the USA. It is not merely that the real economy pays too high a price for the adjustment imposed upon it by overshooting financial markets, it is that there is the continual risk of a major bank or banks suffering such severe losses from their exposure that there is a world-wide credit crunch. In effect the Keynesian diagnosis and prescription of the underlying dynamic of the capitalist economy has moved from the national to the global scale.

We have increasingly to understand that national responses are limited; we have to develop, as a minimum regional and at best global, systems of economic governance. There are a number of possiblities that require serious discussion and debate. We need, for example, a World Financial Authority that regulates financial markets and oversees the adequacy of the balance sheets of international financial institutions; there needs to be a World Central Bank to act as a lender of last resort; the Group of Seven Leading Industrialised Countries need to develop a system of close fiscal co-ordination; and the dollar, yen and euro zones need to be managed so that their underlying economic performance is convergent. Nor should the presumption be that exchange and capital controls are economic 'bads' – they may be vital tools of economic management curtailing volatile capital controls, and give less developed countries in particular policy options that would otherwise not exist.

The idea of a small tax on foreign exchange dealings – the Tobin tax – is now twenty-five years old; the time has surely come for left-of-centre political leaders to discuss whether such a tax is now feasible. It would slow down the exponential growth of foreign exchange dealing and associated speculative capital flows. The status of offshore tax, financial and business havens needs to be withdrawn; these are major means of tax evasion and homes to vast pools of speculative capital. Nor should we shrink from the ultimate aim of organising a single currency for the world, of which the euro is a key building block.

This may seem an ambitious agenda, but it reflects the very large scope of the global change that is happening. The current system suffers from chronic weaknesses, but it offers benefits too. Thus the choice is to do nothing and hope for the best; or do something – and that something has to be informed by a wider vision. What we have outlined is what the vision must be.

The argument is similar over the new concentrations of transnational corporate power. Monopoly now has to be contested and competition asserted on a global scale. The US record of trust and monopoly busting is the example that needs to be followed, but this demands the construction of a global competition authority: national efforts, even those in the USA, are inadequate. This also raises the question of standards of disclosure and corporate governance; there need to be common rules over the construction of company accounts, disclosure of information and the duties of directors. We need to move towards an internationally agreed system of rules for corporate governance. The World Trade Organisation, conceived as a mechanism of ensuring that national markets are progressively opened to all member organisations on the same basis of free entry, needs to be remodelled as an institution that underwrites and polices a basis framework of rules of capitalist engagement, rather than enshrine free trade as an absolutist principle.

From the employment of child labour to the recognition of trade unions, corporations trading in a global market must adhere to common rules of the game, otherwise there will be a 'race to the bottom' in which labour standards tend towards worst rather than best practice – the argument forcibly advanced by Jeff Faux and Larry Mishel.

The same injunction is evident over the environment. The green argument that we only have one world and that it is each generation's duty to hand it on to the next as a sustainable social and natural habitat is no longer the preserve of utopians and environmental zealots; it is the new common sense before increasingly dangerous environmental risks. It may be difficult to reach consensus over the risks posed by, say, global warming but they plainly exist. However, there can be no dispute that the management of the international food chain, ranging from genetically modified food to the consequences of poorly regulated industrial farming that have surfaced over BSE, is a global issue in the here and now. Shortages of water in Africa, Asia and the Middle East are also indisputable. The case for global management and regulation of the environment through a global environmental protection agency is becoming urgent, although as Vandana Shiva dramatises, the issue is not just technical and scientific; it is also a matter of power. The state socialist countries had an appalling environmental record. Internally most Western states now display a much higher level of ecological consciousness than a few years ago, but they have yet to transfer this effectively to a world level. One of the problems is that contemporary shareholder-value-driven capitalism is more careless of the environment than native systems of sustainable agriculture.

This opens up the extraordinarily complex and tense debate over the cultural prisms through which globalisation is interpreted. Through one pair of eyes it is a cynical and destructive plot by the West to impose its values on the world, embodied, as Polly Toynbee writes, in the triumph of Hollywood films, Nike shoes and Coco-Cola, which drive out local cultural institutions, and, more dangerously, locally owned and plural-istic forms of media. But as she quickly adds, the rest of the world hardly needs much convincing to drink Coca-Cola or watch *Basic Instinct*; they enjoy them as much as any American. The issue is not so much the preservation of national cultures in a globalising world, which will necessarily be influenced by other sources and so become much more polyglot; rather it is power and ideology. A global cultural market dominated by half a dozen private broadcasters and publishers will limit political pluralism, and is a developing monopoly that any World Competition Authority must most fiercely contest.

Although this collection of essays did not include any assessment of the security issues raised by globalisation – the focus was on examining the emerging global business civilisation – we are keenly aware that the propensity for conflict, war and terrorism driven by ideological, religious and territorial differences remains acute. Peace is a precious asset: there needs to be a credible deterrent to war – and, if it occurs, a credible means of brokering and policing a settlement between the combatants. What has become apparent over the 1990s is that flagrant abuses of human rights either within any nation state or resulting from conflict between states are no longer acceptable. The Indonesian, Serbian and Iraqi subjugations of the East Timorese, Kosovans and Kurds respectively have been judged to offend human rights – and the internatonal community has responded with military interventions.

This trend will grow more marked, and it is obvious that the current *ad hoc* machinery of hastily assembled international armies and peace-keeping forces, sometimes legitimised by the United Nations and sometimes not, is not as yet adequate to the task. In this field as in the others, we need a clear internationally agreed system of rules whose transgression would trigger a clear international response from a standing supranational, highly mobile military force.

But such a proposal highlights the dilemma behind every proposal we have made. What are the mechanisms of decision-making and account-ability of these global initiatives? Are they to be conceived as forms of inter-governmental colloboration in which sovereignty rests essentially with nation states, or are they the forerunners of genuine global institutions that conform to new rules of cosmopolitan law, democracy and governance – and which will gradually limit and redefine the role of the nation state?

The argument mirrors that over European integration. Sceptics insist that nation states remain the only legitimate political jurisdiction; they are governed by national parliaments answering to national electorates who are united by blood, history, language and culture. The European Parliament, they claim, is a parliament of Europe only in name; it does not speak for a European public nor is there any prospect that it will do so. The EU is simply too variegated, disparate and culturally diverse for that. For the sceptics the idea of European union is a pipedream – Europe must remain a Europe of colloborating nation states.

It is an argument with force, but with a fundamental flaw. Just as we have argued over globalisation, it is a matter of fact that Europe's nation states are increasingly affected by decisions and trends beyond their borders; globalisation is at work on a European scale. It might be the environment; it might be fishing; it might be car exhaust emissions; it might be TV rights for European sports events; it might be the need to develop a European military capacity to intervene in hot spots on Europe's frontiers; it might be the need to find a manageable currency regime – in all these areas a response has to be found that represents more than a brokered position between nation states. There has to be some form of European governance, and some means of holding that governance to account.

The European Commission is Europe's executive directorate; the European Parliament its emerging parliamentary critic and legislature; and the European Council, the decision-making forum for nation states the overarching fountainhead of political and executive power. It is a constitutional structure with palpable weaknesses, but it is the framework of a political constitution for Europe that allows more than colloboration between nation-states. It is a nascent system of continent-wide cosmopolitan governance with mechanisms for proper democratic accountability and continental citizenship.

It is crucially important that the European project succeeds, both in its own terms and as a forerunner of what must eventually be attempted globally. There are the first signs of the EU constructing a genuine civil society that stretches beyond the boundaries of individual nation-states. The principal vehicle are single-issue non-governmental organisations seeking allies to pursue goals that can no longer be achieved successfully within one country; the green movement is one example, Jubilee 2000 another. And there are a myriad of European umbrella associations whose impact is just beginning.

There can be no pretence that national societies and democracies will find it easy or comfortable catching up with the forces of globalisation that are so powerfully operating beyond national borders. But there is no ducking the issue. Although there are differences of emphasis between all our contributors, what we hope to have shown both in our own debates and their essays is that the direction of change is unmistakable, as is the nature of any response. The great national movements for democracy, liberty and social justice that took place in the eighteenth and early nineteenth centuries within nation-states now have to be reproduced globally. Nothing less will do.

Notes on Contributors

Ulrich Beck is Professor of Sociology at the University of Munich, and British Journal of Sociology Visiting Professor at the London School of Economics and Political Science. His latest publications are *World Risk Society* and *What is Globalisation?* (both published by Polity Press).

Manuel Castells is Professor of Sociology and Professor of Planning at the University of California at Berkeley. His latest book is the trilogy, *The Information Age: Economy, Society and Culture* (revised edition published by Blackwell, 2000).

Jeff Faux is President of the Economic Policy Institute in Washington, DC. He is the author of *The Party's Not Over: A New Vision for the Democrats*, published by Basic Books in 1996.

Arlie Russell Hochschild teaches sociology at the University of California at Berkeley, where she also co-directs the Center for Working Families. Her books on the culture of work include *The Managed Heart*, *The Second Shift* and *Time Bind*.

Robert Kuttner is the Co-Editor of *The American Prospect*. His most recent book is *Everything for Sale: The Virtues and Limits of Markets*.

Larry Mishel is Vice-President of the Economic Policy Institute in Washington, DC and the co-author of *The State of Working America 1998–99*, published by Cornell University Press in 1998.

Richard Sennett is Professor of Sociology at the London School of Economics. His most recent book is *The Corrosion of Character*.

Vandana Shiva is a physicist and ecologist. She is the Founder

225

Director of the Research Foundation for Science, Technology and Ecology in New Delhi and a Founder Board Member of the International Forum on Globalisation. Dr Shiva is the recipient of many awards, including the Nobel Prize, and her books include *Staying Alive* and *Monocultures of the Mind*.

George Soros currently serves as Chairman of the Soros Fund Management LLC and of the Open Society Institute. His most recent book, *The Crisis of Global Capitalism: Open Society Endangered*, was published in 1998.

Polly Toynbee is a journalist, broadcaster and columnist for the *Guardian*. She has written books on the NHS, adoption and unskilled work.

Paul Volcker is the former Chairman of the Board of Governors of the US Federal Reserve System.

Index